SURVIVOR
A TRIBUTE TO *Cliff*

TONY JASPER

Marshall Pickering

An Imprint of HarperCollins*Publishers*

To
Frank, Ros, Kerensa, Morwenna, Tasmin Blewett
Margaret Robertson and Sylvia Carter
Stuart, Judith and Lucy Helen Bell

Marshall Pickering is an Imprint of
HarperCollins*Religious*
Part of HarperCollins*Publishers*
77–85 Fulham Palace Road, London W6 8JB

First published in Great Britain
in 1989 by Marshall Morgan and Scott
(subsequently Marshall Pickering)
This edition published in Great Britain
in 1993 by Marshall Pickering

1 3 5 7 9 10 8 6 4 2

A catalogue record for this book is available from
the British Library

ISBN 0 551 02793 2

Printed and bound in Great Britain by
Butler & Tanner Limited, Frome, Somerset

CONTENTS

Introduction   5

1   Year by Year   7
2   Then and Now   21
3   On the Record   39
4   Radio and Television   61
5   Stage and Screen   75
6   On the Road   89
7   In Interview   111
8   Faith and its Effect   127
9   The Final Word . . . from Cliff   151

    Thirty-four Years Of Singles
    and Albums   158

ACKNOWLEDGEMENTS

Thanks are due to many but among them the late Brian Munns, Terri Anderson and Brian Southall of EMI Records, London, the Cliff Richard Office especially Gill Snow, Christine Whitehead, Eileen Edwards, Lyn Taylor, Christine Smith and the book's designer Marian Morris.

PHOTOGRAPHIC CREDITS

Colour pictures: Numbered 1 to 4, Sue Andrews; 5 Dave Clark; 6–8 Sue Andrews; 9 to 15 Paul Cox; 16 Hanne Jordan; 17, 18 John McGoran; 19 Christine Whitehead; 20 John McGoran; 21–23 Gill Jermyn/International Cliff Richard Movement; 24 Grapevine; 25 Sue Andrews; 26 Paul Cox; 27 Music Week; 28 Hanne Jordan; 29 Sue Andrews; 30 Hanne Jordan; 31 Mats Carlsson; 32 Klaus Schultes; 33 Neya Koponer; 34 Sue Andrews; 35 unknown; 36 Hanne Jordan.

Black and white pictures, by page: 12 unknown; 17 by kind permission of Nordoff-Robbins Music Therapy Centre; 18 Hanne Jordan; 26 Grapevine; 29 Paul Cox; 43 EMI Records; 52 Paul Cox; 68 John Farrier; 84 Stephanie Lawrence; 85 Rowan Atkinson; 87 with Dave Clark, John McGoran: with cake, Dave Clark – Alan Grisbrook; 93 John McGoran; 99 Hanne Jordan, smaller picture Harry De Louw; 119 John Farrier; 135 The Star newspaper; 139 Luis Palau organization, photographer Mick Rock; 149 John McGoran; 150 John Farrier; 154 Hanne Jordan.

INTRODUCTION

This is not a re-write of *Cliff*, a book which I compiled with the late Pat Doncaster in 1981, and which made the national top ten hardback listing. Occasionally there is reference to the text of *Cliff* but that is all, and if this is not a re-write, then neither is it an update.

The basic idea of this book is to compile a worthy tribute to Britain's most remarkable pop personality, the only true survivor since pop reared its head with Haley and Presley in the mid-1950s.

There is no story as such; chapter by chapter the different aspects of Cliff's career are covered, and there are tributes from people associated with the many areas of Cliff's life, many of them handwritten, and ranging from the words of the rich and famous to tributes from the vast body of his fans in every walk of life. I have talked with countless people involved in these fields. To end, there is the man himself, looking back over his own career.

The hardback edition of *Survivor* proved an enormous success, reaching number ten in Britain's best-sellers list, and hopefully this new paperback edition will do equally well.

Inevitably the time between the two editions has seen some changes; some people have moved from their jobs, and sadly several have died, not least of course, Freddie Mercury, who was one of the first to send his appreciation of Cliff's career, and George Hoffman, so closely associated with Cliff's work for Tear Fund.

So here we are, after another decade, with Cliff as active as ever, after a recent major British tour that saw its original date sheet extended several times. While his recording activities in the nineties have not touched the dizzy heights of the previous decade, an album of brand new material is scheduled for early Spring, and as Cliff disc-historians well know, a period of inactivity generally leads to another purple patch in his recording career.

Cliff is now into his fifth decade as a music star and personality, and, provided he stays in good health, few, surely, would suggest that he might not survive into the 21st century!

Tony Jasper
1993

EMI MUSIC WORLDWIDE

I first met Cliff in the early 60's when he and The Shadows played Singapore and Malaysia on their premiere concert tour of that part of the world. Then, as now, Cliff Richard impressed everyone he encountered as much by the spell of his enormous creative talent as by the abundance of his personal warmth.

EMI Music is most privileged to have been closely associated for over 30 years with the brilliant career of a truly unique superstar who combines in his work and in his life the commitments of a profoundly sensitive performing artist with a deep sense of humanity, charity and caring for all his fellow beings.

On behalf of my colleagues throughout the world of EMI, I salute Cliff Richard with abiding admiration, gratitude and affection.

BHASKAR MENON
Chairman and Chief Executive
EMI Music Worldwide

Cliff Richard has been a star in Europe for almost as long as he has in Britain. Right from the days when he recorded his hits in German, French, Italian and Spanish, through to 1988 when he celebrated 30 years in the music industry, Cliff has regularly toured and visited Europe.

He is welcomed in all EMI Music's companies throughout Europe as an old friend with a unique understanding and appreciation of the Continental pop market.

Alexis Rotelli
Managing Director - Europe
EMI Music Worldwide

EMI RECORDS (UK)

Overall, I would say that Cliff Richard is a totally unique individual. He has been at the forefront of EMI's success for the last 30 years and has earned a great liking and respect on a personal basis from all of our people around the world who have come into contact with him.

He has been a terrific ambassador for EMI in the countries that he goes to perform in and has never lost sight of the EMI people he has come into contact with. He has frequently shown his appreciation for our people and their hard work and is a firm favourite of everyone. In the world of EMI, Cliff is a very special person and one we all take a great pride in being associated with.

Yours sincerely

RUPERT PERRY

There are few true superstars in the world of popular music and Cliff Richard is undoubtedly one of them.

That success has been achieved not just through his hit records, but also by his determination to succeed and an enormous capacity for hard work, illustrated by his commitment to visiting and touring all around the globe.

He first toured South East Asia in the early 1960's and helped EMI develop in those new markets. Indeed his public stand against record piracy in Singapore was, in part, responsible for the introduction of new copyright laws in that country. Australia and New Zealand have remained loyal to Cliff for three decades and only last year he received a platinum disc for sales albums sold during his Australian tour.

Congratulations and thanks.

David Stockley
Managing Director International
EMI Music Worldwide

1 YEAR BY YEAR

1958 Early in 1958 Harry Rodger Webb became Cliff Richard. The Planets was the original name suggested for his backing group. However, they became The Drifters, unaware that in the USA there was a famous soul group of the same name. Eventually they became The Shadows. Cliff was signed by EMI to their Columbia label on 9 August. His first single (released 29 August) has remained an all-time classic – 'Move It' reached No. 2 in the British charts. Cliff made his television debut on 13 September and began his first UK tour on 5 October. On tour he experienced 'Cliff hysteria' as girls screamed for his attention in the face of their boyfriends' objections. Tired of American pop heroes, British music fans wanted their own, and Cliff was their answer. It was not long before film parts were being discussed.

1959 As in nearly all the years ahead, there were plenty of hit singles with both 'Living Doll' and 'Travelling Light' reaching No. 1 in the British charts. He appeared in two films: *Serious Charge* and *Expresso Bongo*. The then major British teen music paper – *New Musical Express* – gave Cliff his first award: fans had voted him 'Best New Singer'. He bought himself a pink and black motor scooter and from the royalties of 'Move It' could also afford one of the new super hi-fi stereos (with some change to spare). He was hot magazine copy: *Reveille* headlined with 'He Doesn't Try To Be Sexy', while the top-selling *Daily Mirror* called his eyes 'dark, luminous and slumberous'.

1960 There were TV specials, more awards, royal performances and a season at the famous London Palladium. 'Please Don't Tease' and 'I Love You' topped the singles charts. In March his film *Expresso Bongo* opened in the States and he made his first visit to the USA. In this, his last year as a teenager, Cliff enjoyed chart success with five singles, six EPs and an album. British newspapers said that he earned more than the Prime Minister. On his birthday, 14 October, he received more than 5,000 cards.

1961 He filmed *The Young Ones* and the title track gave him another No. 1 with more than one million sales. He became an international star and toured in many parts of the world while his backing group – The Shadows – were fast becoming stars in their own right. Cliff topped the LP charts with *21 Today* – issued by EMI to commemorate his 21st birthday – and The Variety Club of Great Britain made him 'Show Business Personality of the Year'.

1962 *The Young Ones* film was an enormous success in the many countries where it was released. The follow-up *Summer Holiday* was shot, involving over 3,000 miles of travel in five different countries. The album saw the emergence of Cliff as a songwriter – he was co-credited on the massive hit 'Bachelor Boy' – and he was quoted as saying 'It's always been an ambition of mine to write.' He named his favourite male stars as Elvis Presley, Rick Nelson and Ray Charles, while Julie London, Helen Shapiro and Connie Francis were at the top of his list of female vocalists.

1963   Although this was the year that Beatlemania began, Cliff stole the limelight when *Summer Holiday* was premiered on 10 January. Huge crowds prevented him reaching the cinema on time. He embarked on another tour, playing in Kenya and Spain amongst many other countries. In Britain, over 200,000 people saw him play live and he estimated that he signed over 4,000 autographs. He visited the USA again and appeared on the legendary Ed Sullivan TV show.

1964   Cliff starred in another film, *Wonderful Life*, which was filmed in north-west Africa; the soundtrack reached No. 2. He appeared on a number of TV shows in the UK and Europe and starred in a one-hour TV special for ATV with Liza Minelli. He had five Top 10 hits in the UK singles charts (compared to The Beatles' three) and although it was The Beatles who made the headlines, Cliff

Sir Harry Secombe

"It is with great pleasure that I congratulate Cliff, the C. Aubrey Smith of pop. I have been in the fortunate position of appearing with him a number of times, but there are two occasions that I will always remember with particular affection. The first was at the opening concert of the magnificent Sydney Opera House where he was backed by a full symphony orchestra – and he was a huge success. The second time was when he did me the favour of appearing in the opening concert at the Secombe Centre in Sutton. Then he just walked on stage with his guitar and accompanied himself – and he was just as big a success as he was in Australia. The man has a big talent, is professional to his fingertips and is always ready to help a good cause – long may he entertain!"

Harry Secombe was one of the original Goons. As a singer he has made many albums and in recent years has introduced and taken part in the popular British television series Highway.

JOE LOSS LIMITED

Cliff, I've been in the music business since 1926 and I'm sure I'm the longest surviving artist in the record history of E.M.I. So, you cannot claim this record – yet! Obviously I've had so many memories and delights from (my) being part of the music world, I suppose the advent of rock 'n' roll, and the growth of the record as opposed to 'live' music, has been one of the most noticeable things in my career. I remember you making your first record in 1958, and then some more, and more! You have been one of the very few 'lasters' in pop. You have been blessed with good health – save for your back playing up sometimes – and more so with talent and professionalism.

I feel you have been a tremendous credit on every level. You have stayed at the top without blemish of any kind.

So I congratulate you most warmly. Joe.

P.S. If you need a band anytime, the address is above!!!

KENNY BALL

To Cliff
Congratulations
Kenny Ball & the Jazzmen

Roy Castle

Cliff is one of our greatest popular music stars of all time. The grass has never grown under his feet but he is far beyond being a rolling stone.

Roy Castle

One of the 'great' names of British music, especially loved for his famous **Joe Loss Band**. Sadly, since sending this tribute, Joe has died.

Kenny Ball fronted one of the most popular bands during the trad-jazz boom time of the late 1950s and 1960s and had many hits. His music and band remain in demand.

TV personality and pop singer, **Roy Castle**, is a household name, not least because of his courageous battle against cancer.

held his own as a British pop star. He ended the year by starring in a pantomime, *Aladdin And His Wonderful Lamp*.

1965 Elvis was cast aside and individual Beatles ignored as readers of the *New Musical Express* voted Cliff as the World's Top Male Singer. He recorded three TV specials, toured Europe and again appeared on the Ed Sullivan show in the USA. 'The Minute You're Gone' topped record charts all over the world. Although he talked about growing Christian awareness and was attending church regularly, few realised the major change it would make to him as a person and to his career.

1966 On 16 June Cliff appeared on stage at a Billy Graham campaign meeting and spoke openly of his Christian faith. Many of his fans wept when they read this news the following day, fearing the end of his career as a pop star. There was a new film, *Finders Keepers*; he starred in another pantomime, *Cinderella*, at London's famous Palladium Theatre; the now legendary 'Thunderbirds' TV series featured Cliff and The Shadows in puppet form, and there was talk of him touring Eastern Europe and the Soviet Union. It suggested that his fans had wept unnecessarily.

1967 Would he or wouldn't he stay in show business? It seemed the most popular question of 1967. A new film was announced – Cliff would star in *Two A Penny*, sponsored and financed by the Billy Graham Evangelistic Association. There was speculation that he would become a clergyman or a teacher of religious education but Cliff stayed with music and his fans breathed again! However, appearing on numerous religious TV programmes, he condemned pop stars who took drugs, said that premarital sex was unhealthy, and told the Beatles that they were wasting their time consorting with the Marharishi Mahesh Yogi. He performed in Tokyo with a Japanese orchestra and finished the year by landing a role as a straight actor in the TV thriller 'A Matter of Diamonds'.

1968 Cliff represented Britain in the Eurovision Song Contest and failed by one point to take the top place. However, his song 'Congratulations' topped the charts in the UK and many other countries (including Germany where it stayed at No. 1 for seven weeks), and sold over one million copies, giving him his fifth Gold Disc. Cliff played some Gospel concerts, including one at Coventry Cathedral, and a special party was held to celebrate his 10th anniversary as a star. It began to be apparent that Cliff and the Shadows would go their separate ways.

1969 The Shadows toured the UK and Japan with Cliff before they split. Cliff had a very busy year: he worked on a six-part Gospel series for Tyne Tees TV; sang in German when he appeared on a TV programme there; he visited Rumania, Italy, Holland, and Israel where he made a documentary about the Holy Land. He starred in his own TV show on the BBC and the longevity of his career inspired the album *The Best of Cliff*. He continued publicly to support Christian charities and also appeared in a gala at the London Palladium in aid of the Royal Society for the Prevention of Cruelty to Animals.

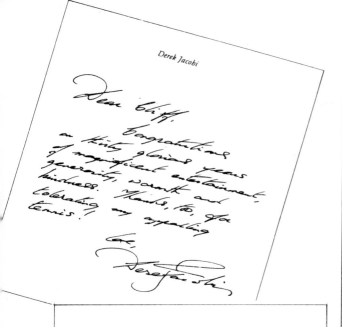

Derek Jacobi

Dear Cliff,
   Congratulations
on thirty glorious years
of magnificent entertainment,
generosity, warmth and
kindness. Thanks, to, for
tolerating my appalling
tennis!
   love,
   Derek Jacobi

Cilla Black

Darling Cliff,
   Thank you so much for
all those super years of
pleasure, entertainment
and sheer ecstasy!! I could'nt
imagine my life without
you cos' you've always been
there and I'm very proud
to have known you and to
think I've even had the
thrill of singing with you
(when are we going to do
it again?)
   Here's wishing you
another Fab 30 yrs, you
look great, you sing great
and I know I should
hate you but I don't,
I luv you, as everyone
does.
   God Bless you Cliff,,
   Yours "Thigh wise"
   Cilla
   X X

Dear Tony,

I'm delighted to contribute my own personal memory
of Cliff to your collection.

It goes back to the 1968 Eurovision Song Contest.
It was the year that Cliff was pipped at the post
by Spain when he sang "Congratulations" for Britain.
He had been a joy to work with during those pressurised
rehearsals at the Albert Hall, and hopes were rising
very high indeed.   I've seen "good losers" before,
but never one who sailed through the experience with
not a flicker of disappointment on his face. I I join
the millions who know him as a great guy - one with
a super sense of humour, combined with tough moral
fibre.

I rather wish I could come up with something different,
but I can't. So there you have yet another warm
recollection of "our hero!"

With warmest wishes, and do give him my love,

Yours ever,

Katie Boyle

How amazing that after
thirty years in the business
Cliff Richard seems to be
more successful than ever!
   Estelle Kohler

During 1989 **Derek Jacobi** starred in King Richard III.

Katie Boyle is one of Britain's best-known television presenters and for many years
she wrote regularly for TV Times.

Cilla came to the fore as a major girl singer of the 1960s, and is these days a major
TV star associated with presenting *Blind Date*.

Estelle Kohler is one of the UK's leading classical actresses and has won many
awards.

A long, long time ago, it started here.

1970   Cliff made two pop albums and two religious albums and although The Shadows occasionally appeared on stage with him, they were not present when Cliff played at the prestigious Talk Of The Town in London. He pursued his straight-acting career by appearing in Peter Shaeffer's play *Five Finger Exercise* and continued to appear on many religious programmes. He was voted both 'Mr Valentine' and 'Best Dressed Star' by readers of the music paper, *Disc and Music Echo*.

1971   Cliff's own TV series ran for the first three months of the year and he also appeared in a TV play. Thirteen years on from his debut, at the age of 31, he was still able to capture the votes of the *NME*'s readers as 'Top Male Singer' and 'Top Vocal Personality'. He toured in Europe and duetted with Olivia Newton-John. He received the Ivor Novello Award for Outstanding Services to British Music. His most successful single was 'Sing a Song of Freedom'.

1972   Cliff was refused admittance into Singapore because his hair was too long and his 1971 single 'Sing a Song of Freedom' was banned in South Africa and Mozambique. He hosted another 13-week series for the BBC and did a 26-date tour of the UK. His single 'Brand New Song' was his first chart miss.

1973   Cliff again represented Britain in the Eurovision Song Contest with 'Power to All Our Friends' – it came third behind Luxembourg and Spain. In terms of sales and the British charts, it became his biggest hit since 'Congratulations' in 1968. He starred in the film *Take Me High* and agreed to play the part of Bottom in his old school's production of Shakespeare's *A Midsummer Night's Dream*. He toured extensively in Europe and Australia and sang in St Paul's Cathedral.

1974   Cliff denied that he had asked Olivia Newton-John to marry him. An 85-track set of Cliff's songs (plus seven by The Shadows), making up six albums, was released. It was revealed that up to December 1973, he had received 19 silver discs for singles selling in excess of 250,000 and 3 gold discs for singles selling more than one million copies. Together with The Shadows he gave a special concert in aid of the dependants of one of the producers of 'Top of the Pops', who had died. He starred in yet another BBC TV series 'It's Cliff Richard'. It was not a good year for his health and he suffered from bronchitis, laryngitis and back problems. His album *31st of February Street* was not as successful as it deserved to be. There was another tour, taking in the UK and Japan amongst other countries. He also undertook a Gospel tour.

1975   Whilst it was not a good year for records, there was no problem in finding radio, TV and live outlets throughout the world. His films were shown on TV in Korea; a double live album was released in Japan; he appeared on TV in Scandinavia; and his concert at the Sydney Opera House was recorded and released as a live album there, *Cliff Entertains*. He also had a 13-part Gospel series on BBC Radio 1. Again he toured extensively and there was talk of him recording in Russia. As with every year, there were countless awards and media specials.

1976   This year saw the return of Cliff to the charts. His *I'm Nearly Famous* album received much praise, and singles such as 'Miss You Nights' and 'Devil Woman' reasserted him as a major recording artist. 'Devil Woman' became a huge hit in the USA and he toured Russia (the first western rock star ever to do so) playing eight concerts in Moscow and twelve in Leningrad. He also played in Hong Kong. In France they released *Cliff Chante En Francais*. On top of all this, he did not neglect charity and religious work.

1977   In terms of records, the highlight was the chart-topping album *Cliff Richard's 40 Golden Greats*. He received the annual Music Therapy Silver Clef Award for his services to the music industry. His autobiography *Which One's Cliff?* was published, and during one hour at London's department store Selfridges, he signed 333 copies of it, setting a new record by beating the previous best of former British Prime Minister Edward Heath, whose total had been 230. There was a visit to India and Bangladesh on behalf of the Christian relief agency Tear Fund. He appeared on American TV in both 'The Merv Griffin Show' and 'The Mike Douglas Show'. In October the fan club organised a National Cliff Week in Britain.

1978   It was the 20th anniversary for Cliff and The Shadows and there was a series of get-together concerts. It was not a year for hit singles but the pace of life for Cliff hardly differed from more successful years. He refuted suggestions that he might

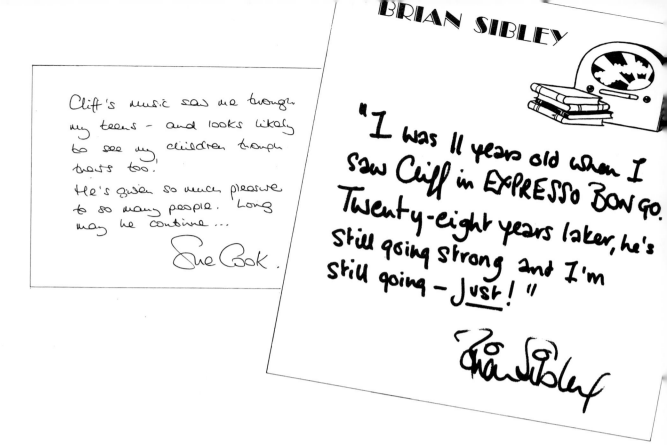

Cliff's music saw me through my teens — and looks likely to see my children through theirs too.

He's given so much pleasure to so many people. Long may he continue...

Sue Cook.

BRIAN SIBLEY

"I was 11 years old when I saw Cliff in EXPRESSO BONGO. Twenty-eight years later, he's still going strong and I'm still going — Just!"

Brian Sibley

retire: 'It's been a fantastic 20 years. People keep asking me how long I think I might go on . . . I'm just looking forward to the next five or six years.' There were countless concerts, including a charity concert at the Ford Motor Works in Essex in aid of multiple sclerosis, and on the religious side he supported evangelist Dick Saunders.

1979 Suddenly it was OK to like Cliff. All kinds of writers and magazines fell over themselves to hail his vocal ability and talent. He achieved his tenth No. 1 record and his first No. 1 since 1968 with 'We Don't Talk Anymore' which also reached the Top 10 in the USA and sold just under 3 million worldwide. His second album of the year, *Rock 'N' Roll Juvenile*, confirmed that he was back in business. There were celebrations for another reason: it was his 21st year with EMI and he was presented with a gold replica of the key to the company's main London offices. As well as the usual media and religious events, he joined in carol singing outside Buckingham Palace with 30,000 people just before Christmas.

1980 The hit records continued: 'Carrie' reached No. 4; 'Dreamin' made the Top 10 and a duet with Olivia Newton-John from the film soundtrack of *Xanadu* reached No. 15. The album *I'm No Hero* received rave reviews worldwide and got to No. 4 in Britain. This success was mirrored in the USA and he appeared in TV specials in Germany, Holland, Australia and New Zealand. He was awarded the BBC/ *Daily Mirror* award as Best Family Entertainer and, best of all, was awarded the OBE, receiving it in person from the Queen. It was the year that Cliff reached 40.

Sue Cook presents various major BBC Television programmes, including *Crimewatch*.

Brian Sibley is one of the most creative and talented of younger British radio and television drama writers and adaptors. He is author of several books.

1981 It was another year of amazing accolades and, amongst other awards, he received the nomination for 'Best Male Singer' in the *Daily Mirror*, and Germany's biggest-selling pop magazine *Bravo* named him 'Top International Male Singer'. On TV, four 50-minute programmes on BBC documented his career. His singles 'Daddy's Home' and 'Wired for Sound' went high into the charts and he undertook a major tour of the USA and Canada.

1982 Once more Cliff toured the world, playing in Hong Kong, Singapore, Thailand, Australia, New Zealand, Kenya, Europe and the USA again. As part of their 50th anniversary, the London Philharmonic Orchestra presented 'An Evening with Cliff Richard and the LPO'. His album *Now You See Me . . . Now You Don't* made the Top 5 in Britain and he had a big Christmas hit with 'Little Town.'

1983 Another historic moment in Cliff's career arrived – it was Silver Anniversary time. His career had spanned 25 years, from 1958 to 1983. His work rate had continued yearly on a major high and although a few records had failed to reach the charts, they were a small fraction of an astounding chart single and album run. Fan club celebrations occurred all over the world. His duet with Phil Everly 'She Means Nothing To Me' was a Top 10 hit, followed by two more chart successes: 'The Only Way Out' and 'Where Do We Go From Here?' As part of his 'Silver' tour he played six weeks of sell-out concerts at London's Apollo Victoria Theatre.

High praise from **Tony Christie** – the man with quite a voice himself.

Nick Kershaw has been a major pop success during the present decade.

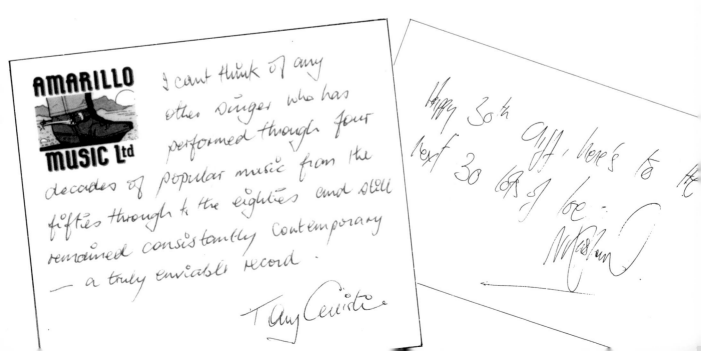

Peter Jamieson is chairperson of the BPI, the governing body of the record industry.

1984 Cliff and The Shadows joined forces once more for a series of concerts at London's Wembley Arena and Birmingham's National Exhibition Centre, and he also did a series of British Gospel dates. Abroad, he visited Japan and Australia. He began playing tennis again after suffering back trouble and took part in his own Pro-Celebrity Charity Tennis Tournament for the second year running. He duetted with Janet Jackson on a single entitled 'Two To The Power of Love' (taken from her album *Dream Street*) and achieved moderate success with his solo singles 'Shooting from the Heart' and 'Baby You're Dynamite.'

1985 There was speculation that Cliff would play a leading role in a West End musical in 1986. He featured as the Bellman on Mike Batt's album *The Hunting Of The Snark*. There was more touring in Europe (including Poland) and more Gospel dates. Although invited to duet with Elton John at Live Aid, he was unable to do so as he already had two charity bookings for that day. However, he did manage to attend the Live Aid party held that evening where he sang one song which was broadcast on TV. His religious work continued and included a visit to Amsterdam where he took part in the Luis Palau mission. Health problems arose again and he had to cancel five British concerts (the first time he had ever been forced to cancel a professional appearance in 27 years!) due to severe laryngitis. Stevie Wonder arranged, produced and played on Cliff's first single from *Time – The Musical*, 'She's So Beautiful.' It was announced that he would star in the musical which was to open in April 1986. In December he appeared in Carol Aid along with Duran Duran, The Pet Shop Boys and many other bands.

1986 Cliff's total involvement with *Time* meant no Gospel tour and no other concert dates. At the end of January he got together with The Young Ones and recorded

16

a special remake of his 1959 hit 'Living Doll' for part of Comic Relief, a project designed to raise money for charity. 'Living Doll' repeated its previous success and again topped the charts. *Time* premiered at London's Dominion Theatre on 9 April and broke all advanced booking records in the history of the West End theatre. Cliff's year-long run completely sold out! Cliff took part in the International Sport Aid day and over 250,000 people were in Hyde Park when he appeared on stage to start his 'workout'. In December he took time off from the musical to open a special Tear Fund/Tearcraft exhibition in London, showing that this charity was still one of his main priorities. He also took part in the recording of 'Live-In World', a Band Aid type collaboration of stars. It was announced that he would leave *Time* in the following spring.

1987   It was announced that David Cassidy would take over the leading role in *Time*. Cliff's departure from the musical on 11 April was followed by a well-deserved holiday. A UK Gospel tour ran the length of June which also saw the first record release of the year – the No. 6 single 'My Pretty One'. This was followed, in August, with 'Some People' (No. 3), both singles from the Top 5 album *Always Guaranteed* released in September. This album has since become the most successful studio recording of Cliff's career. Three warm-up shows at the Wimbledon Theatre were followed by over 50 concerts in 12 European countries. In Denmark Cliff received a platinum disc for sales of *Always Guaranteed* – only the second to be awarded in Danish pop history! In December Cliff became the first artist to sell out six nights at Birmingham's N.E.C. (capacity 11,600!). The last official engagement of the year was his now annual fund-raising Pro Celebrity Tennis Tournament in Brighton.

Cliff and The Shadows have been generous supporters of music therapy and supported financially the Nordoff-Robbins Music Therapy Centre. They've been honoured twice by the Association.

Note the 'hair' (it's still there), the signboard – yes, he's at Wembley for the biggest concert of his career.

1988 A tour of Australia and New Zealand took up the first three months of the year and further European dates took place during May. Recording, planning and promotion for the tour and his forthcoming *Private Collection* album and Wimbledon tennis took care of the summer. Cliff returned from his Portuguese holiday in August for the publication of his Hodder and Stoughton book *Single Minded* and his headlining appearance at the Greenbelt Festival. For the most part, September was devoted to rehearsals in preparation for his 47-date UK tour for which the 200,000 plus available tickets had been completely sold out within 72 hours of going on sale! Stories and pictures of fans camping out overnight were carried in the newspapers of every city he was to appear. **November** saw the release of *Private Collection*, a double album compilation of hits from the past ten years of Cliff's career, and also the release of Cliff's 99th single – 'Mistletoe and Wine,' both of which were topping the charts by the end of 1988. In **December** he compered a Christmas special of the BBC programme *Songs of Praise* that featured the annual Christmas celebrations of the Arts Centre Group. The programme drew 11.5 million viewers and was one of the most successful shows of the Christmas period. There was a celebration charity event with Cliff and special guests, in aid of Great Ormond Street Children's Hospital Wishing Well Appeal at London's Hammersmith Odeon, and the year finished with Cliff's now annual Pro-Celebrity Tennis Tournament at Brighton Centre raising funds in aid of The Lawn Tennis Association's 'Search For A Star' scheme. Cliff topped both the singles and albums chart, to end a marvellous year. He began 1989 in New Zealand.

1989 He began 1989 in New Zealand. A number of major awards came his way, from The Variety Club of Great Britain, The BPI (The 'Brits') (The BPI council special ward for outstanding achievement), the Nordoff-Robbins Music Therapy Silver Clef to Cliff and The Shadows (the only artists ever to win this award twice), Top Male Artist voted by readers of *TV Times*, and at the Grosvenor House Hotel, the *Music Week* Awards 1988 Top Single Award for 'Mistletoe and Wine' and second in Top Album Award for 'Private Collection'.

In April Cliff received a special award for his 30 years in the music business from the Ivor Novello Awards – another major honour.

Apart from the announcement of some club cabaret dates in Britain the major booking was for the first ever Wembley Stadium show for 16th June, that was soon extended over into the 17th.

Cliff Richard is in my opinion one of Britain's finest singers technically & emotionally. 'Rock' the day & met Marie. I've been a fan since to 'We don't talk anymore'. Long may he sing

Love

(signature)

I have been a fan of yours for all 30 years and you were a tremendous influence on my early days as a performer. You would have died if you'd have seen me doing my Cliff Richard impersonation singing 'Please Don't Tease' at the very early Queen gigs. My dream of working with you was finally realised when we sang together at the 'Time' Aids benefit at the Dominion Theatre in April this year. You have no idea what a thrill it was for me.

Keep rocking!

Freddie Mercury

Best wishes from a great admirer.

First with The Police, then as a solo artist, **Sting** is one of rock's most famous artists.

One of the world's most famous stars, **Mercury,** apart from solo projects, is the lead vocalist of Queen.

2 THEN AND NOW

Has so much ever been conjectured over one pop star, as has been about Cliff Richard? Probably not. It has been said that Cliff has had a colostomy, a definite suction of excess fat in stomach, hip and thigh areas, eyelid surgery, permanent eyelash enhancement, varicose and thread vein removal, hair transplantation and a unique treatment for the ageing face. Once he was a svelte, suave and lithe young man, who was loved and admired. Naturally, he is still very much wanted, but the girls who chase him must know that Cliff is now a reconstituted human being, aided in his continuing stage frolics by a pacemaker and continuous injections of collagen!

Thirty years, in pop terms, is a very long time. No one else has lasted the pace with pop as their central pivot. Tommy Steele made his appearance a few years before Cliff but his 'pop' success never went beyond 1961, and if Ronnie Hilton, Ruby Murray and Frankie Vaughan, to name three, can still, in their varied ways, delight and entertain, their pop achievements have long since faded. Throughout the early years the music papers kept celebrating each yearly anniversary until they began to think in five-year periods, but initially they wondered how long Cliff's success might last! The early days of 1954 and 1955, with Bill Haley, then Cliff's own hero Elvis Presley, seemed increasingly to belong to an ancient past. As Cliff's one-time manager of early years, Tito Burns, told me, 'Back in the first days no one thought it would go on like it has and he would become the big star. He was, is, a great boy!'

'He had what it takes,' is how John Foster sees it, some 30 years or so from the day when he asked if he could be Cliff's manager and went to visit the Webbs in their council home in Cheshunt. Foster was among those who attended a special 30 years celebration at the Hurlingham Club after Cliff's London opening of his 1988 British tour that had begun in Dublin and Belfast. He sat at the far end of the room, regaling all who would listen with stories of those momentous evenings at the 2 I's in Soho which proved decisive not only for Cliff but also for Hank Marvin. 'I had gone to hear Tony Sullivan, the best guitarist in England. I sat downstairs. John Littlewood of the 2 I's said he would be in, but at ten to five I was still waiting and I wanted to catch the 5.10 Greenline from Oxford Street. I decided I couldn't wait any longer and said to a guitarist called Hank Marvin, "Do you want to tour?" and he said, "yes" and that was that.'

The late Fifties and early Sixties saw nothing of the current desire to analyse, dissect and evaluate pop music and its stars. Pop stars were entertainers, and they did just that. They were not social and political observers and commentators, nor, like some current pop stars, were they students of Jung and recipients of analysis. They may have had a religious faith but they did not talk about it, and most certainly if they were gay then they adopted a pretty girl or two to keep fans oblivious of the truth. For the most part

When I was a mere teenage undergraduate, I was summoned to do my first TOP OF THE POPS with "Everyone's Gone To The Moon". Nervous as a kitten, I trembled my way through the mime of the song and, at the end, was horrified to hear not so much as a clap or a cheer from the rehearsing technicians in the empty studio. "What have I done wrong?" I wondered (it didn't take me long to discover that this reaction is standard practice during rehearsals). Suddenly a tall, good looking young man walked up to me, took my hand and shook it. "Hi" he said "I'm Cliff Richard. I absolutely love your record. It's the first one I've bought in ages. Best of luck with it". He turned and walked away. I've loved him ever since.

Jonathan King

Cliff - we were a hoot and a holler away from paradise when my Dad drove us back from town in his silver-grey Mayflower with the red upholstery, and I took you out of your cover and lovingly laid you on the turntable of our nearly-new radiogram. Remember? And do you remember when I came to see you in The Young Ones at the Odeon Leicester, taken by my big sister to my first grown-up movie? And afterwards in the street, reluctant to go home, we filled in a questionnaire to say that, yes please, we would like to have a youth club, just like that one. For some reason it never happened, and we were stuck with the village hall and Reverend McCandless. Ah me, the exquisite agony of those days. Did I love you more than Bobby Vee, or the same? The two of you vied for my attentions on my bedroom wall, but I just couldn't bring myself to disappoint either one of you. I'm sorry if I've caused you pain. Congratulations and jubilations - rock on, Dreamboat.

Lou Wakefield

Music pundit, TV star, newspaper journalist with *The Sun*, hit-maker under many names, record company owner, **JK** is quite something.

Lou Wakefield has found considerable stage, television and radio success as a writer, director and actor.

the press at this period was unconcerned with raw facts and they convived to preserve show-biz myths.

Overall, Cliff was part of the early pop syndrome – the show-biz aim to make people happy, a period when everyone liked to be liked and the music 'biz' perpetuated a fun feel, even if beneath the apparently artless and guileless front there were shady deals, bad contracts and exploitation of artists. Few music stars received media maulings, though Haley and Presley did, and the Fifties early rockin' Cliff received a few roastings.

It's annoying for present-day appraisers of British music history to find Cliff relatively uncomplicated. Rather than praise Cliff, they often prefer to postulate gripping scenarios which, if they do not fall into the medically reconstituted Cliff image, centre on his ageing, being an 'old man' in pop terms. He is criticised for not causing 'change' to the music scene whatever the chosen decade – and Cliff does, after all span four and soon five – and for lacking a rebellious temperament. Cliff's deep Christian convictions of 20 or so years seems less interesting than some Sixties thoughts of his that he might make contact with his father through a spiritualist séance. They seem unhappy with his account of his physical youthfulness as being the result of years of disciplined living, with early nights, careful diet and proper exercise. Cliff seems to have failed abysmally to measure up to many a critic's criteria for being a rock star – especially the emphasis upon a working-class background, though Cliff's background in fact was more working-class than even Lennon's. There are no dope arrests, drink and driving offences, running off with someone else's wife, lewd public behaviour or insulting remarks to authority figures. Cliff has been a good boy, disappointing all those who either wish to indulge in their own fantasies of what being a rock star involves, or cannot conceive that there can be a good boy who is not boring. Said Cliff, 'There's this fake thing about the rock 'n' roll image that you have to swear and spit at your audience. I'm an enigma only because I don't fit the bill. I'm not mentioning any names, but I don't mess up the first-class cabin of a jumbo jet with marmalade and I don't throw TV sets out of the window.'

He did cause some early havoc in theatres, but deep down Cliff was never a wild figure. 'At home there was always discipline,' and he tells of how coming home late one night, he was locked out and had to find shelter in the coal-bunker until his father decided he had learnt his lesson. When Cliff found early fame and some money, he quickly moved his parents out of their council house and into a semi-detached North London residence before he bought a large family house in Essex. Although at one time he had a flat in London's Marylebone High Street, he would always return home, until

Sue Townsend's books on Adrian Mole have topped the British best selling lists.

Carole Hayman is an actress, playwright and top ten selling author.

MYTHS OF THE EARLY SIXTIES

They were halcyon days; we could smoke ourselves stupid on 'Senior Service' in complete ignorance of the big C waiting to grab hold of our innocent lungs. We could eat several lightly boiled eggs for breakfast and then have poached eggs for tea and scrambled eggs before going to bed. Nobody had heard of Cholesterol let alone know how to spell it. We thought, that butter and cream were good for us. We thought our legs looked good in American Tan stockings, and we truly believed that when Johnny Ray cried on stage he was overcome with an emotion too powerful to control.

We expected daily that the Russians would drop an atomic bomb on Leicester. We hurried home from school so that we could eat our tea before we died.

We went out to a youth club on sunday night dressed in a gingham skirt with a hoop of plastic in the hem, white high heels, the aforementioned orange stockings and a frilly white blouse. We demurely carried a straw basket over our white gloved wrist. We thought we looked mature and desirable and were astonished that the local sports jacketed youths did not swoon and fall at our winkle-pickered feet.

'Speed' was going downhill on our bicycles and 'pot' was what our mothers put jam in.

The vicar who ran the youth club informed us that we were teenagers and tried to enthuse us into exuberant displays on the dance floor. He swayed to the music inside his cassock and one embarrassing Sunday night he clapped his hands. We danced rigidly with eyes cast down. When the music stopped we sneaked and went to the lavatory to re-bouffant our hair, with sharp up and down movements of our pink plastic combs.

But, after hearing 'Living Doll' only three times on the youth club record player we were singing to the words. At first we loosened up on the church hall dance floor. We were taken in by his touch thought Cliff was an American. We were taken in by his Elvis Presley appearance, his black leather jacket, and his 'soundalike' accent.

Then the story broke that he was English and lived with his mum and was polite and nice.

We were only a <u>little</u> disappointed.

Sue Townsend

CAROLE HAYMAN

Dear Tony,

The Summer I was fourteen, Cliff was on Radio Luxembourg all day long. Me and my cousin played my tranny in the back of the car as we were driven through Cornwall. We preferred driving in her parent's car , as her father was a little deaf, mine would invariably say, 'Turn that bloody row down'. Little did he know he was spurning Pop's most enduring Giant! That Summer was hot and beautiful. The beaches and rocks of Cornwall burnt us brown (my nose peeled three times), we both fell in love with the same boy. I never knew his name (probably because of my peeled nose) and he wasn't specially good looking, but he walked along the wave edge with his tranny swinging and Cliff singing 'Got a rovin eye and that is why she satisfies my soul' and filled us with our first longing to be his, or anybody's, Living Doll.

Lots of love,

eventually he would find another family in Bill Latham and his mother Mamie, whom he came to love dearly.

And when it came down to it his mum worried over him and his two sisters missed him terribly. However, as Dorothy Webb was to concede, 'Despite his fame, he remains as always – a warm-hearted, affectionate boy with no airs or graces.' Those were her words in 1959. She sees no need to change them now, something quite evident to the milling guests at the Hurlingham Club as EMI and friends celebrated his 30 years in the business, and she gladly embraced her son. Of course she has little intimate memories that few others can share. 'When he was a boy he slipped on a patch of oil on the floor

Cliff Richard Movement - USA

All of us here in America would like fans everywhere to know, as well as Cliff himself, is that he means every bit as much to us as to any of his other fans and that we intend to continue supporting him as much as we possibly can. We are proud to share with Cliff fans everywhere our mutual affection for this wonderful man.

Sincerely,

Dixie Gonzalez,
President, CRM-USA

Dixie Gonzalez has held numerous important fan club posts with the US Cliff Richard fan club.

and fell, striking his head heavily. He was knocked completely out, and he bore the scar of this accident on his brow.' And did you know that his favourite toy from the time he learnt to walk was 'an ancient HMV portable gramophone, and he would wind it up himself and would always choose the same two records. The titles, I remember, were "Jersey Bounce" and "Shorty George".'

Soon after savouring early pop fame, Cliff would have less time for his nearest and dearest, and he would relish the attention of fans – 'their screams can be sweet music in my ears,' he said in early days – but even then his attitude towards his fans was not

24

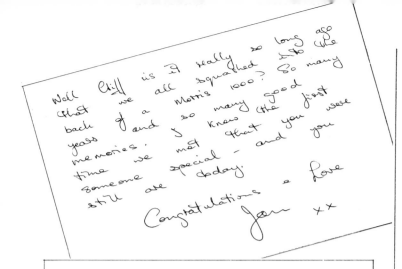

Well Cliff is it really so long ago that we all squashed into a Morris 1000? So many years back and so many good memories. I knew the first time we met that you were someone special – and you still are today.

Congratulations & love

Jan xx

THIRTY YEARS at the top is an incredible time! Our star did it! Cliff entered the music scene in August 1958, and now thirty years later he's even more popular than in 1958! What to think of venues like the National Exhibition Centre of Birmingham where all four concerts are sold out in a few days time? And what to think of having top-ten records in the charts (like "Some people") after nearly thirty years? When I first started a Cliff Richard Fan Club (for Dutch fans) back in 1961 I could not forsee that after 27 years I still would run one, the ICRM! And he don't seem to stop. When you see Cliff on stage you even can't believe that it is really his 30th year. Perhaps it's true. 30 years ago Cliff Richard did not exist and so Cliff must be 30 years of age! Thanks very much Cliff for those great 30 years, but we all hope you are able to continue for many years to come. Good luck and see you!

Anton

ICRM-Secretary

My job has given me the opportunity to work with many artists from Scott Walker to The Temptations, from Joe Cocker to Paul Young. The nicest person that I have ever met in the pop world is CLIFF RICHARD, he is as sincere and genuine as the press picture him.

With warm Christian greetings,

Christine

Christine Whitehead

Unlike many stars Cliff has not deserted Britain. However many times we have met Cliff or seen him in concert the thought of the next show always creates a nervous excitement in us which once again only proves what a great star Cliff is.

Diana Duffett
Cliff Richard Grapevine

Jan Vane was the first Cliff Richard Fan Club Secretary in the days when there was an 'official' club and is a great friend of his family.

Among other things **Christine** runs the Cliff United fan club and produces an excellent monthly magazine.

Grapevine is one of several successful nationwide Cliff fan clubs.

Anton Husmann founded the International Cliff Richard Movement. Countless Cliff fan groupings worldwide belong to this movement.

Fans are chums and friends – with Diana Duffett of Grapevine.

that of many rock stars. Hank Marvin has said, 'I never saw him try to take advantage of any of the girls who flocked backstage, and I think that was because he had a great deal of respect for his own sisters and his parents. A lot of people might mock the fact that he restrained himself, but I always thought it took more strength to do that than to abuse the privileged position he was in, like others did.'

The respect that Cliff has shown to his fans is one of the reasons why he has retained their affection over the years. Eileen Edwards, who runs one of Cliff's largest fan club branches, has been a fan since she was 12 years old. Inside the theatre during his performance fans come and bring flowers, cakes, and small mementoes to the front, and in an appropriate moment or song, Cliff will graciously take these expressions of love and thanks. Your sophisticated hardened rock commentator finds all this unbelievable. Gill Snow, long-time frontline assistant-cum-secretary in the Cliff Richard Organisation, says he keeps some gifts, perhaps one cake from the many, and shares it with the guys backstage; the rest go to those in need. Fans come in all ages, sometimes it's become a generation matter, as middle-aged women come to remember the old days, with their teenage daughters in tow.

In the rather more august circles of the music professionals there is universal respect for Cliff's dedication. His career professionalism will be seen in other relevant chapters, but in personal terms all speak highly of his overall attitudes. Ted King has been a DJ for

Radio Luxembourg and British Forces Broadcasting, and lays claim to have been the first DJ to spin a Beatle record. 'I had left Lux and Cliff was at the Palladium with The Shadows. I went backstage to say hello. A well-known star of the time came into the dressing room where there were also lots of young ladies. He told a rather blue story. Cliff rounded on him and said, "I will not have it in my dressing room, cut it out or get out." DJs spin records all day long and don't always worry what they are playing, but I always felt good at playing Cliff; he's such a nice guy.'

Ron White, the executive responsible for the A and R department at EMI, who was also general manager of the company, tells me, 'Cliff has always been the same courteous person, no matter how rapidly he grew. Unlike so many shooting stars he has always kept his feet on the ground. I think I admire him most for fighting the temptations that were put in his way at the beginning of his career. He could so easily have succumbed to drink, drugs and easy sex, which were certainly offered in the beginning. He has a great sense of humour and sense of family. It was wonderful to watch him with his mother and sister when they attended the various EMI publicity functions. The family were always invited to those affairs and Cliff always made sure that they were comfortable and well looked after before he got involved in the event.'

Brian Southall is now Director of Public Relations and Communications, EMI World-wide, but during the Seventies he was Cliff's press officer. Cliff was never fond of those newspapers that had an obsession with his private life and, according to Southall, 'their unique ability to misquote him'. His solution to the problem was not to talk to them and Cliff is a man, who, once he has determined a course of action, will steadfastly stand by his decision. Southall sees Cliff's clear-sighted determination as instrumental in his longevity. He recalls travelling to see Cliff in Belfast on one of his regular gospel tours. 'He played a solo set, as his band chose not to travel to Northern Ireland. It was a day spent in the company of armed soldiers and the concert began in mid-afternoon for security reasons, but Cliff was never not going to do the show . . . that would have meant giving in to outside forces and disappointing his fans.'

Peter Vince, one of the star engineers at EMI, and still very much part of that famous recording studio complex, can recall people having to go and stop Lennon walking off the roof of the building, so drugged and so high was he, but with Cliff there was never anything like that. 'Alas, for some, Cliff is too good to be true; it just happens that he is a nice guy. I never heard him swear and he would apologise when he was wrong, and never adopt a prima donna image. I have been in the studio with him countless times, and in the cafe that was near the Abbey Road complex, and never known him turn nasty.'

Vince exhibits great affection for Cliff and some of this comes through Cliff's personal attitude. 'He has always stuck by me and others will say the same thing. At Christmas I always got something from Cliff and he has carried on doing this. The scale may be less from years ago when we worked closely with each other but he still remembers and it means a great deal to me and other people.'

Radio One's Controller Johnny Beerling is another who is enthusiastic in applauding Cliff's essential 'niceness and goodness' and sees it as one element in his survival. He talks of the Richard charm, ultimate professionalism, spectacular achievement and adds, like others, that 'Cliff's always seemed too good to be true,' but notes how he has worked hard at improving what were some of his deficiencies, such as the way 'he would gabble, speak too fast, run words together when he was talking on radio.'

Songwriter-producer Alan Tarney is backed by many others when he adds to all this Cliff's ongoing enthusiasm, something that has not been jaded by age. For Cliff, unlike some very famous artists, the primary motivation for the constant recording and touring is not to pay tax bills, or maintain a very high standard of living. He is as enthusiastic now as he was in 1958. He still wants to see his records in the top ten, and is genuinely pleased to receive yet another award, whether it be for the best-dressed British male or for making people feel good. 'It's so catchy,' says Tarney of this continuing Richard love for what he does. 'In a way, for a producer and songwriter he is a dream. He has such a good voice and technique. He sings a song the way you think it will sound, you don't have to spend hours coaching him, persuading him. When he senses something is good he can't wait to record it, he almost wills a record into its final form.' Cliff, for Tarney, is someone who immediately understands a song, and attacks it, finding his way round it remarkably quickly.

That is a view shared by other Cliff songwriters, for instance Guy Fletcher and Doug Flett. Apart from the obvious fact that they enjoy writing for Cliff because it automatically means some form of financial success, there is from them the same professional respect, and I detect here, as with others, that they are genuine fans of Cliff. Doug Flett recalls the time they called at the Peter Gormley office with a new song that they hoped Peter would pass on to Cliff. 'Peter merely said, "he's in the back room with Hank, so try your luck." ' This they did. 'You can always tell with Cliff, he has this sixth sense that something is just right and on this occasion it took all of three minutes for him to say he would record it.' The song was 'Through The Eyes Of A Child' and it gave Cliff a Top 20 hit early in 1970. The best-known song they've written for Cliff has been the 1973 Eurovision entry 'Power To All Our Friends'. Says Doug, 'I remember he was terribly disappointed that he didn't win, as we all were. On the other hand it was in the Top 5 in 14 countries. I can recall that Cliff was terribly apologetic, as though it had something to do with him.' Fletcher comments, 'I think he's unique, I don't want to compare him with anyone.'

Some might say the word 'fan' is inappropriate, when it relates to the reaction of other artists, yet most professionals would confess that there are those they admire, and in terms of their profession these are the ones who perform well technically. From innumerable conversations with fellow artists it is obvious to me that in any poll conducted among singers, songwriters and producers (with the precondition that they began their career before the Eighties) Cliff would most likely come out on top. Many of these artists have their own story to tell, and some have done so here in their tributes.

Closest of all to Cliff have been The Shadows, backing group and friends since the first years. They gave Cliff stability and when this was combined with their own zany humour aiding and abetting his, it was a winning stage partnership that would extend beyond recording and 'live' concerts into pantomime and film. Says Cliff, 'I guess I was one of the first to use a group as more than just backing. In the early days we never discussed ending the relationship even if with all our success people kept thinking it would end. Certainly we discussed *not* ending it hundreds of times. I remember we made up our minds that we would never part because it seemed silly to break up something that was so precious to us and the fans.' This working relationship was pretty exceptional though outside work there was not a great deal of mixing. But of course they were often together for extremely lengthy periods when they toured the world. Brian Bennett tells me that, 'there were so many terrific times and when I get asked to sort out individual happenings I sometimes get a blank, and it was some time ago! There was no time for egos, and anyway that would get boring amongst people working closely together. We were never treated by Cliff as though we were some accessory to his own success.'

Brian, discussing relationships within the group and with Cliff says, 'It was important we didn't spend lots of time together, too many groups do this and so they never come together feeling fresh, like the beginning of a new school term! I think we were so different as people and that helped.' And how does he view Cliff, apart from all the usual things that people say? 'Well, he has remained single and so that has made a difference;

Looks a trifle like Leo Sayer here, he jumps in photos too.

the rest of us have had relationships and families. He has the extra time for doing things. He is the kind of person who fills every hour. He doesn't throw tantrums; argue, yes, but that's quite a different thing. I think Cliff has found enormous happiness. Here he is, 30 years and still going, everything nonstop and I'm sure he is ever progressing onward, and most important, forward.'

Throughout the 1960s the main British music paper was the *New Musical Express* with a circulation passing 300,000. The news editor and feature writer was Derek Johnson. The Johnson of the late Eighties is overflowing with memories of early Cliff and The Shadows. Should Johnson have made certain overtures, then the Cliff story might have been considerably different.

> Bandleader Eric Winstone, for many years the doyen of dance music at Butlin's in Clacton, phoned to tell me there was a promising young singer performing in the camp's new Rock 'n' Roll Ballroom who was looking for a manager. I drove down to have a look at him and, although impressed by his enthusiasm, I was doubtful about his long-term potential. After all, at that time there were scores of young rockers trying to make their presence felt, on the crest of the Presley wave. Who could tell which of them would strike it lucky and, even then, how long it would last?
>
> So I passed up the opportunity, and that was probably the biggest mistake I've made in the whole of my career. Because the lad I could have taken under my wing was Cliff Richard, accompanied by his group, then The Drifters.
>
> I was to see a lot of Cliff in the years to come. And to this day, he still chides me good-naturedly about that boob.

The *NME* and Cliff had a lengthy period of accord, though not without occasional acrimony, and Johnson, doubtless with countless thousands, recalls the many annual Poll Winners Concerts at the Wembley Arena, then the Empire Pool.

> One year, the bill also featured The Beatles and The Rolling Stones – what a show it was! When three such major attractions appear in the same concert, there's usually an argument about who should be the closing act, but none of them fancied it in this case – they all wanted to get away before the end, to avoid being mobbed when the audience turned out. I felt sorry for the group who landed the task of closing the show, because they were a total anti-climax.

Johnson's popularity with Cliff and The Shads was clearly shown when they all turned up at his wedding reception and laid on a brilliant act for the guests.

He would also spend time with The Shads and Cliff while they were filming in Sitges, near Barcelona, and he recalls the time when they all decided they would go to a bullfight: 'Cliff hadn't seen one before and was reluctant to go, but eventually he did so because he didn't want to spoil the party. But he walked out, sickened, after the first bull was killed. And I have to confess I joined him.'

Keith Skues encountered the Cliff and Shadows team when he was broadcasting for the Africa Forces Broadcasting Service, based in Nairobi. The boys came to Kenya in 1963 for a concert to support underprivileged children. Skues remembers that nothing was too much trouble for Cliff. 'He gave me at least three hours of a very busy schedule to record a marathon interview. The Shadows also participated. The two big names in Kenya in the early 1960s were Elvis and Cliff. There was no chance Elvis would visit, but Cliff did and won the hearts of every teenager, black and white, in the country.'

Thinking back, from the vantage point of some 25 years later, as a writer and broadcaster who has seen many come and few remain in the volatile world of pop, Skues says:

> He looked good. He sounded good. He was a polished performer. He had a varied offering. There was a genuine air about him. He was in no way snobbish. He had professionalism. He had time for everyone – broadcasters, listeners and the general public.
>
> By 1963 I had worked with many big names in the pop world, but none were so charming and professional off the set as Cliff. He had my highest admiration then and today I have not in any way altered my feelings.

It is Cliff's 'family' image that appeals to many people when they finally come to ponder some of the underlying reasons for Cliff's success and, more so, his career longevity. There is, as already mentioned, his loyal mum, proud as punch of her son, his three sisters, who look rather like him and still obviously find it all exciting that their brother should be someone so special. For his eldest sister, Donna, especially, it's a long way back to the time when she would have a hot meal ready for him and the boys when they returned to his flat in Marylebone High Street after an exhausting gig and accompanying travel. 'She took her duties so seriously, keeping the flat clean, sewing and mending for me. She got tired but she was happy.' Donna was useful beyond measure when it came to songs. Tito Burns or Norrie Paramor would send over tapes of new tunes and Donna could take down the lyrics of a number having only heard it twice.

Cliff's mother's attitude to her famous son is not wholly adulatory: 'Now I'm the one who criticises him most, although I know he doesn't accept criticism from me. I think he knows in show business that you've got to be criticised but I don't think he likes it. I think that is a weak point in him. He gets terribly annoyed if someone is criticising him completely wrongly.'

His close friend Bill Latham would add another Cliff trait: 'He's an exceptionally good talker; he fires words out; he's not so good at listening.' Of course, listening is never easy for someone who is blessed with a very quick brain. Hanne Jordan, photographer, journalist and eventually friend of Cliff's says, 'I like quick thinkers; in this business to survive you have to be one, and Cliff is such an example. I have seen him moody and sometimes he forgets he has a smile but not for long; he makes life easy for those working with him. He is never without an answer and I have been to many press callings in many countries. I have never seen him thrown. You know he is always concerned and wants to please. But he is nobody's fool.'

Another member of the inner sanctum is Gill Snow. Her association with Cliff goes back to 1972. Originally she joined Tear Fund and worked with Bill Latham, who was at one time director of this relief agency, whose work and association with Cliff is described in full later in this book. Then in 1978, she moved into the Cliff office. Gill says, 'He's someone with an equable character, incredibly patient with people. I have seen him really hustled sometimes, especially at the stage door, but even here he

That nice teenager first met in 1957 is still the same approachable
gentleman thirty one years on. Thanks,mate, for the memories
and the friendship. Oh, and the beans on toast are always available
at our house...

JOHN FOSTER

John Foster was Cliff's first manager, the man who touted his wares when Cliff was unknown.

doesn't forget common courtesies. He's easy to work for, although the job can be very demanding.' She has observed some changes in Cliff over the years. 'I think he calls the tune much more, and he will say no, although normally I think we can assess the things he will want to do. He puts his foot down a lot more! I know it may sound corny and the kind of thing I should say but I can only say it is true, it is a privilege to work for him. And people do stay around.'

In her last remark Gill approaches the essential reason for Cliff's ability to stay around. Talent yes, most certainly, oceans of the stuff, but many profusely talented artists have come and gone. Yet Cliff continues to work with people who have known him for over 25 years, something unique in the music business. These people have become another family to add to his long-time friendship with Bill Latham and, until she died Bill's mum Mamie, often referred to by Cliff as his 'second mum'. There is Peter Gormley, the guiding hand since 1961; and David Bryce, at first road manager for The Shadows and later moving into all areas that have involved Cliff, from chauffering to light shows, and now, with Peter Gormley's partial retirement, Cliff's manager. Here, you have two exceptional men.

In 1961, for a variety of reasons, Cliff's management structure was typical of the frenetic

Haven't had a hit record, but I have been with
EMI 3 years longer than you - Best Wishes always,

Vic Lanza

Vic Lanza was Senior A&R Manager with EMI records until his retirement in March 1989. EMI has had continuous artist relationship with Cliff since 1958.

32

pop scene, with good people coming and going, and Cliff soldiering on. Cliff still had his mates from those early changes of managerial cast, and not all had become lost because of disagreement, but the entry of Peter Gormley was manna from heaven. He was quiet but forceful, well able to appraise and see through the thin veneer of truth that sometimes seems to hover over popland. Gormley was already managing The Shadows so it was automatic after Tito Burns and Cliff's dad failed to see eye to eye that he should be the candidate and winner. Originally Peter was a journalist, after which he went into film journalism, and eventually to entertainment, where he met Frank Ifield. Frank's early bow in on EMI's Columbia label was rather subdued, but once his 'I Remember

---

NICK PAGE

I'm not qualified to make musical judgements.
Cliff shows supreme professionalism, undiminished
creativity and unerring instincts in his work.
He knows what he wants to say, and is able to
say it honestly, directly and compellingly.

All this would ensure that he is held in
respect. The fact that he is genuinely and
widely loved stems from deeper personal
qualities, such as his warmth and generosity.

Whether in public or in private his genuineness
shows through. He is a man of integrity — and
as those of us of his generation would want to
affirm, a <u>young</u> man of integrity.

God bless you,
Yours

Nick   *or more Officially Nick Page.*

Nick Page has fronted countless radio programmes and is well known in Christian arts circles.

You' hit the top spot in 1961 there was no stopping him for a while. And while Ifield exploded into the big-time, The Shadows were running strong, as was Cliff. Peter suddenly had a trio of hit-makers.

Frank told me in the autumn of 1988, 'It was tremendous. Obviously Peter was elated. At first I didn't get to meet Cliff but I do remember feeling very embarrassed on one occasion. Some kids had won a magazine competition to be with me and we would go and meet Cliff in his dressing room, for they had been given seats to see his show at the Palladium. I didn't fancy the moment when I would meet Cliff and the young people might realise that I didn't know Cliff, for they assumed I must. Well, we got there, and Cliff greeted me like a long-lost friend!'

Doug Flett would see Peter as a 'great man, full of integrity, good for Cliff,' while Alan Tarney sees him and David Bryce both exhibiting the same gentle, persuasive and forceful management. 'The whole organisation has been fantastic. Why are so many

THERE ARE MANY SINGERS IN THIS WORLD.
THERE ARE MANY PERFORMERS. THERE ARE FEW
GREAT STARS. EVEN FEWER CAN CLAIM TO BE
ALL OF THESE THINGS. CLIFF RICHARD IS ONE
HIS ENTHUSIASM AND PROFESSIONALISM A
TOTALLY INFECTIOUS AND THIS COUNTRY CA
COUNT ITSELF PRIVELEGED TO HAVE SUC
AN ARTIST.

A UNIQUE TALENT.

Possibly someone famous! We're still working it out

Cliff my Dear, congratulations on your 30 years in Show Biz.. What a bright light you have been, heres to 30 more years. With Love.
Ruby Murray.

Cliff Richard has been, without doubt, a driving force and a great ambassador for Great Britain in the pop world for the last 30 years - an exceptional man with an exceptional career!

Kind regards,

Marty Wilde

Ruby Murray was one of Britain's major recording stars of the Fifties. She continues her entertainment career.

Marty was one of Britain's most successful pop artistes in the late 1950s-early 1960s. He is the father of delectable Kim Wilde, now a major world pop star.

34

careers short? Simple, see what's behind them. I'll tell you what's so amazing about these two and the others who have been with Cliff for so long – they've been devoted to Cliff. They all work to keep him at number one. Peter and David have never flagged to keep him at the top. And all this must have given him so much confidence and allowed him to get on with things.'

Vince recalls how Peter would pop into the studio at EMI, to see how things were going. 'He would listen for a moment, say, "I don't think much of that" or "That's not very good, you know where I am." ' Peter for a long time had a flat near the Abbey Road studio complex, within yards of the famous Zebra crossing, immortalised in a Beatle album cover, upon which numerous Japanese and Americans walk every summer so that they might be photographed and, as a sideline, cause traffic tailbacks. 'Peter has been a powerful man in quiet way, often of few words, and he might merely say something like "great new single" and it was the way he inflected his speech that told you if it was that good.' Vince smiles when he recalls how Peter would use the word 'Look' and people would not be too sure whom he was directing this word towards. 'He would go straight to the point. He liked a song to have a melody and if not, he would just say "no tune"; he had the first say in those days. But he was never nasty, even if what he said might be upsetting, following upon lots of effort.' While it was useful to Peter that he lived next door at 1 Albany House, (not now) it had a bonus for the boys 'He was among the first to have a colour TV and we would go round and squint, perhaps it was the set's tuning!'

The combined efforts of Peter Gormley and David Bryce also win applause from David Winter, the Head of BBC Religious Broadcasting, a great friend of Cliff's and the man who was influential in the eventual direction of Cliff's religious commitment in the Sixties. Winter, surveying Cliff's career, and Gormley and Bryce's part in it, says, 'It's been quite amazing, the length of time must be unique in pop history. But if you are going to write of what they've done you should not forget Norrie Paramor; he was a second father to Cliff.'

Paramor is mentioned later in the book but suffice to say here that he was one of the great figures of EMI recording. His daughter Carolyn (Carrie) Ledingham recalls,

I was 12 or 13. I was very into pop music, and with Dad being who he was I was close to what was happening in the music world. EMI was a very successful company. I can remember Dad talking about him, jiving with the door handle to 'Move It', and wondering if it was better than Elvis, for I was a great Elvis fan. I went to Butlin's, later to Cliff's house and I remember we had some lovely gatherings at home with Cliff and others, including Vera Lynn, and Dad would play the piano and everyone would sing along. And people would let their hair down. They were not big organised dos that you associated with hotels and such like where the pop industry was always holding receptions, just homely and terrific. Nothing disruptive, just great fun . . . It was all very friendly in those days. I don't know if it's the same now.

Cliff would come to her engagement party and then her wedding. She remembers her engagement party: 'My husband-to-be had the same initials as Cliff, and I recall when

Cliff arrived he walked in and saw the cake with the big letters CR, and said 'that's for me?' in a voice that suggested he thought it was, he was funning around.

Cliff was different from other rock stars she met, 'Some you felt were a bit stuck-up, even boring, not so Cliff, for he was always so friendly and natural. I'm sure it's one of the reasons why people have wanted to work with him and of course why he has lasted so long. I really don't think there's anyone quite like him. I think he has deserved everything that has come his way.' And her thoughts would be echoed by many over the years and presumably as long as Cliff decides it's worthwhile continuing his career.

Lynne Kitt, President of the Cliff Richard Movement of New Zealand, says, 'He has endured because he has earned the respect of his admirers. One returns to concerts time and time again because one has learned they will be superb entertainment. One buys new recordings because one recognises the true craftsmanship which has gone into them. One has really to hold affection for the man behind all that, because he is honest; he really does care, and his attitude is a breath of fresh air in the often rather sordid and hyped pop/rock world.' She sees Cliff as someone who is totally professional without being 'slick', and has noticed a change in recent time, 'In latter years Cliff has presented each song as a separate entity and become quite theatrical (and convincing) with each performance.'

When I met Helen Meyers, the Australian Fan Club President, in London, she remarked that Cliff has no difficulty selling out in Australia, for he has been one of the major British pop stars on the Australian scene for a long time. But why has he lasted for so long? 'Well, he is a great performer, quite spectacular, his music is so great and of all artists I know he has this lovely rapport with the audience.' Thousands of miles away from Helen and Lynne is Bridget Bowles, secretary of the Cliff Richard Fan Club of London & Surrey. Bridget says Cliff has lasted so long because 'it must be that he enjoys what he does. It soon becomes very apparent when boredom sets in, the quality and quantity goes. The other priceless quality Cliff has is the ability to change and learn new techniques – an all important talent in the world of entertainment where trends are constantly changing. He has not stagnated but has learnt, no doubt by listening and working hard. However, this brings us round to complete the circle because his love for rock 'n' roll has given him the incentive to look at what he does and ask questions about his own performance in live concerts and recordings.'

Not unexpectedly, critics have been fascinated by Cliff's career longevity. Some have seen his approach as 'either very naive or expertly disingenuous' and at least one writer, Susan Hill, says 'talking to him is like banging your head against a cotton-wool wall.' She believes perhaps this is all part of the 'survival' mechanism:

> Success when very young, a cocoon of wealth and spiritual security, an army of materially protective managers and executives who buffet him from grubby reality. Many pop stars boast about how long it is since they travelled by bus or tube, but it must be a long time since Cliff even spoke to a nasty or unfriendly person (journalists excepted). Everywhere he goes, people are pleased to see him.

Personally, I think there is a germ of truth in what she says, but no more. My overall impression of Cliff, when compared with a general view gained from interviewing many pop stars from the late 1960s onwards, is that he has a greater sense of reality than almost any of the others. In his case, for instance, a sense of realism has come from his religious and charitable expeditions, and certainly in those first times, the change of managers, the death of his father, his very basic questioning of religious precepts have hardly allowed him to become cocooned.

I would rather plead the case that can be drawn from some of the preceding copy, namely that he has been fortunate in finding two exceptional men to guide his career, Peter Gormley and David Bryce. Gormley and Bryce are not wishy-washy individuals, nor have they been people embued with an over-protective zeal; and they do lend the blunt word when they feel it is needed. But it is true that Cliff can both break through normal pop star conventions and at the same time follow them. Susan Hill's article in *Melody Maker* of 3 November 1979 did not please some Cliff followers, because of its critical and cutting edge, but I read it also as one that paid him intelligent respect. She instanced well the way Cliff can break general taboos, for example at 1 a.m. one morning, when an 'earnest-looking' German teenager suddenly appears and asks if she can talk with him. 'Quite unselfconsciously, and with polite patience, he listens to her stilted questions and gives serious, detailed answers.' How many other stars would make themselves publicly available to meet the ordinary fan? He follows pop conventions on occasions doubtless, punishing himself, giving interview after interview and perhaps saying little that is new and different. I can remember an editor of a music paper once saying to me something like, 'Why do you want to interview him, what's new?' Perhaps little on that occasion, other times something. Who knows? Certainly, it seems true to me that, if someone is to last in the fast changing media personality world, then invariably at times the shutters must come down, the 'autopilot' must run things, and though the words may flow fast and furious, they've been said before. Susan Hill admits 'Cliff seems to know himself very well, which isn't to say that he shows himself, despite all the chin-grasping candour and intensity . . . he knows just what to say, how to protect himself, when to stop.'

Some will say his consumate professionalism carries him through, sometimes at least, as Russell Davies wrote in the *Sunday Times*, 29 November 1981: 'Today, the Cliff Richard stage performance is a sort of lively professorial demonstration of past styles, and very well done. Having acquired the versatility of a session-singer, he can manage most sorts of material . .'

Cliff's sheer professionalism is obviously one answer to the question as to why he is still at the top. But for many it is Cliff the person, first and foremost, who holds so many good memories for them. As his first-ever fan club secretary, Jan Vane, says, 'May he continue to make as many people happy in the future as he has done in the past.'

Billboard
Billboard Limited

All of us at Billboard have watched Cliff Richard's distinguished career with great interest and admiration over the years. He is a true professional, dedicated to his art of entertaining the public and preserving the highest musical standards and personal integrity. He is a living embodiment of all that is best in the world of show business; and a welcome demonstration that sometimes nice guys do come first.

Mike Hennessey,

Mike Hennessey,
International Editorial Director.

MUSIC WEEK

If ever there was an award – voted for by dealers – to the most consistent selling artist over the past 30 years, Cliff would win by a mile. In whatever direction his career has developed he's always been a nice little earner as well as presenting the most wholesome and professional aspect of pop music to the public across several generations of fans.
One note of jealousy – I would wish to look that good after 30 years in the music business.

David Dalton

Editor, Music Week.

for THE RECORD

The loyalty shown to Cliff Richard by several generations of record buyers must make many retailers wish more artists had such longevity, popularity and credibility. The problem is that Cliff is unique,

John Tobler
Joint Editor,
For The Record,

March,1989

3 ON THE RECORD

Since this is basically a happy story, it would be pleasant to begin this chapter of Cliff's vinyl triumphs with a scene of tranquil harmony. But Cliff's first recording was a nerve-racking affair. It was agreed that 'Move It' should be one of the two titles, the other being 'Schoolboy Crush'. But then it had to be decided which song should be the 'A-side', the one that DJs should play and of which the media should be aware. That was indeed a vexing enough problem, but there was another to frazzle the nerves even more.

This other problem was simple. When they pressed the first test copies it was noticed that the credits had one major mistake: the artist was listed as Cliff Richards. When Harry R. Webb became Cliff Richard, it was guitarist and songwriter Ian Samwell who realised that most people would assume that it was Richards and not Richard and that this would mean that they would then have to correct what had been said or written. Indirectly, this would get his name known and talked about. But for the record company to have fallen into the trap? That was another thing. Stan Edwards, one of Cliff's early managers, was one of the few to have a copy. Sadly, this treasured object is now in three pieces, having been sat on by a young Edwards many years ago! The name was corrected to Richard on subsequent copies, and everyone got it right eventually.

As to the problem of the title A-side: the first promptings were towards 'Schoolboy Crush', for 'Move It' had been a late consideration. Neither of the original 'demo' numbers, 'Breathless' and 'Lawdy Miss Clawdy', were favoured by Norrie Paramor, recording manager for Columbia, part of the HMV group of labels. When Norrie took both recordings home he found that his daughter had other views. Young Carolyn heard a test disc of metal thinly coated with shellac, not intended for too many spins, and wore it out. She went for Ian Samwell's song 'Move It'. So did Jack Good of the new ITV television show 'Oh Boy!' Others shared their judgment and enthusiasm and it should be added that Norrie Paramor was not opposed to the choice. In July 1958 he told Pat Doncaster of the *Daily Mirror*, arguably the first national journalist to pick up on Cliff, 'I just can't see the kids giving up these personalities with a beat.'

However, it was expected that the first plays would be for 'Schoolboy Crush'. So it was that a young Cliff playing at Butlin's gathered with group and friends in a holiday

Mike Hennessey runs the British office of the American magazine *Billboard*, the world's leading journal in music entertainment.

David Dalton edits Europe's leading music industry paper *Music Week*.

John Tobler is a prominent British music journalist and author and is Joint-Editor of the trade paper *For The Record*.

chalet to hear the record played on Radio Luxembourg. To their surprise, the Luxembourg disc jockey played 'Move It'. Norrie's daughter was thrilled; so were the boys. It had an immediate impact upon the listener and sales were to become more than a trickle. Mickie Most, one of Britain's best-known record producers, recalls 'Move It' well. Cliff kept filling the 2 I's coffee bar juke-box with coins to hear the record. Opposite the 2 I's was another cafe with a juke-box, and Cliff, with some help, would arrange for both to be playing his record at the same time, doubling the volume and making his sound crash from one side of the street to the other! He rather liked the whole thing, did Cliff.

Obviously, 'Move It' was a very good record, but even if it excited the likes of Jack Good, no one thought it would come to be seen as a classic record, or that it would sound just as lively and vigorous some 30 years onward. Nobody thought about the future in those days; each step was taken as if there were to be no others. Each moment was for enjoyment, but certainly Cliff could hardly contain his excitement when his very first disc eventually reached number two in the charts.

That was something no one could ignore, although record veterans were as well used to one-hit wonders then as they are now. All the same, it meant that Cliff was news, and this brought him enormous media attention, so much so that Cliff on one occasion collapsed into bed, failed to wake up to the alarm the following morning, and even found himself telling his mother, 'Mum, I can't stand this life any more. If it's going to be like this I'd sooner go back and get my old job at the factory.' Cliff, talking about 'Move It', said: 'It was luck, I think, because my second record was awful – "High Class Baby".' He was to rerecord 'Move It' in 1983 for the Silver Anniversary set: 'I wasn't going to do it, but my band said, "If you are going to do old rock and roll, you have just got to

'Early' words on Cliff from his beloved **Norrie**, producer of so many hits.

Carrie is the daughter of the late **Norrie Paramor** and the girl who suggested Move It should be the first A-side of a Cliff record.

```
                    "C L I F F"
                  by Norrie Paramor


Columbia, and from the outset I developed a strong liking for Cliff's

singing, personality, and indeed for Cliff himself.  I have met his

parents and sister, and believe me they are a really nice family.

Cliff always pays attention to what his father and mother say, and

he has a great quality of humanity which is a rare commodity among

some Artistes these days.  Yes I am glad I signed Cliff Richard for

Columbia.  This is easy for me to say of course as Cliff has been

such a tremendous success on records, but had his success been not

so strong I would still have been glad Cliff was on Columbia.
```

It seems hard to imagine that 30 years have passed since I 'jived' (with the door handle!!) to the strains of "MOVE IT". The long professional association enjoyed by Cliff and my late father resulted in an enduring friendship, which extends to our whole family, who join me in wishing you continued success Cliff - here's to the next 30 years!

Carrie

do 'Move It'." They reminded me once again that "Move It" was the very first British rock song.'

Obviously, by 1983 Cliff was very much aware of the longevity of his career and of the record feats that were unique to him. However, 1958 was just a start, albeit an impressive one. It hardly needs saying that Cliff is out on his own when it comes to the question of which British recording artist has had the most singles released, the most albums issued, the most chart successes in both areas, and the longest recording career. He simply routs the opposition in these categories. And even outside his central areas Cliff can make unique claims. For instance, he has recorded hit duets with no fewer than five artists, and no other singer has had hits with more artists.

Cliff was the first British artist to have a record that immediately went to number one. This same record, 'The Young Ones', was the first in British record history to have a prerelease order in excess of 500,000 copies. And then again, he had at least one Top 10 hit every year between 1958 and 1970. Here, the only person who can challenge him is Elvis Presley, and even the king of rock 'n' roll could only extend his Top 10 success for 11 consecutive years, from 1956 to 1966. Apart from Elvis, there is no artist, no act in British record history who can even begin to touch Cliff. That conclusion does not come from bias; it is plain and simple fact. And it is quite remarkable.

By the end of 1988, Cliff had had 99 solo singles and 52 albums released, but it should be said that these figures represent the UK only. Elsewhere, there have been other releases and collections, and in British terms the album total does not include special compilations, some of which appeared for the religious company, Word, and others which were box-set issues, for instance, for EMI's World Records company. None of the latter include otherwise unreleased material. There must be many who would appreciate an issue of Cliff recordings only marketed in such countries as Japan. For dedicated fans, the ultimate in live recordings is *Live in Japan 72*. Another useful release is *Japan Tour 1974*, which was made available on import and so is not as valuable.

Although the factual data is most impressive, it should not be assumed that Cliff is the richest star as far as recording profits are concerned, he probably comes considerably down the earnings table. The really huge earners are those who write hit songs, and who preferably have had two of their compositions, one on either side of a single, to pick up all the royalties; those who have written all the songs on an album; who have produced and possibly arranged the music on their records; and, most importantly, who have enjoyed considerable American success. On this basis, it can be seen quite clearly that Cliff does not meet the requirements. He has written rather more songs than people give him credit for, but few of these have been hits. His financial take has been as an artist. His USA track record has not been without some high chart positions, but it is a pale shadow of his attainment in Britain, and indeed in some European territories. The lack of real recognition in the States has had severe side-effects, taking from Cliff the possibility of huge earnings from concerts and, more so, from paraphernalia, the latter now being in many instances a higher earning area than any other, including record sales. All this doesn't mean he is poor; to suggest that would be absurd. His record royalties have been wisely invested, but compared, say, to a Paul McCartney or Elton John, Cliff is a relatively low earner.

Behind the impressive Cliff statistics there lies, not unexpectedly, many a story, and not all of Cliff's recordings have fetched untainted praise from the man himself. But, while he may believe his second single 'High Class Baby' was awful, the view is not shared by all. He was somewhat surprised during a 1983 interview with the knowledgeable Capital DJ, Roger Scott, later of Radio One, to hear Scott say he thought the song terrific, and that he had loved it just as much, if not more, than 'Move It'.

In early times, as often happens, there was a degree of uncertainty about what to release, and even when decisions had been made, they might be reversed. At one time, the fifth Cliff single was down as 'Choppin' 'n' Changin'', coupled with 'Dynamite'. As it happened, 'Dynamite' became the sixth single, but was coupled with the catchy song 'Travellin' Light'. Around this time Cliff and The Drifters had made their first LP, simply called *Cliff*. It was released on 10 April 1959, cost 34s. 1½d (about £1.70), and had a dreamy coloured picture of Cliff on the cover. Thirteen of the songs featured Cliff, and there were three by The Drifters. In those far-off days companies believed that an album could contain a large number of tracks. The Drifters also had a single available, entitled 'Feelin' Fine' coupled with 'Don't Be A Fool', with vocals by Bruce Welch and Hank Marvin.

Stan Edwards remembers the recording session for 'Choppin' 'n' Changin'' and 'Dynamite'. It was a long affair. Although the rehearsal studio was pretty large, the full amplified sound let loose would completely drown Cliff's voice, so he had a big task in keeping the right key and concentrating on the phrasing of the lyrics. An initial rehearsal had lasted four hours. The actual session to lay down the tracks was quite a marathon, and even by the tenth take Choppin' was not the right sound and Cliff was drinking plenty of water and perspiring freely.

Edwards recalls: 'Halfway through the fifteenth take, the words left his mind completely, and with a look of sheer amazement on his face, he waved the boys into silence, saying something like "I've forgotten the lyrics", or words to that effect.'

This moment heralded another 'tea' break, to the pleasure of Bruce Welch, who, it seems, in early times favoured the word 'Tea' at all times and in all places. Bruce would shout 'Tea' at the top of his voice whenever the situation seemed apt. In this instance, Edwards says, the Welch remedy worked, for once back in the studio from the canteen, a new vitality could be noted and the eventual playback was considered fabulous. 'Dynamite' proved less of a problem: it took five or six takes, no more, and a day that had begun early in the morning closed at 12.45. The next move was an oft-repeated one after recording sessions – all retired to a slap-up feed at Cliff's favourite West End restaurant, the Lotus House in Edgware Road. It appears that the Bruce Welch cry of 'Tea' was to be heard but this time it was Chinese! On some occasions, relief from the day's recording stress was found in taking a trip to the coffee bar at London Airport and observing the first transatlantic arrivals – it was somewhere to drive to and it provided all-night liquid refreshment.

For Cliff, it was vitally important that he should get his first records as right as he could.

I had to prove I wasn't going to be a one-hit or a few hits artist, like so many. I mean I was thrilled to become an 'overnight sensation' and I really did worry when

Record face travels.

'Move It', for instance, made number two. It made the next few records that much more important . . . I determined from early on that there must be plenty of hard work. Life became a whirl and the pace I was set was terrific. My schedule was packed with one-night-stands, variety, television, broadcasting, rehearsals, photographs and press interviews. Wow! it went on and just goes on. I had these recording schedules.

Oh, yes, I mean recording is one thing but at the same time we had to find songs and I had to learn them. I mean, remember I had to learn some new numbers for 'Oh Boy!'. I can remember being annoyed in those days by people who wrote that I never rehearsed. I quoted Bernard Bresslaw and said that anyone who believed that was a 'nut case'! Fortunately everyone was so friendly in recording, Norrie, the boys, engineers, and so on.

Although people often talk of Cliff rock 'n' rolling – as indeed he did on 'Oh Boy!' and on tour where he caused havoc – fairly early on he was singing ballads. His third hit single 'Livin' Lovin' Doll' had 'Steady with You' on the flip and his second recorded ballad was 'All That I Need'. But, like 'Choppin' 'n' Changin'', it failed to make the singles release schedule, and while 'Choppin'' did appear in the album *Me And My Shadows* in October 1960, this second ballad appears to have been lost. But why did he record ballads and how did he feel at the time?

Well, for one thing I discovered I could sing something else other than rock 'n' roll. I love singing ballads but when I did the first album I wasn't sure that I could do that sort of stuff. Up to that point the only people I heard doing it were Bing Crosby and Frank Sinatra, and I thought they weren't in my field. So when I discovered I could sing ballads, I did so. It was obvious for me to show off a bit and say . . . I can do rock 'n' roll but I can do ballads as well, and then that sort of crept into all albums. Later, people would say why didn't I record tougher tracks. This particularly was so after the *Nearly Famous* album and people said I was making harder music.

There was another reason – it was the done thing at the time for pop stars to find themselves on all kinds of family shows and invariably to gravitate a little toward being all-round singers.

People were pushed in that kind of direction. Also I found if I hadn't felt like that, which I did, the films *Summer Holiday* and *The Young Ones*, brought us an audience that demanded more rock 'n' roll! And anyway then, and always, you have to face the fact that a record company isn't going to want me if I'm just going to make records that don't sell, even if I thought they were the most wonderful records in the world.

I think my career has been a mixture of both feelings, but on something later, like *Rock 'n' Roll Juvenile*, I was stating for the first time: look this is completely what I want to do.

Apart from British releases, a very good collection of early Cliff rock 'n' roll tracks is found on a Swedish album *Cliff Richard – 20 Rock 'n' Roll Hits*. 'Hits' is perhaps not the right word, since many of the tracks on this album are from the lesser-known B-sides. The album contains a recording of 'Dynamite' that is not the same as the British released single, and some tracks have been culled from early albums. Many of Cliff's early albums that have been deleted in the UK are available as imports from Holland and Belgium. EMI in Britain have reissued much early material, sometimes in advantageous form for the consumer. Their Music for Pleasure label issued *Listen To Cliff*, which consisted of the original album of that name, plus the 1962 release *32 Minutes and 17 Seconds*. Other MFP reissues are *Everyone Needs Someone To Love* (originally titled *Love Is Forever*), and *All My Love*, the MFP version of the 1965 album *Cliff*. Both of these were later deleted but were reissued in Belgium. For newer fans unfamiliar with Cliff's earlier material, catching up would involve considerable financial outlay, so extensive was his output from the Fifties onward. *40 Golden Greats* is the most obvious retrospective set, including singles from 'Move It' to 'My Kinda Life' from 1977. It duplicates much of three earlier compilations – *Cliff's Hit Album, More Hits by Cliff* and *The Best Of Cliff*. However, one early compilation set more or less survives, namely *The Best Of Cliff Volume 2*, only three of whose tracks appear on the *40 Golden Greats*. Many would choose *Me And My Shadows* as the best of the early recordings, and only one track from this appears on the *40 Golden Greats*. Original copies with a green label are worth between £20 and £30. The film soundtrack albums have all been reissued.

In common with many artists of the late Fifties and early Sixties, Cliff had material issued in EP form. Some of this was nothing more than the breaking down of an album into a number of releases, but this was not always the case. Here, one of the best collections is on an album released in New Zealand, *Rock With Cliff Volume 2*. The title is deceptive, since it is not wholly composed of rock numbers. It's ideal for early fans with scratched or worn records.

Early in 1982, EMI reissued 12 early Cliff singles, with the original B-sides and original labels but with new picture sleeves. Finally, in this survey of early recording availability, mention must be made of *The Rock Connection*, released in 1984. Five of the tracks were originally included on the *Rock 'n' Roll Silver* album and all of the first side, save for the old Rick Nelson song 'Never Be Anyone Else But You', is from that source.

Cliff, 'Yes, that's right, it was like a double hit, because he did an up-tempo hit on one side and a ballad hit on the other.

'I wanted to do some quieter stuff on the rock album, because everyone thinks that rock and roll is just a tempo, in fact it's not, it's a whole musical culture, and out of it came great little ballads like "Never Be Anyone Else But You". Mark Griffiths, my bass player – he is also a guitarist – said "I have got this great idea, if we did that song, I have got this lovely guitar riff that we could play on it" and he played it to me and it won me over immediately.'

At the Greenbelt Festival and on tour during the autumn of 1988, Cliff featured a charming version of the 1957 Charlie Gracie hit 'Fabulous'. I was with Cliff and his group when they were developing and finally rehearsing their version of this oldie, and with this, as with many early songs, such as Nelson's, Cliff displayed an amazing memory for the lyrics. 'It's because back in the late Fifties we were on endless coach tours and used to sing and play along.'

Cliff, surveying the early recordings and their success, adopted a rather laid-back explanation. 'I reckon it's fairly easy to make hit records once you've got the formula. You just get a good song, make an interesting sound, and it's there. But it is up to the individual performer to make something of himself – to choose records that will help, not hinder, his long-term prospects.'

That was his opinion in 1961, after he had parted from his manager Tito Burns on the premise that Burns thought in the short term, whereas Cliff was developing a sense of a long-term, though still lucrative career. But certainly there was plenty of discussion as to what would be recorded and released in early times.

'Our stuff was basically youth music,' is how he once described the early records; but even if it had the right appeal, and even if much of Cliff's brief analysis of the nature of a hit is accepted, there is in his case a unique factor: his own voice. David Winter, who, in 1967, wrote the perceptive book on Cliff *New Singer, New Song*, comments:

His voice is light baritone to tenor in pitch, comfortable in the octave below middle E. Within that range and a few tones on either side of it, it is flexible and accurate. In effect he has two voices. His 'ballad' voice is soft and confidential, lingering over certain phrases and employing an occasional glissando with great effect. The crooner's trick of making the hearer wait for the expected note while he toys with the one above or below it, has been regularly employed by Cliff since his first song in the ballad idiom, 'Steady With You'.

On the other hand his 'beat' voice is full throated, exciting and spontaneous. Like the great jazz singers, he appears to improvise runs and inserts ejaculations and shouts in response to the music itself. In the early rock 'n' roll numbers the pace of the performance added to the magnetism, the voice throwing out words and phrases in a steady stream while the backing rocked and rolled along.

There is also a quality of clarity about Cliff's voice: you can actually follow the lyrics, and it retains today a remarkably youthful quality of tone.

Perhaps the best way to describe it is by saying that his voice is likeable, warm and engaging. Without great range of tone or pitch, it is still a performer's voice, an excellent medium for expressing mood or emotion.

The period from 1958 to 1974 contains a great deal more than can be described in one chapter. Singles, EPs and albums flowed, none without success – and probably none without a story. One fascinating moment in the life of the single 'Gee Whizz It's You' clearly shows its popularity. The song is found on the album *Me And My Shadows*. EMI UK had no intention of releasing this as a single, but they did make it available in the export market. Cliff fans found it could be ordered from dealers and, notwithstanding the extra cost, so many ordered it that it made the UK top 20.

Then there was his visit to record in New York and Nashville in August 1964. This was the time when Beatlemania raged through America. When Cliff arrived in New York he could not have been unaware of Beatle fever and the huge queues for the Beatle film, *A Hard Day's Night*. And his departure for America almost coincided with press reports on The Rolling Stones' recording sessions at the Chess Studios in Chicago. Their record 'It's All Over Now' had been the first major result of this visit and in August 1964 an EP of five songs from that recording arrangement was released. As Cliff set out for America he was also aware, with wry amusement, that the British music press was trumpeting the arrival of the *new* Cliff Richard, one Simon Scott, who showed some physical similarities to Cliff. Scott, who was Indian born, was 18, the same age as Cliff had been when he signed his first contract, and almost the same height, a little below six foot. Scott had had his first disc released, called 'Move It Baby', and was booked into the Stones tour in America, scheduled for the autumn.

In the meantime, the original Cliff was working with Epic producer Bob Morgan, with Norrie Paramor and other British people in attendance. Groundwork had already been done, for in June, Morgan had flown to Britain and with Cliff routined around 12 new numbers, including three songs by the then very hot songwriter Burt Bacharach. 'I had no idea what the Americans wanted,' says Cliff, 'I only knew what I liked doing and which suited me best of all. I just hoped that some of the results from the recordings later would be successful.'

Bob Morgan's verdict was: 'He's a tremendous performer and terrific material to work with. He's very co-operative in the studio, and frankly I think his voice is sensational. I think Cliff has a long-term future in this country.' He also impressed the head of Epic, Sol Rabinowitz, who said, 'I was very surprised at his versatility.'

The Barron Knights have had many hit records in which they have parodied other artists and their music.

Simon and **Rob** form **Climie Fisher**, one of the best and most successful new acts of the Eighties.

Cliff's recording of Bacharach sent the American songwriter jetting across the Atlantic to discuss music publishing with Cliff's one-time manager, Franklyn Boyd, who ran Aberbach Music. An early result of the American sessions came in September 1964, when the Bacharach song 'It's Wonderful To Be Young' headed a new EP. This Bacharach song became the theme title song of Cliff's movie *The Young Ones* when it was retitled in the States to avoid confusion with *The Wild Ones*. In the UK charts, Cliff was running strongly with the slow number 'The Twelfth of Never', previously recorded by Johnny Mathis and Elvis Presley.

In 1966 Cliff surprised many people by recording a Rolling Stones song. Some thought it inappropriate, because few kind words came his way from the Stones camp. Be that as it may, Cliff recorded 'Blue Turns To Grey'.

The song was picked out of a bunch of demonstration discs which had been lying around our agent's office. We were about to put it on – it was a case of something to do – when we realised the song's composers were Mick and Keith. I remembered then it had been recorded by a group called The Mighty Avengers. We were after a good up-tempo thing in the modern idiom, too. It was a nice song.

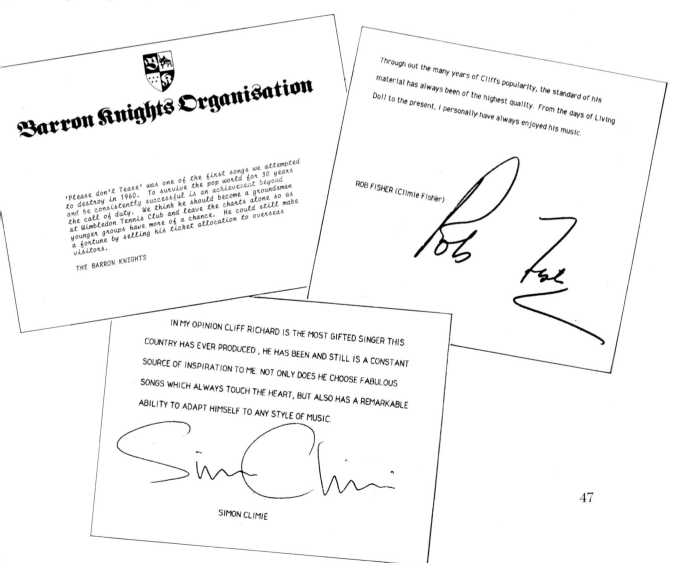

Barron Knights Organisation

'Please don't Tease' was one of the first songs we attempted to destroy in 1960. To survive the pop world for 30 years and be consistently successful is an achievement beyond the call of duty. We think he should become a groundsman at Wimbledon Tennis Club and leave the charts alone so as younger groups have more of a chance. He could still make a fortune by selling his ticket allocation to overseas visitors.

THE BARRON KNIGHTS

Through out the many years of Cliffs popularity, the standard of his material has always been of the highest quality. From the days of Living Doll to the present, I personally have always enjoyed his music.

ROB FISHER (Climie Fisher)

IN MY OPINION CLIFF RICHARD IS THE MOST GIFTED SINGER THIS COUNTRY HAS EVER PRODUCED, HE HAS BEEN AND STILL IS A CONSTANT SOURCE OF INSPIRATION TO ME. NOT ONLY DOES HE CHOOSE FABULOUS SONGS WHICH ALWAYS TOUCH THE HEART, BUT ALSO HAS A REMARKABLE ABILITY TO ADAPT HIMSELF TO ANY STYLE OF MUSIC.

SIMON CLIMIE

47

Cliff also recalled that it was one of a few songs in his career that stood out on first hearing: 'That's unusual. At the time I can only remember songs like "The Twelfth Of Never", "The Minute You're Gone" and "Wind Me Up" having instant impact.' But hadn't the Stones' criticism of him rankled? 'I wasn't bothered with that. It's the type of number that interested me, not who wrote it. Actually I had liked most of their stuff. "As Tears Go By" and "Play With Fire" were particular favourites, and though on first hearing I didn't like "19th Nervous Breakdown" I ended up liking it, for it had lots of excitement and a good sound, and that's what counts.' 'Blue Turns to Grey' reached number 15 in the charts.

The records of the period 1958 to 1972 had one thing in common – this was the era of Cliff and Norrie Paramor, an unprecedented partnership of constant success between recording artist and producer. Paramor was more than a producer. He was a musical arranger and a skilled orchestra conductor.

When his relationship with Cliff drew to a close, the reason for the break-up lay in various areas. Paramor was embarking on a new era for himself with an appointment as principal conductor of the Midland Light Orchestra. He also felt that a younger person might guide Cliff into new and exciting areas, and there was a general feeling that Cliff might experiment with new producers.

Cliff, speaking of Norrie, said 'He was like a father figure to me. We had great freedom with Norrie, which a lot of producers don't allow their artists. I never remember us *having* to record anything, except one song, and it was a million seller. That was 'Livin' Doll'. We didn't like it, and it was Bruce's idea to do it in country and western style. We were on tour somewhere.'

Cliff remarked that, 'production is a creative thing, like writing and performing. Norrie gave me 15 years of consecutive hits.'

Retrospective accounts of this partnership between Cliff and Norrie often tend to fall into the trap of imagining that there was an overall similarity in material. It suits the simple thesis that Cliff's early material was of one kind, and then another era dawned in late 1975. Obviously there was a marked change in Cliff's recordings from the mid-Seventies but certainly the earlier recordings had plenty of variety. In no particular time order, and chosen purely at random out of a heap of record release notices, there is, for instance, 'I Ain't Got Time Anymore', a rather more serious affair than some releases, penned by Mike Leander (later associated with Gary Glitter and The Glitter Band) and Eddie Seago. 'I'll Come Runnin' Babe' was another song that certainly represented a change from the bulk of pre-1967 material. This song and the record's flip, 'I've Got The Feelin'', came from the prolific pen of Neil Diamond, and both were beaty and fast numbers, produced with Leander. There was 'All My Love', an Italian song; a romantic number that came with an attractive B-side, 'Sweet Little Jesus Boy'. There was 'The Joy Of Living', a social-minded number co-written by Hank Marvin and singer Paul Ferris. In the single, 'The Time In Between', Cliff used an up-tempo bossa nova rhythm for this French song, backed by The Shadows and Norrie Paramor's piano. At the time Cliff said, 'I know an up-tempo bossa nova sounds strange, because a bossa is usually regarded as cool and swinging. Well, this song is loud and swinging. It's probably one of the best records I've made.' And it should not be forgotten that with Norrie at the

3

4

1 At full throttle: energy and power!
2 Fierce and flamenco.
3 'It's important, this line . . .'
4 'Every beat of my heart, for you.'
5 Pacing the boards in *Time*, and keeping fit!   *overleaf*

6 Obviously born to 'rock 'n' roll'.
7 'Hey, you know, I enjoy this!'
8 Body, face, gesture and microphone control: all part of the Cliff 'art'.

6

helm Cliff recorded in numerous languages. He learnt the words and pronunciation through sheer hard work.

However, Norrie was listed as co-producer with Dave McKay for the first single release outside the Cliff-Norrie partnership. And disaster struck. 'Brand New Song' was the first single to miss even a top 50 entry. Fortunately for Cliff, 1973 was Eurovision year, and he was able to bounce back quickly before too many people could assail the headlines with claims that his career was on its way out.

There were still some unsettling times ahead. 'Help It Along' barely scraped into the top 30; 'Take Me High' fared only slightly better. Better times shone briefly with the Top 20 song '(You Keep Me) Hanging On', but then came another chart miss with 'It's Only Me You've Left Behind', followed by the furore over his 1975 recording of 'Honky Tonk Angel'.

There was general amazement that Cliff should have recorded a song about a prostitute, and consternation reigned. When he realised what the song was about Cliff immediately told the press, in response to their probing, 'I hope it's a flop.' He was asked what he thought the song was about. He confessed, 'I knew honky tonks were something to do with bars but I completely misconstrued the meaning. OK, some people might say I'm naive. Obviously it's very embarrassing for me.' The press could not resist some ironic humour with the *Daily Mail* saying 'Mr Richard's fears that this record is actually going to do quite well will be realised by the end of the week. It might even counteract the harm done to him by Mary Whitehouse's fervent cry that he is 100 per cent wholesome.'

Cliff could not get the record withdrawn, but he spurned chances of promoting it on radio and television and it didn't reach the charts. Apart from the subject matter, his vocal could not be faulted and it was actually a rather good record. Cliff comments:

People said I had it taken off the playlists but I didn't. The thing is I said, I hadn't realised that a Honky Tonk Angel was . . . well we know now. I've got the song on my jukebox and I recorded it in all innocence. I play it to myself at home cos I think – it was produced by John Farrar, Bruce Welch and Hank Marvin, and it was a bit of a marathon for me trying to please three producers, so I have fond memories of it – I rate it as one of my best records. So I decided I wouldn't sing it anymore live; that's all, really.

Since Cliff was busy, it perhaps was less worrying to him than to some friends and critics who wondered if his end might be nigh. His 1974 album, *The 31st Of February Street*, had not received the response it deserved, although it's always been one of Cliff's favourites. In retrospect, the album surely laid the foundations for the new and seemingly rejuvenated Cliff, who, unknown to many, was busy towards the end of 1975, along with Bruce Welch as producer, recording another pearl album of his career, *I'm Nearly Famous*.

I'm Nearly Famous was recorded in the Abbey Road studio where the Beatles put together their million-selling hits. In one magical evening three hits were spawned – 'Miss You Nights', 'Devil Woman' and 'I Can't Ask For Anything More, Babe'. Arguably it was one of the finest recording evenings in contemporary music history.

John Perry was there to record back-ups.

It was an amazing time. Bruce was determined to drag Cliff into the twentieth century and here were a bunch of songs of high quality. Cliff and the others had previously heard the songs in demo form and had gone through them at Bruce's flat in Hampstead and later at David Bryce's residence. So it was not a 'starting from scratch' situation, but for all that it still took some magic to record these songs, in such a short period of time, and still satisfy the perfectionist nature of both Cliff and Bruce.

Perry expresses enormous pleasure at Cliff's vocal ability. 'He can do clear vocals any time of day, even morning, when most people have hardly a voice. I remember once at a BBC session at the Delaware Studios in Maida Vale, it was early morning, I was spluttering and here he was with lovely dulcet tones taking things in his stride. It makes it great for anyone to work with him.'

Perry was elated with 'Miss You Nights' and 'I was very excited about "Devil Woman", this was very contemporary and the riff was good. Terry Britton wrote it. Around this time he was the cat's whiskers, with some lovely songs, and it was an exciting song to do. Bruce, here and on the others, was an ideal producer, knowing when to and not to give room. You know; there was an air of determination and being there in the Beatle studio heightened things for us all. Perry calls them songs that send tingles down the spine. 'It was an outstanding night.'

Dave Clark, famous long before *Time*, for his group the Dave Clark Five, which accumulated 22 hits, is another who is in love with this period of Cliff's career. He stresses, 'Cliff is someone who, when he believes in a song, then makes it the most important thing at that moment.'

Cliff, speaking of this time, says, 'I think on *31st* it was a progression into something else, away from the albums I'd done in the past, which were just a string of songs. It's not as though I've never been able to do it. You've got to use that kind of voice for that kind of song.'

The album *I'm Nearly Famous* provided an embarrassment of riches and posed the question of which ones would make singles. The three songs 'Miss You Nights', 'Devil Woman' and 'I Can't Ask For Anymore Than You' all made the UK Top 20 and in some ways, even more important, the song 'Devil Woman' gave him his first US Top 10 hit, and a taste of success for Elton John's Rocket label in America.

Cliff noticed that he had now become very much 'in' with people who had previously regarded him as somewhat passé, or even a little quaint.

I didn't feel that my career at this point was on the slide, whatever some people suggested, but it had certainly stopped moving in any direction, other than straight. And I was still having record successes, remember. I think I was becoming more interested in acting than I was in singing. So I came to the point where I had to make a decision, and then I had to say to myself, 'Right, either I follow my instincts towards the drama, or to the even greater instinct that is making me think again of finding my roots musically.' So I didn't toss the coin – but almost like that. Because it was really close. But the thing came down in favour of music.

A very early tribute from **Ian 'Sammy' Samwell** who wrote 'Move It', and other songs.

Cliff undoubtedly wanted to make something happen again in his long musical career and once again he moved away from what might be called middle-of-the-road music. ' "Devil Woman" to me is classic rock, and I happen to be lucky enough to have that in my sweaty mitt before I recorded it. I did, and it changed everything for me.' 'Devil Woman''s success, both in sales and also in critical acclaim, had Cliff reflecting on the strange fortune that attends artists — when you have a hit, then people start to notice things that have in reality been present for some time: 'For years I had been singing falsetto on stage, but no one wrote up on it. It took the album for them to realise, but all the loyals would have known!'

EMI, under marketing manager David Munns, deservedly won the *NME* award with Cliff's album, for the best marketing campaign of 1976. At this stage, in most histories of Cliff, everyone rushes to the glorious peak that made the Seventies so splendid for Cliff, namely his return to top the single's chart and to make another album, brimming with so much good material.

I'm Nearly Famous was followed in 1977 by *Every Face Tells a Story*, which deserves more than a passing mention, although this writer cannot summon up the same enthusiasm for the 1978 album *Green Light* which, with its inability to spawn good singles,

Stock, Aitken and **Waterman** have become the biggest hit writing team of the Eighties decade with a success record that has been quite amazing.

As Cliff Richard fans, we never thought the day would dawn when Cliff would want to work with us. It is a great honour for us that in the 80's he would want us to write a song for him.

MIKE STOCK

MATT AITKEN

PETE WATERMAN

51

'I once had a hundred sheep, thirty cows, ten chickens...'

almost heralded a mini-crisis and the suspicion that 1975-76 might have been just a brief remission in what was perhaps a terminal musical patient.

Every Face Tells a Story did have three hit singles, although only 'My Kinda Life' made the Top 20. But even if the album did not have any real stormers the total product made the Top 10.

But there now came a momentary stop to innovations, for 1978 was the twentieth anniversary of Cliff's career. The past was recalled, and he reunited with his friends, The Shadows with the resulting album, *Thank You Very Much*. Long-term fans swooned again and former teenage fans, now women in their late thirties, rushed to the front with flowers and cakes and became young again. Without wishing to take away from the splendour of the reunion and the joy surrounding the occasion, it was a nuisance incursion, but then that is the way of major anniversaries. After all, many had written him off as the man who sang 'Congratulations' and 'when I did "Devil Woman" they went gulp! so I like to keep up front,' was his response, but here he was in 1978 back with the old songs of past times.

52

Separating *Every Face Tells a Story* and *Green Light* was the chart-topping *40 Golden Greats*, which brought together all the big hits from 1958 onward. There was also a religious album *Small Corners*.

Mike Smith, ex-Radio One, has said that Cliff's 'new musical creativity was reached in 1979 when he released an album with the splendidly cheeky title *Rock 'n' Roll Juvenile*.' That album contained one of his finest tracks – 'We Don't Talk Anymore'. It topped the UK charts and once more revived his American dreams when in the States it reached the Top 10, and began a series of regular Billboard listings for Cliff in the USA. 'We Don't Talk Anymore' was an Alan Tarney song. When Cliff heard it he says he had a feeling that only comes once in a while, for the something special. It gave him 'goose pimples' and, together with producer Bruce Welch, he rushed into the studios and spent a total of some 48 hours until the song came in the way that seemed just right. Because the song happened this way, it had not originally been planned for the album, but obviously, if for commercial reasons alone, it would have been folly to leave it for later or to risk missing it altogether.

'We Don't Talk Anymore' was a five-million seller, a worldwide smash and, of course, was helped in sales by American response. It was another classic pop single and the music world resounded with praise. The single had a lovely drum sound, some memorable synthesising, a good tune, a catchy riff and vocals that rode very easily. It also translated – somewhat to Cliff's surprise – into disco territory. Cliff was into the world of 12″ singles, and as contemporary as the next artist. For Cliff, there was the thrill of topping the charts for four weeks, coinciding with his topping the bill at Greenbelt and, of course, it was his 21st year as a major pop star. It could not have been better.

Rock 'n' Roll Juvenile took over a year from conception to recording to release. Cliff wrote the title track. He wanted an album based on rock 'n' roll, and characterised by enthusiasm, though it might be said that the title track had more of the old flavour of rock 'n' roll than the other tracks.

'I wanted to say that rock 'n' roll progresses, it becomes something else which is just as good. It doesn't grow old. I wanted an album with energy, which I felt the punk lot had, and I had felt that perhaps my records lacked spontaneity and energy.'

Again, Cliff was pretty elated with the response, which was a gut feeling that he was as contemporary as the next artist, whatever their age. 'People said to me it was great to hear tougher tracks, that I was making harder music. I mean in the beginning, when I was first listening to music, I was attracted by the sheer rawness of rock 'n' roll.'

This successful album reached number three in the album charts and spawned other British hit singles, including 'Hot Shot'. But obviously it was his first number one in 11 years that created the most excitement.

One beneficiary of Cliff's sudden leap to top the charts was the annual Christian-based Greenbelt Festival. The 1979 event was held at Odell, in the beautiful countryside of Bedfordshire. It was the first time Cliff had starred at this event. Some 15,000 people saw him on August Bank Holiday Saturday, when, a little after 10.30 p.m., Cliff ran on to the stage with cheers ringing in his ears as he opened with 'Hot Shot'. There was much cheering and clapping when he sang 'We Don't Talk Anymore': it was number one for that weekend. He danced about on stage, waving his arms in the air in a triumphant gesture, and it was plain that he was extremely happy. Later, as an encore, he came back and gave the crowd an extra long version of the song and here, as in its first outing, the gathering sang along with the chorus. Radio One had decided they would present a special for Bank Holiday transmission and during the show DJ Richard Skinner gave the first airplay to two tracks from *Rock'n'Roll Juvenile*: 'Doing Fine' and 'Carrie'.

Cliff's next album, *I'm No Hero*, reached number four and contained the Top 10 single 'Dreamin'' and 'A Little In Love' which reached number 15. This was still a peak time for Cliff, for three major single hits followed: 'Wired For Sound' (the album title track, which reached number four), 'The Only Way Out', and the magnificent 'Daddy's Home', which just failed to make number one.

Wired for Sound saw a continuation of Cliff's relationship with Alan Tarney. The hit singles have already been mentioned. Among the other album tracks, there was 'Better Than I Know Myself', a song that Cliff had introduced during his 1981 Gospel Tour. There was a somewhat Elvis Costello feel in 'Oh No Don't Let Go', plus some Caribbean rhythm, and there was arguably his heaviest track up to this date, 'Cos I Love That Rock 'n' Roll (Too Much)', which had a powerful fuzzed guitar and an avalanche of sound that at one point removes Cliff's vocals to second place. It had a much slower pulse rate than *I'm No Hero*; it contained more ballads, and in presentation it returned to a style familiar to fans, with a photo of Cliff on the front and back of the album sleeve.

Apart from the useful compilation, *Love Songs*, Cliff's next album outing was *Now You See Me . . . Now You Don't*, which came out in August 1982. This was basically a Gospel album and featured songs he had already performed during his concerts. The title track contained the arresting lyric line, 'I'm in vision, I'm on stage, I'm seventeen, I Don't Look My Age!' Reaction was rather subdued, but the album did contain a song destined to remain an all-time favourite. This was 'Little Town', a shortened version of the familiar title 'O Little Town of Bethlehem'. The familiar carol's lyrics were set to a completely new tune and arrangement. The mix of early chiming piano, an orchestrated crescendo, trumpet fanfare and tubular bells, plus the use of former Kings singer Nigel Perrin, to add a choral touch in the last verse, and the merging of all into the chorus 'Twinkle Twinkle Little Star' – all of these made for an excellent record. When it was released, many tipped it for the Christmas number one, but it had to settle for the surprisingly low position of 11.

Cliff, speaking with Michael Aspel, agreed that it seemed an inevitable single, but it had taken a long time to see the light of day, and he admitted: 'I've never sort of sat down in July and said "let's do a Christmas song".'

He told Michael that the song had been given to him almost 18 months before it was recorded. 'I thought, well I'd like to do it, but it just didn't feel right for me to do at that time, but I knew we'd do it. So this July when we recorded the album, I said, "look there's a song here: if we do it, it's got to be a Christmas single, and we've got to go all out to make it feel and sound wonderful".' Budget considerations were pushed to one side and 'we got in the 24-piece brass section, Tony and Nigel to aid me on back-ups, and when it all ended, I was really thrilled, because it did sound like a Christmas song. I didn't think there has been a real Christmas hit for some time. I mean there are hits

Three decades of Cliff in the profession, and he still looks so young!

Looking back over the years that I have known Cliff, when I went from Studio Producer to Editor, then Executive Producer and finally, Head of B.B.C, Radio 1 Music, he was always there, always at the top of the professional tree - changing styles as styles changed. Cliff was ever searching for the best material, always giving his very best performance. Listening to advice, following some of it, and digging his heels in when necessary!

Whenever someone writes in tribute to an artist, a host of adjectives spring to mind. In Cliff's case, it was easy for me. Professional, Conscientous, Caring, Humorous, Loyal, Dedicated, Enthusiastic. These factors quite apart from being immensely talented, artistic and empathetic! Cliff is truly unique,

As an artist, that he isn't 'moody', 'edgy' , 'bombastic' or 'anxiety-ridden', is not to say that he hasn't had to lick his wounds in private from time to time.

In my group of adjectives I left out the word 'honest' - it didn't seem to fit there, but it does here. Cliff's honesty shines through.

For those of us, who have basked in the reflected glory of the artists in whom we've had faith, Cliff really does stand head and shoulders above the many others.

Oh yes, I left out the most important word "humility".

DOREEN DAVIES
HEAD OF RADIO 1 MUSIC,
B.B.C, (until Jan.'88)

Cliff!

It hardly seems possible that over thirty years have passed since I sat at the controls in Studio 2 as you sang your way into the charts with "Move It". That session has always had a special place in my memory because your first hit record also happened to be the first hit I engineered. Although very different, our careers were launched at the same time!

The question that we are most often asked is "What is so-and-so really like?" There was never any hesitation in answering this question about you. You are exactly the way you appear to be on stage, on screen or wherever: just a very nice young man. I have only the fondest memories of how pleasant it was to work with you, and, of course, The Shadows! We had a lot of laughs, I remember.

Anyway, it's nice to know that you're still out there making hits.

CONGRATULATIONS !!!

Doreen Davies had a life-long career with the BBC, especially in the field of popular music, and was for many years Head of Music at the BBC's Radio One, and an Executive Producer.

Malcolm Addey now works in the States but he was for many years a major figure at EMI's Abbey Road studios.

over the Christmas period – we had one in "Daddy's Home" – but I think Johnny Mathis had the last one with "A Child Is Born".'

Cliff felt there was nothing to lose, 'and as a Christian it would be great to have a record out – even if only Christians bought it. Because everyone enjoys that time of year.'

Appetites had been whetted for 1983 by news of Cliff's musical flirtation with Phil Everly, one half of the famous Everly Brothers. Cliff had always expressed his admiration for the early music of both Little Richard and the Everlys. 'I have been inspired incredibly by them – probably why I am a vocal group at heart!'

Cliff had asked for Phil to star with him in a special concert that had taken place in the spring of 1981 at London's Hammersmith Odeon, which was filmed by the BBC as part of their semidocumentary series on Cliff. In this concert, the two performed two Everly Brothers classics, 'Dream' and 'When Will I Be Loved'. In May of 1982, Phil returned to the UK from his Los Angeles home to record the song 'Louise' and it was during this visit that plans were made for the two to record material later in the year.

In the autumn of 1982 they recorded a ballad entitled 'I'll Mend Your Broken Hearts' and eventually the single 'She Means Nothing To Me'. Musicians taking part in the session included guitarist Mark Knopfler, drummer Terry Williams, both of Dire Straits, and well known pop star, musician and keyboardist Pete Wingfield. Both songs appeared on Phil Everly's next album. Early in 1983 the single reached the Top 10. While the Everly duet, released on Capitol, was still selling, EMI was busying itself with promoting Cliff's version of the old Buddy Holly hit 'True Love Ways'. This was culled from *Dressed For The Occasion*, which was issued in May, and contained material Cliff had recorded at a charity concert at the Royal Albert Hall the previous November, with the London Philharmonic Orchestra in attendance. And just to keep the pot boiling, Cliff was busy working on his new *Silver* album, with some tracks earmarked for production by Bruce Welch and Mike Batt. He also aided the gospel singer Sheila Walsh on her single, 'Drifting', even down to appearing in the video. Cliff, along with Craig Pruess, produced Sheila's *Drifting* album.

Silver, of course, celebrated Cliff's magical 25th year at the top. The single to coincide with release was 'Never Say Die', his 87th and a Top 20 hit. There was also a limited edition box set, with a second album, *Silver Rock 'n' Roll*, not available separately. Its ten tracks had been selected by Cliff and produced by his band, Thunder, and it included a new recording of 'Move It'. There was a booklet containing specially commissioned photographs of Cliff by Lord Snowdon. *Silver* contained two hits, the already mentioned 'Never Say Die' and 'Please Don't Fall In Love', written by Mike Batt. This last was a veritable tear-jerker and recalled some of those early sixties-style songs. 'Love Stealer', with its heavy beat and fast up-tempo, was a song rumoured to have been coveted by rocksters Iron Maiden. 'Hold On' was arguably a potential hit single, with its electronic sound and fine sax solo. 'Ocean Deep', possibly evokes most memories from fans, especially as it has lasted in live performance and has been accompanied by a magnificent light display. The song was the longest on the album.

Rock 'n' Roll Silver contained a laryngitis-hit Cliff singing 'Donna', found originally on his first album. There was the famous Elvis hit of 1957, 'Teddy Bear', and a song from Cliff's record history, 'It'll Be Me' from 1962. Little Richard's 'Lucille' from 1957 opened the second side. Of the other tracks, three particularly catch the ear: his version of the old Ricky Nelson song '(There'll) Never Be Anyone Else But You', Gene Vincent's 1956 bopper 'Be Bop A Lula', and another Little Richard belter, 'Tutti Frutti', first heard in 1957. The record was dedicated to Norrie Paramor and was recorded at Strawberry Studios. Plaudits came from far and wide but there was pleasure in the Richard camp at seeing some excellent US reviews late in 1983.

The last year of the seventies and these first years of the Eighties were tremendous times, during which there seemed to be record action on all fronts, allied to video and television support. And 1984 proved no mean year, even if the singles 'Baby You're Dynamite' and 'Straight From The Heart' proved disappointing affairs.

The big occasion of 1984 was to be a series of four reunion concerts, two in London and two in Birmingham, with Cliff and The Shadows. Within two days of a half-page advertisement in a Sunday newspaper, enough ticket applications had been received to sell out double the envisaged number of shows. A Wembley spokesperson at the time exclaimed: 'We have never had such a massive response in such a short space of time.' The response meant that in the end there were four nights at Wembley and five in Birmingham. To mark the occasion, EMI issued a compilation album simply titled *Cliff and the Shadows*.

Towards the end of 1984, EMI issued *The Book Connection*. The 15-track set included reworkings of some old hits, such as 'Willie and the Hand Jive' and 'Be Bop A Lula'. Cliff's hit with Phil Everly, 'She Means Nothing To Me', was also featured. For fans, it was something of a disappointment, considering that so many of the songs were available elsewhere.

The musical *Time* was to present Cliff with a lovely song 'She's So Beautiful' from Stevie Wonder, on which Wonder played. Dave Clark, creator of *Time*, had had the good musical sense to realise that Cliff's vocal could make it a thing of beauty: 'A really good combination to bring those two together. Stevie had already laid down the backing and I thought Cliff perfect for the vocals. We did them at Abbey Road, in London, the scene of so many Beatle recordings. With someone like Cliff you know you will get 110%.'

Cliff also released 'It's in Everyone of Us' from *Time* as a single. Although many thought it would give him a Christmas hit, in view of the lyrics, this was not to be, nor was there much joy in his last of his three songs from *Time*, 'Born To Rock 'n' Roll'. Clark comments, 'It was a very commercial number but for some reason the BBC did not play it, and without their support it's virtually impossible for a record to take off. I found it hard to understand, especially such an attitude to Cliff . . . He is our most successful singles star and he should be treated accordingly.'

Cliff also joined in the minor controversy. He was quite bitter about the treatment he received from BBC's Radio One: 'I was really disappointed. They didn't even pay me the respect of 28 years of presenting them with hits in their shows. I was really angry.'

Fortunately Cliff survived the lack of response, to these singles both from radio and sales. His detractors in the producer ranks of radio stations, especially Radio One, suddenly became admirers when he surfaced in mid-March 1986, along with the comedy outfit The Young Ones, to record afresh his 1959 hit 'Living Doll'. Once more he was trendy, the 'in' man of the moment, as it became the fastest selling single since Band Aid shot to number one in Britain. Cliff, Hank and the others were not to make a penny, since all profits went to the Comic Relief charity. Asked why he recorded with The Young Ones, Cliff replied, 'They approached me with the idea and I liked it. I didn't see very much of the TV series and some of what I did see was ridiculous. I didn't mind the Cliff Richard jokes. It was quite flattering to be filtered into scripts.' He talked of having 'great laughs' with them in both radio and video recordings.

His Comic Relief single was not the only unusual happening for fans during this year. There was also his single with Sarah Brightman, which took the record public by surprise. The song 'All I Ask Of You' came from Andrew Lloyd Webber's musical *The Phantom of the Opera*, then just about to open, which would star Sarah and the amazing Michael Crawford.

The single's reviewer in the magazine *Cliff United* appears to have been somewhat taken aback at what he was hearing. Gary Miles told readers: 'On first hearing, I thought,

Good Grief Cliff – what have you done – going back to the late '60s, early '70s style. But, I have to admit the more you hear it, the more it grows on you. And, now I have to admit I actually like it. Lushy, romantic, I can see a lot of guys going out and buying it for their girlfriends.'

But why had he done it? To Cliff, it's an irritating question, the kind of thing journalists ask, which provokes the response, 'Why do these people pigeon-hole me?' Admittedly there must be few pop artists, apart from Cliff, who both can and are willing to make such transitions in style and sound. Here was Cliff passing from The Young Ones to singing with someone trained in classical arts. But this is what he did, and there is no reason why someone of his talent shouldn't pull it off. As to the accompanying video, some thought it rather overdone. It was a view with which Cliff had little sympathy; he thought the Ken Russell video was the best he had ever done. Also at this time, an Elton John single with Cliff made its appearance on Rocket. 'Slow Rivers' struggled for life, partly because this was not a terribly good time for Elton. Had it been released in 1987, among Elton's other successes, it would doubtless have gained the popularity and sales it deserved.

The 1987 album was *Always Guaranteed*. It seemed as a title a very reasonable statement about both Cliff's record work and his live performances. The album produced three very fine singles – the exquisite 'My Pretty One', 'Some People' and 'Remember Me'. These and 'Two Hearts' (released in 1988) formed a first-class video, *Cliff Richard Video EP*, released in March 1988. *Always Guaranteed* became a British 500,000 seller. The cover looked ordinary until, in a bright light from some ten feet away, it could be seen giving a shadowy 3-D profile of Cliff in a dreamy pose.

By this time in record history the CD had arrived and *Always Guaranteed* was marketed by EMI in a limited CD edition, taking the form of a numbered, boxed set. Inside there were four postcards, an autographed colour print, a poster/calendar and a one-sided 7″ of 'Another Christmas Day'. There was an engraved message from Cliff on the other side.

Personally, I was surprised and disappointed that the third single from the album 'Remember Me' did not become a major hit, rather than a mere top 40 entry. It had a great sense of life and vitality, although it might be said that the overall sound was a little too familiar. It was this single that had 'Another Christmas Day' for its flipside. Cliff had performed this Yuletide special during his Gospel tour, the preceding June. The 1988 single release from the album, 'Two Hearts', was a damp squib in spite of enormous expectations from those connected with Cliff. This song had once been recorded by David Cassidy, the man who took Cliff's place in *Time* and, of course, a major star in the previous decade's pop annals. There was an excellent video that showed Cliff with a 12,000 audience in Birmingham, and it was a pity that the single's sluggish sales and lack of real chart penetration prevented many people from seeing the video.

So 1988 seemed somewhat lacklustre, and British fans awaited the compensation of a British tour that began late September in Dublin. They learnt there would be no new album to accompany the tour, but there would be a personalised Cliff selection of favourite recordings from the Eighties, under the title of *Private Collection*. And there were numerous rumours as to what the 99th and 100th singles might be. In some quarters there was much debate as to how many singles Cliff had had released, not counting his recordings with other people, and there were some frantic recountings and listings of titles.

But one thing is obvious, whatever the number of titles and their comparative chart success, there is simply Cliff's amazing track record that will soon span four decades. He is the record survivor, and an amazing amount of good music has come from him in a variety of record forms. What, though, remains to be achieved? Two somewhat contrasting views have been given me by Mickie Most, one of Britain's best-known record business personalities, and Cliff himself. Most says:

> Anyone who survives four decades is unique. To survive the Sixties was a tough job, with the Liverpool sound and the mass of groups. So many of those with him from the Fifties did not. He survived flower-power, metal, glam rock, junk, the punks, the disco scene, the technical bods, computer music, you name it. He's stayed in there. He's won more Derbys than Lester Piggott and not gone to prison!

Most prefers Cliff with harder music and if he has to name 'duff' Cliff, then he would illustrate his point with a song such as 'Goodbye Sam, Hello Samantha', 'I think he has done some wimpey songs. I think Cliff has to avoid the temptation that comes the way of many artists and that's to choose the undemanding material, the stuff you can do with your eyes closed.' Most believes there is considerable unexplored territory in the Cliff vocal region. 'I think it would be interesting to see Cliff produced by people who are involved with artists like Alexander O'Neal and Michael McDonald. He has a more black voice than people have heard, I mean urban black music.'

Cliff feels that any soul quality in his voice already finds expression through songs that allow outlet for this and any other facet of his vocal ability. His response to Most's suggestion was:

> If I get a song I sing it my way, and sometimes the song will dictate this. You can't, as it were, suddenly pretend you're a soul artist. I mean, I am not black, and out of all the musical forms that are there it is one very much based on communal experience and upbringing. However, when I've sung, say, 'Lawdy Miss Clawdy' or 'Devil Woman' then I believe there has been a certain soul feel. To be honest, I've never been a fan of soul music.

Cliff's 30-year recording career was triumphantly crowned by the fantastic success of his Christmas song 'Mistletoe and Wine'. By the beginning of December 1988 it had moved into the Top 10, and rose to reach the coveted position of the Christmas Number One single. At the same time the album *Private Collection* was soaring up the album charts, and that too had reached the Number One position before the end of the year. Cliff's choice of 'Mistletoe and Wine' demonstrates yet again his instinct for picking the right song at the right time, and this splendid double success proves that his magic as a recording artist is as potent as ever.

And the future? No one I've talked with, and these cover many varying aspects of show business, can foresee a day when Cliff will cease recording. Perhaps the style may change, the songs might become less demanding – who knows? Dave Clark simply says, 'Cliff at 60? No problem.' And the man himself? He told me, 'So long as I am in love with music.' I can't see his interest declining. Not at all.

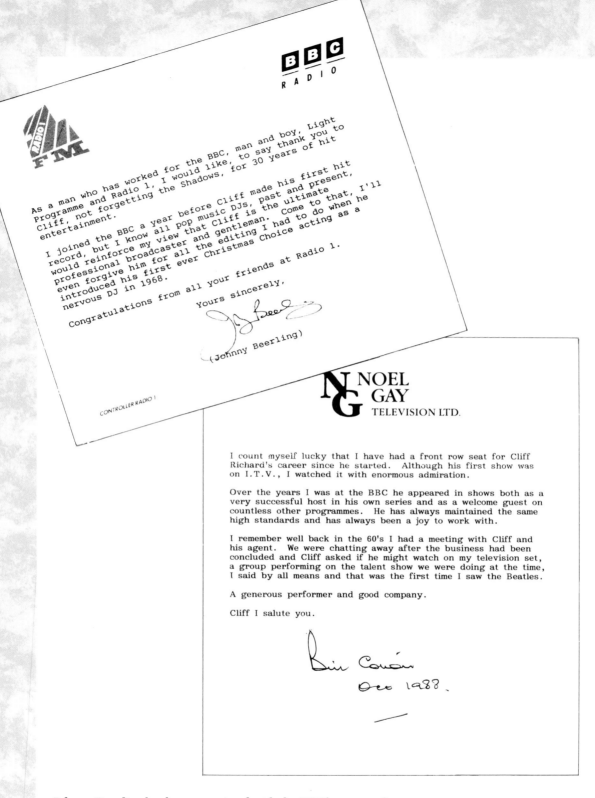

BBC RADIO

As a man who has worked for the BBC, man and boy, Light Programme and Radio 1, I would like, to say thank you to Cliff, not forgetting the Shadows, for 30 years of hit entertainment.

I joined the BBC a year before Cliff made his first hit record, but I know all pop music DJs, past and present, would reinforce my view that Cliff is the ultimate professional broadcaster and gentleman. Come to that, I'll even forgive him for all the editing I had to do when he introduced his first ever Christmas Choice acting as a nervous DJ in 1968.

Congratulations from all your friends at Radio 1.

Yours sincerely,

(Johnny Beerling)

CONTROLLER RADIO 1

NOEL GAY TELEVISION LTD.

I count myself lucky that I have had a front row seat for Cliff Richard's career since he started. Although his first show was on I.T.V., I watched it with enormous admiration.

Over the years I was at the BBC he appeared in shows both as a very successful host in his own series and as a welcome guest on countless other programmes. He has always maintained the same high standards and has always been a joy to work with.

I remember well back in the 60's I had a meeting with Cliff and his agent. We were chatting away after the business had been concluded and Cliff asked if he might watch on my television set, a group performing on the talent show we were doing at the time, I said by all means and that was the first time I saw the Beatles.

A generous performer and good company.

Cliff I salute you.

Bill Cotton

Dec 1988.

Johnny Beerling has been associated with the BBC's output of pop music over many years and is the current Controller of Radio One.

One of the greats in British television, **Bill Cotton** has been Head of BBC TV's Light Entertainment.

4 RADIO AND TELEVISION

Cliff arrived at a fortuitous time in the history of British radio and television exposure of pop music. The speed of his transition from a comparative nobody to a national personality was greatly helped by the advent of two much loved and remembered shows. Both were considered in varying degrees as 'shocking', for they swept away the remaining cobwebs of dusty radio and television that reflected a postwar clinging to the past and took no account of a booming prosperity that would release hordes of hungry and affluent teenagers who wanted their own music and their own heroes, and in their own style.

In the late Fifties, the best music for young people came from outside British shores. Its centre was in the small principality of Luxembourg. The famous radio station was exciting because it brought on its airwaves American-based pop music. And it played records. In Britain, the BBC radio pop outlet played a few records on shows that, more often than not, featured live music and a sound orientated toward older people. BBC television, toward the end of the Fifties, did produce '6.5 Special', but Luxembourg had real DJs and not just staff announcers spinning the discs. In the late Fifties Keith Fordyce, Jimmy Savile, Alan Freeman, Pete Murray, Jimmy Young and David Jacobs were among the familiar voices to be heard. They created a surge of interest among British young people for the new so-called 'irreverent' music that came from the likes of Presley, Haley, Jerry Lee Lewis, Eddie Cochran, Chuck Berry and Fats Domino. For a teenager like Cliff Richard, British radio and Independent television by and large lacked the right spirit and drive.

Things were about to change, and for a British youngster with his first record, soon to be hailed as a classic, this could not have happened at a better time. The two new shows of 1958 featured British artists and steered away from worshipping at the American shrine of pop. The first years of rock 'n' roll had been dominated totally by American stars. Tommy Steele was then the only British rock artist with a name that made sense to young people, and arguably the first British star to undergo teenage pop treatment. All this was helpful in setting the scene for Cliff, although the media insisted on endless comparisons between him and Steele.

ABC television's 'Oh Boy!' provided the TV spot of the time for Cliff. Its producer Jack Good went for a raw energy and excitement. When he heard 'Move It', he was enthralled, enchanted and, better still, immediately driven to sending out the search parties for British youngsters with rock 'n' roll records that could compare with the Americans. Admittedly, Good had his doubts until he met Cliff, for he could hardly believe such a record would also bring him a star who both fitted the bill and looked the part.

He knew this promising youngster would need to have his rough edges smoothed, yet in so doing it must not take away his style, which was undoubtedly individual, even though it owed a few things to his hero Elvis Presley. Good found Cliff shy and diffident, hardly then possessed with a strong personality, obviously inexperienced, yet at the same time imparting a genuine enthusiasm, warmth and, yes, charisma.

'Oh Boy!' had found a somewhat eccentric young producer in Good, and indeed his team averaged 27 years in age, something unique in those days. It was also unusual for the producer to pick artists, choose the song numbers and exercise responsibility over all programme areas.

Rehearsals were long and arduous. Good was a perfectionist, determined that the acts he booked would give of their best, and more. Sunday, 7 September 1958 saw the first run through of 'Move It', which had been released in August. A 90-minute rehearsal was followed by some work on another song 'Don't Bug Me Baby'. Finally the viewing public saw the programme transmitted at 6.00 p.m. on Saturday 13 September from London's still extant and magnificent Empire, Hackney. Some five million watched Cliff, who appeared along with Ronnie Carroll, the John Barry Seven and Marty Wilde.

Good's shows had a little more decadence, rowdiness and gut feel than, say, those other popular shows '6.5 Special' and 'Thank Your Lucky Stars', although both of these had their own charm. Good made teenagers feel that the music belonged to them and ought not to be handed down from on high by adults who neither comprehended nor liked the new beat sounds. Cliff was an essential ingredient of the Good movement; there to supply a few jerks and hip swings that would draw endless rapturous squeals from the girls. Cliff would soon learn a greater degree of showmanship, lose some of the early wild gyrations, the forced lip curl and sneer, and be more relaxed, with a greater degree of flexibility in presentation.

For a totally new recording artist like Cliff, the show was to prove an invaluable experience. Apart from anything else, he learnt the importance of togetherness even with fellow artists who, like himself, chased chart positions. Good said in those far off days, 'The show has the friendliest cast ever. Whenever anyone on the programme is making an appearance elsewhere, the rest of the cast invariably turn to cheer him up.' When Cliff played his first variety event, both Leslie Cooper, 'Oh Boy!''s movement man, and producer Jack Good were there to advise him on stage demeanour and general presentation.

Good found Cliff 'easy to rehearse. The main thing is he had a strong sense of rhythm. Cliff didn't read music very well, but Cliff does read the top line, and always knows the key in which he sings.'

While 'Oh Boy!' launched Cliff upon young viewers of the time, in radio terms its equivalent was 'Saturday Club'. It was one of the BBC's early attempts both to understand the new pop music and to attempt an appealing form of presentation for youthful listeners. It was launched in October 1958. The show ran for two hours and it soon became the record pluggers 'must' show, with every star of the day booked in and generally enjoying increased record sales as a result. British artists to the fore were Lonnie Donegan, Tommy Steele, Anne Shelton, Frankie Vaughan, Billy Fury, Anthony Newley, Chris Barber and, of course, Cliff. For Cliff, as for Marty Wilde and the John Barry Seven, the show was his broadcasting debut, and this is also true of The Shadows. Much of the show was prerecorded. This was because it needed a lot of work, for in general the booked

Alan (Fluff) Freeman

the year 1959, London had become my home for the last
...ths, and with the odd stint on Radio Luxembourg & the
...ight Programme under the belt, I knew I wasn't returning
...ssie as planned!

There was this lad by the name of CLIFF RICHARD!
...s kind of impressed but not terribly moved by "MOVE IT"
...to my horror to this very day, was heard to say on a
... show that "LIVING DOLL" probably wouldn't sell a copy"!!!

So much for "SMART ARSE FREEMAN"!!!!! But for
...e last thirty years, how all of us have wanted to somehow
... a part of that quite stunning "Cliff Richard Success" yes?

I thank him for not only the chance to play his
...any manifestations on vinyl, but for the great example he set
...s all over the years....to remain, for all his talent,
...very warm...very caring & very involved with Humanity!

Happy 30th Young Cliff! There 'aint nothin' like
the real thing! And if you re-record "Living Doll" yet again,
"CAN I SING IT WITH YOU"??????????

Cheers!
Fluff!

BBC

BRITISH BROADCASTING CORPORATION

Jimmy Young asked me to send this to you:

"To get to the top in our business isn't easy. To
stay at the top in our business is rather more
difficult. To stay at the top in our business for
30 years is extremely difficult. To stay at the top
in our business and continue to turn out hits is
superhuman.

And to do all that and still continue to look as young
as Cliff does, shouldn't be allowed. A professionals
professional and always such a nice guy with it.

Congratulations,"

Yours sincerely,

(John Gurnett)
Senior Producer, Jimmy Young Show

CLIFF RICHARD.

Cliff is part of British Pop Music. An obvious thing to say ? Perhaps,
but how many other entertainers swiftly come and, as swiftly, depart. If we
check back through the thirty years we celebrate here, how few have stayed the
course, re-entering the charts year after year, and being regularly booked for
shows and movies to which we all go.

Another thirty years Cliff. No problem. Good luck.

Simon Dee
SIMON DEE

DAVID JACOBS

I have known and admired Cliff since the
start of his career and now, three decades
later I admire him even more, he is a
great credit to the profession and indeed
to himself. I'm proud to know him.

DAVID JACOBS.

Alan Freeman has an enormous TV and Radio pop presentation credit list and is
one of the really great names in his field.

Jimmy Young is one of Britain's best known radio presenters. He was formerly a
very successful pop recording artist.

Simon Dee became one of the best known names in British pop presentation on
radio and TV during the 1960s and still presents for national radio, BBC Radio 2.

David Jacobs is one of Britain's most famous DJ's, and radio personalities.

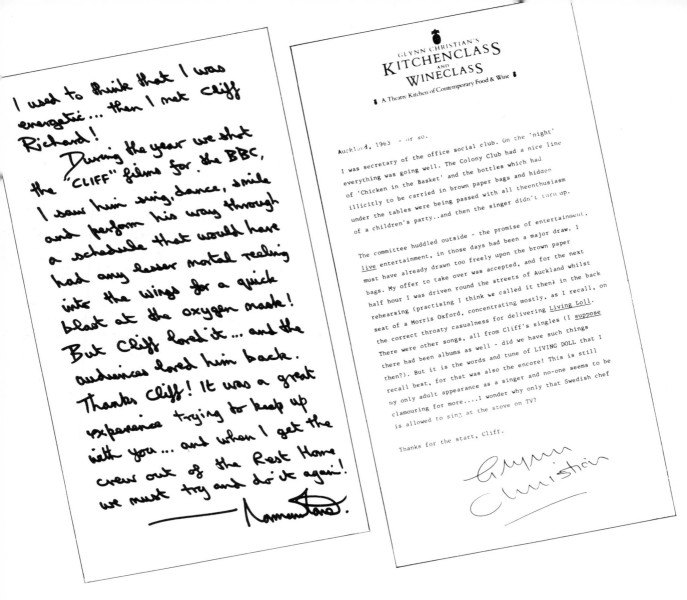

I used to think that I was energetic... then I met Cliff Richard!

During the year we shot the "CLIFF" films for the BBC, I saw him sing, dance, smile and perform his way through a schedule that would have had any lesser mortal reeling into the wings for a quick blast at the oxygen mask! But Cliff loved it ... and the audiences loved him back. Thanks Cliff! It was a great experience trying to keep up with you ... and when I get the crew out of the Rest Home we must try and do it again!

— Norman Stone.

Auckland, 1963 - or so.

I was secretary of the office social club. On the 'night' everything was going well. The Colony Club had a nice line of 'Chicken in the Basket' and the bottles which had illicitly to be carried in brown paper bags and hidden under the tables were being passed with all the enthusiasm of a children's party..and then the singer didn't turn up.

The committee huddled outside - the promise of entertainment, live entertainment, in those days had been a major draw. I must have already drawn too freely upon the brown paper bags. My offer to take over was accepted, and for the next half hour I was driven round the streets of Auckland whilst rehearsing (practising I think we called it then) in the back seat of a Morris Oxford, concentrating mostly, as I recall, on the correct throaty casualness for delivering Living Loll. There were other songs, all from Cliff's singles (I suppose there had been albums as well - did we have such things then?). But it is the words and tune of LIVING DOLL that I recall best, for that was also the encore! This is still my only adult appearance as a singer and no-one seems to be clamouring for more....I wonder why only that Swedish chef is allowed to sing at the stove on TV?

Thanks for the start, Cliff.

Glynn Christian

Norman Stone has become one of Britain's brightest and most talented TV producers.

Glynn Christian is renowned for his television culinary exploits. He has his own 'Kitchenclass and Wineclass – A Theatre Kitchen of Contemporary Food and Wine' school in London.

groups played and sang live. The programme producer was Jimmy Grant and its compere was Brian Matthew.

Cliff enshrined the spirit of young people with these words from that time: 'I'm so wrapped up in what I'm doing at the moment that I can't think further ahead than my next record . . . I suppose I'm typical of people of my age. I'm still very young. I don't want to be tied down too much. I've had a lot of luck very early in life, and I want to enjoy it while I can. I want to go out and have fun and, believe me, I do.'

64

Radio and television studios became a second home. Perhaps his instinctive taking to television, with immediate booking for the 'Oh Boy!' series of late 1958, was instrumental in Cliff's first gift to his parents from earnings derived from 'Move It' – a television set!

Soon he would be found gracing radio and television shows that offered him record exposure, including 'Parade of the Pops', 'Easy Beat', 'Pop Inn', and 'Thank Your Lucky Stars'. He would join the team of 'Juke Box Jury' to give his opinion on new record releases. He would contribute material to other entertainment shows of the time, including 'The Billy Cotton Show' on BBC1. He would record special material for transmission on Radio Luxembourg and, just prior to the Beatle invasion, Luxembourg for the first time devoted an entire 'ABC Of The Stars' to Cliff, something never accorded any other artist. He would also be interviewed for Radio Free Europe.

Both BBC and ITV were to give him major television shows, with the Beeb eventually giving him a number of series during the Seventies. ATV let him loose for a 'Cliff and The Shadows' show and then gave him three one-hour specials. He would frequently appear on the popular ATV show 'Sunday Night At The Palladium' and outside Britain he was in constant demand, especially in Germany, Belgium and Holland. In 1965 he appeared in the States on the very prestigious 'Ed Sullivan Show'.

Along the way Cliff worked with a select number of artists, of whom one was Una Stubbs, who appeared with Cliff in the early Sixties films *Summer Holiday* and *Wonderful Life*. She joined him in pantomime, and in the Seventies she would be with him for most of the series that came his way courtesy of the BBC. Although not a card-carrying Christian, she would appear with him and The Settlers in the late Sixties series 'Life With Johnny', produced by Tyne Tees. And there were several general shows in this decade in which she appeared with Cliff.

At the outset of 1968 Cliff appeared on the extremely popular 'Dee Time' television show. Then in Germany, and singing in German, he contributed 'Don't Forget To Catch Me' for the popular 'Golden Shot' TV show. In March of that year he was singing the six short-listed titles for his attempt to win Eurovision for Britain. He appeared on the Morecambe and Wise show at the end of March, and on 6 April he came second at Eurovision with 'Congratulations'. May saw him in his own BBC television show and later that month he took part in the BBC Light Programme show 'Any Questions?'. In June came the ITV programme 'Big Show' and the popular 'Talk Of The Town'. Another visit to 'Juke Box Jury' came in July; then came an appearance with Keith Skues on 'Saturday Club' in October; choosing his favourite discs for the BBC Light Programme show 'Off The Record'; being interviewed by Adrian Love for the BBC's World Service; recording his chart topper 'Congratulations' for the 'Top of the Pops' Christmas show, and recording material for Scottish TV. It was a busy media year, but most years have been that, at least during the Sixties and Seventies, and simply because whatever form is chosen Cliff brings to it the assurance and professionalism loved by producers. To book Cliff means things will go right, it's as simple as that really.

But what was the most novel event of the decade? For that, we must go back in time. In 1960 Cliff found himself cheerfully accepting the prospect of being marooned as a castaway for Roy Plomley's legendary BBC radio series 'Desert Island Discs'. Cliff's selection of eight records on 31 October was this:

> 'Beat Out Dat Rhythm On A Drum'
>   (from the film *Carmen Jones*) – **Marilyn Horne**
> **'Tammy'** – **Debbie Reynolds**
> **'Heartbreak Hotel'** – **Elvis Presley**
> **'My Funny Valentine'** – **Dakota Staton**
> **'How You Say It'** – **Lena Horne**
> **'That's My Desire'** – **Dion and the Belmonts**
> **'Rock Around The Clock'** – **Bill Haley and the Comets**
> **'Am I Blue'** – **Ray Charles**

His luxury item was a guitar and the book he chose was
Johann Wyss's *Swiss Family Robinson*

It was, shall we say, his most unexpected booking of the decade. Doubtless in 1970 he would have chosen different titles. Certainly when he was asked for a list he might have composed in 1988 he told the always excellent *Cliff United* magazine:

> **'Heartbreak Hotel'** – **Elvis Presley**
> **'Sailing'** – **Christopher Cross**
> **'I Honestly Love You'** – **Olivia Newton-John**
> **'Money For Nothing'** – **Dire Straits**
> **'Your Song'** – **Elton John**
> **'Another Tear Falls'** – **Gene McDaniels**
> **'Devil Woman'** – **Me!**
> **'Fabulous'** – **Charlie Gracie**

His luxury item was still a guitar, but his book choice was now a set of the *Narnia Chronicles* by C. S. Lewis.

There was no let-up for him from the media during the Seventies, and there were a number of particularly interesting moments. Early in 1971 he provided the commentary for 'The Lollipop Tree', a programme in BBC2's 'The World About Us' series. It told the story of a home for 80 children at the foot of the Himalayas, where Cliff's aunt once taught. His own BBC TV series, that ran for 13 weeks from January, saw Cliff singing songs way beyond his record catalogue. He was joined by friend Una Stubbs plus the newish group Marvin, Farrar and Welch. On August Bank Holiday Monday, BBC1 screened *Getaway with Cliff*. This was a film shot entirely on location in France, when Cliff was in that country during the previous month. Olivia Newton-John was one of his guests. Songs were sung against varied physical backcloths and included Cliff with guitar singing 'Fire and Rain' as he walked the streets of Biot, and Olivia rendering 'Love Song' in a modern art museum near Nice. Both were seen walking the beaches at Juan Les Pins. The 1971 Eurovision winner, Severine, was seen singing 'Un Banc, Un Arbre, Une Rue'.

Cliff was on BBC1's 'Nationwide' in September 1971 and 'Ask Aspel' the following month, and compered 'Music for Sunday' on both Radio 1 and 2 on Sunday mornings. Cliff, with Tim Brooke Taylor and Olivia along with two Scandinavians Pekka and Laitho, starred in a co-production between the BBC, SR, NRK and YLE television a film called *The Case*, shown both on BBC and Swedish television. It took 10 days of filming and had a somewhat complicated plot. Cliff commented, 'They just shoved a black case in my hand and I ran from place to place.' At least, it kept him in trim. With Una Stubbs expecting a baby and Hank Marvin not wishing to be a resident guest, there were forced changes to the BBC1 TV series 'It's Cliff Richard', scheduled for 1972. Dandy Nichols, famed for her role as the long suffering, though far from defeated, wife of Alf Garnett in the BBC TV series 'Till Death Do Us Part', appeared for a while, but with Una's son Christian safely born she returned to the series. The New Seekers were special musical guests and sang the songs short-listed for Britain's entry to the 1972 Eurovision Song Contest. Among other guests were Labi Siffre and Elton John. The series gained two million more viewers than Cliff's 1971 effort.

Cliff, not without protests and discontent from some quarters, represented Britain in the Eurovision contest for the second time in 1973, and appeared for six weeks running on Cilla Black's BBC1 series singing the prospective songs including the eventual selection 'Power To All Our Friends'. Sadly, Cliff did not triumph on the vital night in Luxembourg and ended a mere third, even though experts rated the song as the strongest UK entry since 1967 when Sandie Shaw was victorious with 'Puppet On A String'.

Recalling and linking his two stabs at Eurovision, Cliff says, 'I was terrified then (1968) but this time I knew what to expect.' He confessed that it was awful sitting backstage and hearing the various jury results come in. He returned a disappointed man and said, 'Maybe I'm getting too old for song contests. I feel it would be unwise to appear again in a contest like this for at least five years. Then I'd be 38 – a bit of an old age pensioner for song contests, I think!'

In 1974 came more television, with 'The Cliff Richard Show' from the London Palladium, a special guest appearance on 'Look – Mike Yarwood', 'The Nana Mouskouri Show' and another series of 'It's Cliff Richard' for the BBC. Cliff had a yellow jacket plus a multicoloured tie, with his fringe parted in the middle, for Nana's show. His most unusual appearance on the box was for 'Play It Again, Stewpot'. Here Cliff was impersonated by a puppet that sported a purply flowered shirt and purple trousers.

His new series of 'It's Cliff' saw the emergence of the Nolan Sisters, with Cliff mostly relying on Sixties material. Lyn Paul was guest soloist on the second of the series, Dora Bryan and Labi Siffre the special guests the following week, and on programme four, Ireen Sheer and Aimi MacDonald. And so the series continued, with Cliff into a green jacket and white trousers by programme five and Olivia starring in the sixth and last show.

ITV's bustling and somewhat fun-crazy 'Saturday Scene' provided presenter Sally James with the chance to interview Cliff in April 1975. She discussed with Cliff his four and a half song-writing contributions to the album *31st of February Street*. He recalled he had written some songs previously, particularly the popular, 'Bachelor Boy', along with the Shads. He recalled the writing of 'On The Beach' and 'Don't Talk To Him' with Bruce. 'I stopped writing because I got more interested in singing and then, of course, when the Shadows were together they used to write; it kind of cut me out a little bit – not that I minded.'

'I keep telling the salesroom, my sofa and fireplace are not for sale.'

Cliff guested on Pete Murray's 'Open House' radio show in May 1975, where he talked of his general popularity in France, although he had not had hits there, save for one that he recorded in French – the well known song 'La Mer'. He also talked of his family as a close-knit group, discussed the weather, and talked over some old songs.

In 1975 came more of 'It's Cliff' with the extended title of 'It's Cliff – And Friends'. The show continued into the new year, with Adge Webber, Richard Kerr, Olivia Gray, Cotton Lloyd and Christians, Superior, comedians The Black Abbots, Les Brian, George Moody and Skyline among his guests. Obviously, there was an emphasis on general entertainment rather than merely the music scene. It must have seemed to some that Cliff was gradually moving away from the overall pop chart scene, but any such thoughts were soon proved unfounded, for his chart single at the beginning of 1976 was the gorgeous 'Miss You Nights'.

For his 'Top Of The Pops' performance in January 1976, on the show compered by Tony Blackburn, Cliff wore a dark suit with thin white stripes. A few weeks later, he appeared on the powerful ITV show of the time, 'Supersonic', and this time wore a white jacket and trousers and a green shirt. He was again on 'Top of the Pops' in late February, and for Cliff's fashion addicts, this time it was all new once more – a dark green suit, white shirt and green-and-black tie. 'Miss You Nights' had considerable radio exposure and should have gone higher than position 15 – it is surely one of his all-time greats. It was to be followed in the charts by another much favoured Top 10 hit, 'Devil Woman'.

The end of the Seventies saw the usual yearly flourish of major show bookings. He appeared on the colourful 'Tis Was' and underwent the usual rituals of the show, which included having something squashy stuffed in his face and cold water poured over him. Radio One broadcast the Cliff story in the first of a series that was called '20 Golden Years'. Dutch, Korean and Australian film and television concerns were among the international audience seeking his attention. The decade ended on a most happy note, for he was back on top of the record world, thanks to the number one hit 'We Don't Talk Anymore', and even the *NME*, finding its way out of the punk era, had time to stop and approve a rejuvenated Cliff.

Una Stubbs, looking back at her association with Cliff in the Sixties and Seventies, has nothing but the most enjoyable of memories. Speaking particularly about the various BBC series of which she was an important part, she comments: 'They were particularly popular programmes, but if they gave the impression of being almost ad-libbed, I can tell you they were tightly scripted.' Una's main role in these shows was acting with Cliff in a number of sketches. 'The audience loved them and seemed to like the fact that I got Cliff in the end! They didn't seem to be jealous.' She remembers another occasion at the Palladium when 'we kissed rather a lot and then the kids did squeal!' Una also contributed dancing skills that had been acquired during her early career; indeed originally she had been engaged for this ability when the casting was made for *Wonderful Life*.

I did not sing with Cliff. I'm a disaster when it comes to singing. Obviously things went wrong during rehearsals and I remember the time when Cliff pleaded with the producer to keep in the show something that had misfired but which we thought was great. However, it wasn't to be. I think the producer thought it might seem a bit like the popular 'Laugh In' show of the time where they showed a series of how things can go wrong.

She regrets that their time together had to end.

It was a great run and such fun. Both of us had lots of things happening and he would be tied up with tours and recordings and so somehow, as it often happens, time marches on. But we have kept in touch and when we meet up it's as though it was yesterday that we were together. We've simply got on so well. I suppose it was at a time when we were very young, finding success, seeing everything as new and exciting and we built up a good relationship, companionship really.

Moving to the Eighties, there were to be considerable changes, for there would be no entertainment series on television, but there were documentaries and major guest appearances on a number of radio and television chat shows. Doubtless, many of his new teenage followers are unaware that he was a regular TV performer with his own show, unlike in the Eighties when he has been seen as just a major music star who finds himself invited to 'chat' on the leading television talk shows. To an outsider, it must appear strange that someone like Cliff does not present his own show, either one with guests and with conversation dominating, or a contemporary music-styled show. The oddness of the situation is made more surprising by the very simple fact that there is always a need for shows that can draw an audience.

Certainly, Cliff's presence has not been lacking from our television screens. In radio, he has met problems, although this is not to say it has been a closed area; far from it, for there have been lengthy and engaging interview-music spots with people such as Mike Smith, Simon Bates, Roger Scott, Roger Day and Dave Lee Travis. Cliff has maintained close friendly associations with certain DJs, but there has been a feeling on the part of some – not just younger DJs but also some older ones who are striving to maintain their own declining youth – that really it's about time Cliff settled for the 'oldies' rather than a young audience. For some DJs, it is because their own 'image' comes first – they believe that their imagined legions of fans will think less of them if they should play a new Cliff record release. Others think there should be less heard of Cliff, in person or song, simply because he is getting older. This is just nonsense for kids of today do not seem to have an 'age' consciousness, and quite happily raid, listen and dance to music of other decades.

In the end, the only real question is whether the music of a Cliff, a Phil Collins, a Paul McCartney, a Bob Dylan or a Mick Jagger makes sense now. A particular new release may not do so: indeed, sometimes it didn't when they were much younger. But to say a Cliff record should not be scheduled in, say, Britain's Radio One playlist because Cliff is heading toward his 50th birthday is patently crass and stupid.

Undoubtedly, as he gets older, Cliff will face the matter of relevance, but it should also be remembered that even stars in their twenties in the fast moving world of pop have to meet the same question, and in even more insecure pastures than Cliff's; for the ethos surrounding a star, from the record company perspective, may purely be one of having obtained two hit singles and one big selling album, and no more. Cliff's larger battle lies in keeping up his own enthusiasm and desire to continue with hectic recording, touring and PR schedules. There is no sign whatsoever that he is fed up with any of these, although the latter can be a chore, as it was when he was considerably younger.

His television interview appearances fairly brim with the energy that has always character-ised his work. And he always looks good and is assured and personable. This tribute cannot, by virtue of lack of space, print the many television and radio interview transcripts that I have, from Britain, the continent, Australia, New Zealand, the States, and else-where, all of which display an increasingly cogent, intelligent, life-imbued person, whether the host be Wogan or Dame Edna Everage!

The Eighties have seen a number of major Cliff documentaries on radio and television,

Thirty years ago Radio Luxembourg was – as it is now –
at the forefront of British pop. It was the first
radio station to play Cliff Richard's debut EMI
single. Thirty years later we are both still going
strong!

Maurice Vass
Managing Director

Maurice Vass is MD of Radio Luxembourg whose programming is widely heard throughout Britain.

none more detailed and well assembled than those presented by BBC Television in 1981 and produced by Norman Stone. Cliff would rather see them as 'mini' documentaries since, in essence, they consisted of Cliff in conversation, some music, and talk with others about his music and life and so forth.

Certainly, he appreciated them. The series called 'Cliff' consisted of four programmes, each 50 minutes in length. The first, 'Rock 'n' Roll Juvenile', viewed his music career. The second 'Why Should The Devil Have All The Good Music', centred on his Gospel music. The third, 'Travellin' Light', covered his recent tour of the United States, while the fourth, 'My Kinda Life', was a film portrait. Producer Norman Stone said he had tried to make the programmes 'starkly visual but distinctive' and certainly not 'one long concert'. More than 40 interviews were recorded by researcher and interviewer Steve Turner.

Another highlight of the Eighties in the television field was a series of interviews and appearances on American television, as part of a further attempt by Cliff to realise his heart's desire and mean something to the American music public, or, in less complex terms, to establish himself in both the singles and album charts in the States. On January 7 and 8, 1982, consecutively, he appeared on 'The Mike Douglas Show' and 'The Dinah Shore Show'. His main promotional focus centred on his major European hit, 'We Don't Talk Anymore'. But naturally the Americans seemed more fascinated by his new, seemingly ancient and historic, appendage, his OBE.

Dinah: Now let me tell you a remarkable thing. Cliff Richard has been awarded the OBee . . . it's the OBE . . . its, well . . . you explain. . . .

Cliff: It's the 'Order of the British Empire' . . . and, of course, I was 'Off Broadway' when I got it.

71

From here the conversation turned toward his Indian birth and childhood. Cliff talked of the British Raj and the British Empire. A further historic and profound moment came a little later:

Dinah: I read in your biography that you are single now.
Cliff: Well, I always have been. I've been single all the time.
Dinah: You've never been married???

The Mike Douglas Show also began with the matter of that OBE.

Mike: What happens . . . I mean, do you actually go to the Palace?
Cliff: Yes, I have been there a few times, but that's not the thing. It's when they give you that little medal . . .

The conversation then turned to Cliff's career with Douglas commenting: 'You have had more hits than virtually anyone that I have had on this show. It must be in the *Guinness Book of Records* . . . 70 hit records.' Cliff responded with great mental agility and quickness of thought: 'I think the Guinness Book of Records should say that, after 21 years, I'm still the best unknown in your country.' Later Cliff recalled his American visit of 1960 and how he thought then he could take America, until he saw how big the place was.

Douglas was not the last major American chat show host to interview Cliff, for in March of the same year he appeared on the 'Merv Griffin Show'. Here, the immediate conversation saw Cliff recalling his 1960 visit. Griffin expressed his astonishment that Cliff should have been on the 'Biggest Show of Stars' for 1960.

Griffin: You date back to 1960?
Cliff: I go back even further.
Griffin: But you still look like a kid!
Cliff: I was a child star!

He talked of Cliff's Christian experience and then switched back to music, with a remark that amused Cliff:

Merv: The Beatles were fans of yours, Elvis Presley was a fan . . .
Cliff: Oh! I don't know about that . . . but it sounds good though. I like it, but I'm not quite sure whether they were fans.

The next year, he was back once more in Los Angeles. He appeared on the Griffin show once again, but also on the 'John Kelly Show'. The 'John Davison Show' and Dionne Warwick's 'Solid Gold Show'.

Shortly after this book is published, it seems likely that Cliff may well be back on television screens with a new format show.

I haven't avoided a TV series during the Eighties. The right thing hasn't come along. I haven't wanted seaside and summer specials or the kind of thing where you say, 'Hi, I'm Cliff Richard. On my show tonight is . . . and here they are to sing their new single . . . Nor have I wanted a re-run of the old ideas that were OK, yes, years ago. Not now.

R A D I O W A V E S

Like everyone else, I know that Cliff has given us some of the finest British records ever made. But alongside his music making I think that British radio has an awful lot to thank him for: Cliff understands that radio is the finest medium yet invented for the sharing of music and for strengthening that all important link between an artist and his audience. Over the years it has been my good fortune to produce many Cliff Richard radio shows and to get to know a little of the man himself. No other artist of his stature is as professional in his media dealings or in his enthusiastic approach to programme making. The sadness is that his ongoing success has stimulated more than a fair share of media sniping - the joy is that I know he'll be 'Wired for sound' for many years to come and that millions of us will still want to be listening.

Tim Blackmore
Programme Director
PPM Independent Radio Production

BBC
T E L E V I S I O N

For almost ten years I produced "Top of the Pops" weekly, and during that time I had quite a few traumatic moments with unruly and inexperienced people. However, there were also many happy and exciting times with some marvellous artists - none more welcome or greater than Cliff Richard. The praise one would wish to heap on him sound nothing less than fulsome - every hit, and there were many, had a superbly worked out routine which he always performed with energy and excitement. Never late and ever co-operative over all arrangements, he was a pleasure to work with - a true professional.

Those of us who know him personally feel - that besides a natural talent and charm, he is one of the most sincere, hard-working and intelligent people in showbusiness.

Yours sincerely,

(Robin Nash)
Executive Producer
Light Entertainment (Comedy) Department

Tim Blackmore has been an Executive Producer for Radio One, Head of Music at London's Capital radio station and is now a director of PPM.

Robin Nash is one of the BBC's most famous light entertainment producers and was for many years responsible for the high viewing figures that have come the way of *Top of the Pops*.

And he has veered away from the sort of show that might seem like a 'Top of the Pops', but featuring only his hits.

> I don't want the typical Saturday night variety show either. I don't know really! I did enjoy the show with Norman Stone some years back. There it had an ethos I liked – it was to tell people what it's like to be me, come around with me, talk with those around me and catch some of the atmosphere, the boring bits and the great times. And it was done with some speed, weaving in and out of things. All I know is that whatever I do it must be exciting.

This author wondered why he had not got into the 'chat' show area. Cliff's answer: 'I'd talk too much!' I recalled something Tear Fund's founder George Hoffman once said to me, that when they had gone to film Cliff as he toured parts of the Third World they threw away their prepared scripts, for they realised he was animated, excited and rational enough for them to take a film without being hedged in by words and directions. He was let loose to see, react and comment, as he walked ahead of cameras and overall film crew, and this made for exciting and spontaneous watching.

'Well . . .' said a dubious looking Cliff in response, 'OK there, but not when you have a series, for you do need guidelines, not only for yourself, but for all the others who are involved.'

So what will it be? 'I have ideas. If I tell you, someone else might pinch them!'

Whatever they are, we can expect the result to be exciting and professional as ever.

73

The Stage
and
TELEVISION TODAY

Cliff has always remained at the top, in the biggest halls, theatres and other venues.

Why ? Well, I suppose that is the magic of Cliff. But only in part At least some of his lasting success must be due to his sheer professionalism, which is something those of us involved with the theatre and light entertainment fields, as distinct from pop, prize above everything else - the ability to always give a good show, regardless of the conditions. I saw Cliff at Chiswick Empire when he was starting out 30 years ago, and I have seen him many times since, at the Talk of the Town, in pantomime at the Palladium, in a Graham Greene play at Sadler's Wells, at the Albert Hall and, of course, in 'Time' at the Dominion, and he has always been the same, superbly professional. You don't have to be a fan of Cliff's to admire him, and this may also have something to do with his approach to life in general as well as with the quality of his work.

In over 30 years around this business I have never heard a word against him - and never expect to do so.

PETER HEPPLE
Editor: The Stage and Television Today

Peter Hepple edits Britain's foremost magazine of theatre and club entertainment, *The Stage*. The journal also covers radio and television.

5 STAGE AND SCREEN

Musical movies seemed to be on the wane during the very early Sixties. Before then, there had been an average of 50 or 60 a year. But rising budgets had curtailed former unbridled enthusiasm, and box-office success was guaranteed only to films like *South Pacific, Can Can*, and *The King And I*, now reissued in an even-wider screen print.

Both in career terms, and in market possibilities, *The Young Ones*, arguably Cliff's greatest film, happened at the right time. It was released in 1961, and there was a niche available for something that would catch the flavour of the day. *The Young Ones*, with its fun, jollity and endless energy, caught the innocence, newness and naivety of the time. Its title tune was an anthem for youth, so far removed from the cynicism, aggressions and blatant generational conflict espoused in The Who's admittedly glorious shout of 'My Generation' in 1965. It was youth with freedom, money and a sense of adventure, of a Britain breaking free from the straitjacket of postwar rationing and austerity. For adults, it had a good message, that youth was not unthankful for the sacrifices that had been made by parents and grandparents. This was an attitude that was fast dying out. Soon, youth would be demanding more, and rounding on their elders with accusations. They would point to those in power who were busy planning World War III, polluting the planet with nuclear dust, disturbing the earth's ecological balance. Young people would pour scorn on the hypoctrical adult lifestyle which criticised youth culture but was itself imbued with worship of alcohol and tranquillisers or, as The Rolling Stones put it 'Mother's little helper'.

The Young Ones stands as 'the' film musical of the 1960s, and unlike the Beatle films, it demanded more of its central character, and on reflection it seems to stand the test of time better than films built around the Liverpool four or Elvis Presley. Certainly this view, held by many, has been expressed by Alan Sievewright, who, at the suggestion of director Sidney Fury and choreographer Herb Ross, was engaged as the consultant designer on *The Young Ones*. Apart from finding Cliff marvellous to work with, Sievewright, now a rather grand figure in film and opera circles, sees *The Young Ones*, and Cliff's subsequent films in the Sixties as classics.

The Young Ones, particularly, holds up very well. It all seems very simple, but simple things are difficult to achieve. It projected an exuberance and really it was this film that set Sidney and Herb on to their now very illustrious careers. No one thought Cliff a great actor but he was damn good, and there and then, and since, I have had to take my hat off to him. Cliff had to work very, very hard. He was carefully choreographed to seem better than he was, cleverly constructed to make him better. I doubt if Cliff had ever kicked his legs in the air save on a few pop songs but here he was with dance routines among professionals.

The great thing about him then, and obviously since, lies in his commitment. He was very much at ease. I don't think the Beatles were, in their films, and the Beatles were always Beatles, up to high jinks and games, no more. They took hold of Cliff and made him play a role, something the Beatles did not. It wasn't just a case of Cliff getting up and singing some songs.

And you have to remember Cliff was 21, not 17, and there is an enormous difference in those ages at that time of life. He had to jump back and think what it was like to be 17. His instincts were right and you can't teach that.

It was freelance stage producer Kenneth Harper, of the Grade organisation, who decided there should be a musical film. Harper was not a brash style of producer, but a very distinguished Englishman. Sievewright remarks that it all might have been an absolute disaster. 'And they had terrible problems finding the right kind of girl to play opposite him. In the end the choice was right, in the experienced Carole Gray.'

For Cliff, the film was a welcome relief after the somewhat irksome process of his earlier filming in *Serious Charge* and *Expresso Bongo*: 'In those two I felt awkward and very ill at ease and so embarrassed whenever I had to face the camera. But when I started to make *The Young Ones* I knew I was going to have a ball.'

Cliff hit it off with Sid Fury, himself young and keen enough to inject the film with something extra-special, all certainly far from a production-line job. But Cliff was daunted initially by the film's demands: 'When I read in the script that I had to dance, boy, was I scared! I just didn't see how I was going to get away with it. I'm no Gene Kelly. I prayed for a great dance choreographer. Well, my prayers came true. It was Herbie who gave me every confidence when it came to dance routines.'

He had another worry – Robert Morley had been cast as his screen father. 'He was one of the best actors around. His experience frightened the life out of me even before we started playing the scenes. I didn't see how I could possibly share an acting scene with him.' But Cliff now says, 'He was marvellous and gave me so much help.'

The first of his films, *Serious Charge*, had seen him playing Curley Thompson, a guy whose brother was the gang leader of speed-crazy kids who were supposedly misunderstood by adults. The film had gained an X-certificate which meant that most of his fans, being under 18, would not have been allowed to see it. He had been praised for his performance, even if it had been relatively unpolished. However, it was enough to persuade British producer Val Guest to offer him the leading role in the screen version of the London stage hit, *Expresso Bongo*. Guest, apparently, was quite unprepared for the reception that greeted Cliff in his first starring role. Certainly the film whetted Cliff's appetite for more, and in a moment of sudden reflection he said at the time, 'One can never tell how long rock 'n' roll will last and, frankly, I would like to have some acting experience behind me as well, so that at a moment's notice, I could work before the film cameras.'

The film was a penetrating glimpse into coffee-bar society of the time; as the publicity notice said: a 'modern fable of how Johnny Jackson, a likeable but unscrupulous citizen of the square mile of song known as Soho, promotes and exploits young Bongo Herbert.'

One unnamed writer of the time wrote in the popular *Hit Parade* magazine:

The thing that may well stand out in your mind when you eventually see *Bongo* will be this. If Cliff's acting is rated as high as his singing, it will without a shadow of doubt put his name before all other contenders for the title of British king of rock 'n' roll. In fact, as the result of distributing the film overseas, it may well help Cliff to begin challenging Elvis for the international title.

Francis Cross, writing in the *New Musical Express*, saw Cliff as a smoother actor from the previous film, and certainly the only one with 'the faintest idea of how to handle a musical number.' Cliff sang three songs in the film, 'Shrine On The Second Floor', 'A Voice In The Wilderness' and 'Love'. *Serious Charge* had, of course, spawned his first-ever million-selling single, 'Living Doll'. Sievewright would place both films very much behind *The Young Ones*.

I think we set out to make it all very glamorous. I don't know what I expected in Cliff. All I knew was that here would be this popular pop star and I had to fit him out as a teenager, take him back a few years. I recall he had a few henchmen around this time for he was so popular and needed some kind of protection from fans who would innocently tear every piece of cloth from him!

Sievewright remembers Cliff's preoccupation with his legs. 'I remember he asked me if he had short legs. Well, I said, it depended on how we would approach proportions. He wasn't a small person, after all. Anyway, I got together with Cecil Gee, very much the go-ahead men's shop in those days if you were up with fashion, and designed accordingly. He was very co-operative.'

Cliff's enormous popularity was made very plain to Sievewright.

We rehearsed in a hall around Tottenham Court Road, in London. It wasn't long before the fans got to know of the venue and anyway Cliff had this pink cadillac which he parked outside! There was one day where there was an enormous crowd. I was dark-haired in those days, so we did a swop over. He would take mine and I, his. So I disguised myself as best I could and really got mobbed and almost got ripped into pieces. When the girls realised, they were absolutely livid!

Later, of course, the iron gates of Elstree kept out the curious and fanatic.

For Cliff, *The Young Ones* came in a difficult year. There were management problems and, more important, there was the death of his father, and for a brief while filming was stopped. But in those days there was a great deal of camaraderie. And at the end of it all, Cliff said: 'I don't look upon *The Young Ones* as being just a personal success, but a success for everyone who worked on it, because if it had not been for their help, well, I don't know what would have become of me in films.'

Summer Holiday and *Wonderful Life* would follow pretty close on the heels of *The Young Ones* and arguably drew larger audiences, but then it might be said that the standard set by the first musical paved the way for a wide acceptance of what was to come.

Certainly there was no diminishment in the fun stakes. Una Stubbs starred in both films and, indeed, she can thank *Summer Holiday* for launching her out beyond a previously restricted world of dancing. 'I knew little about Cliff when I went to audition. I

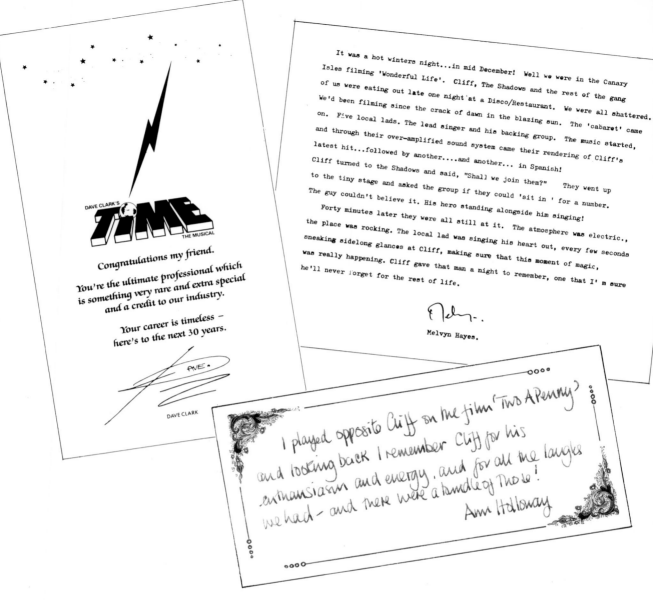

It was a hot winters night...in mid December! Well we were in the Canary Isles filming 'Wonderful Life'. Cliff, The Shadows and the rest of the gang of us were eating out late one night at a Disco/Restaurant. We were all shattered. We'd been filming since the crack of dawn in the blazing sun. The 'cabaret' came on. Five local lads. The lead singer and his backing group. The music started, and through their over-amplified sound system came their rendering of Cliff's latest hit...followed by another....and another... in Spanish! Cliff turned to the Shadows and said, "Shall we join them?" They went up to the tiny stage and asked the group if they could 'sit in ' for a number. The guy couldn't believe it. His hero standing alongside him singing! Forty minutes later they were all still at it. The atmosphere was electric., the place was rocking. The local lad was singing his heart out, every few seconds sneaking sidelong glances at Cliff, making sure that this moment of magic, was really happening. Cliff gave that man a night to remember, one that I' m sure he'll never forget for the rest of life.

Melvyn Hayes.

I played opposite Cliff on the film 'Two A Penny' and looking back I remember Cliff for his enthusiasm and energy, and for all the laughs we had — and there were a bundle of those!
Ann Holloway

suppose there was something about me which appealed to them and I ended up with a screen test and I was very pleased to get out of the chorus. It was my career break.'

She talks of a tremendous sense of togetherness amongst the cast. 'I think it had something to do with the fact that we were very young and we were all going somewhere. I can remember having so many good times. There was a spirit of companionship and trust.'

She thinks it important to note that *Summer Holiday*, like the previous musical, was pre-Beatles and pre-Stones.

I think there was very much an up-coming Sixties feel but with a Fifties morality. It was all good and wholesome; not goody-goody, mind you. I remember my first impression of Cliff was that he was a nice guy, funny, kind and he could be very witty.

78

...is always full of joy and enthusiasm. He takes time down. He always has time... Cliff and is genuinely interested in you and your family and what they are all up to. A thoroughly nice person bursting with talent; and a shining faith which is beautifully enduring. He has certainly been chosen and carefully placed by God very near the limelight & he shirks that responsibility never.

Love, Dora

I consider myself so lucky to have met Cliff never mind, working with him for ten years... he is a life enhancer.

Una Stubbs
x x

Dora Bryan has had hit records but is best known for countless TV and theatre credits, not forgetting her film work.

Una Stubbs appeared in film and television series with Cliff, and is a major theatre star in her own right.

Dave Clark headed the famous **Dave Clark Five** of 1960s pop fame, has done much more, including being the man behind the major musical Time.

Melvyn Hayes the famous British film and stage actor, particularly known for his role in the major TV series.

Ann Holloway is a famous theatre and film and TV actress.

I remember we all laughed a lot on the set for *Summer Holidays* but then whenever I meet Cliff now we laugh a lot. Everything was so positive and it was not a cynical time.

For Cliff there was one odd side to the filming of *Summer Holiday*: much of it took place in Greece, and he arranged for his mother and two sisters Joan and Jacqueline to have a brief holiday. He found them a bungalow on one of the beaches near Athens. However, filming commitments meant that he saw less of them than he might have done in England.

'I used to telephone them every day to see if they were enjoying it. They might have been a thousand miles away for all I was able to see them. They were on holiday – I wasn't.'

His most intriguing experience of *Summer Holiday* lay in his learning to drive a large

I don't want to put this too strongly, but I think it's fair to say that Cliff Richard ruined my teenage years. It wasn't really his fault, but from the moment I saw *Summer Holiday* I became completely obsessed with the idea of going abroad in a double decker London bus. And since I was only 13 at the time, my parents wouldn't let me. Instead we had the usual fortnight in Tenby with the rain belting down, no-one my age within 50 miles and not a bus in sight. (And before the whole of Tenby writes in to complain – the place was lovely. It just wasn't a bus.) My mum and dad were very understanding ('Now dear, you can't always have everything you want' and 'Life isn't like the cinema – just imagine the diesel fumes') and wisely thought my fantasy would fade into oblivion as quickly as Mr. Richard himself, the latest in a long line of teenage heart-throbs. Well, my obsession did fade (though not until I was at least 16, I might add), but the great Cliff is still going strong. And what's more, still winning fans and making hit records. The secret of his long-running success has always fascinated me.

Bridget Rowe
Editor *Woman's Own*

Bridget Rowe edits one of Britain's best selling women's magazines – *Woman's Own*.

London double-decker bus which he accomplished to his satisfaction. There was also Trudy, a St Bernard dog, who was so large that she worried some Greeks who were not used to dogs of that size, some even believing she was a lion! Trudy intruded into the film at points where she had no contract. Eventually, she was taken home by film producer Andrew Mitchell and later had a role in the film *French Dressing*.

Cliff was busy filming *Wonderful Life* in the Canary Islands when he heard he had won first place in the *Motion Picture Herald* survey for the most popular British film star. He spent two-and-a-half months escaping from the winter of 1963–64, a season only slightly better than the terrible British winter of the previous year. Away from the filming there were plenty of late night raves in a small club a few hundred yards from the official hotel residence. However, true to form, there was no staying up until the early hours if he had to be up early next day for filming.

Once more Cliff was called upon to dance. The dance director of *Wonderful Life* was Gillian Lynne. Asked for her opinion on Cliff the dancer she says:

He has an inborn line in his movements – roughly that means his body maintains a series of clean-cut, symmetrical positions during a dance routine. Again, he has a natural sense of phrasing. Though that, too, is hard to explain to a non-dancer. I can give the broad illustration that a dance sequence has to be phrased in the way a song must be phrased – if it's sung by someone like Sinatra. Thirdly, Cliff's dancing is greatly helped by his sense of rhythm.

She remarked that, before the location work, there had been a month's general training for all the *Wonderful Life* dancers. Cliff had been asked and had willingly joined in the training sessions, more often than not turning up ahead of time.

Cliff's favourite memory is of travelling from the filming centres on a minibus with The Shadows and an English nurse Jennifer Gretton, who had been living in the Canaries

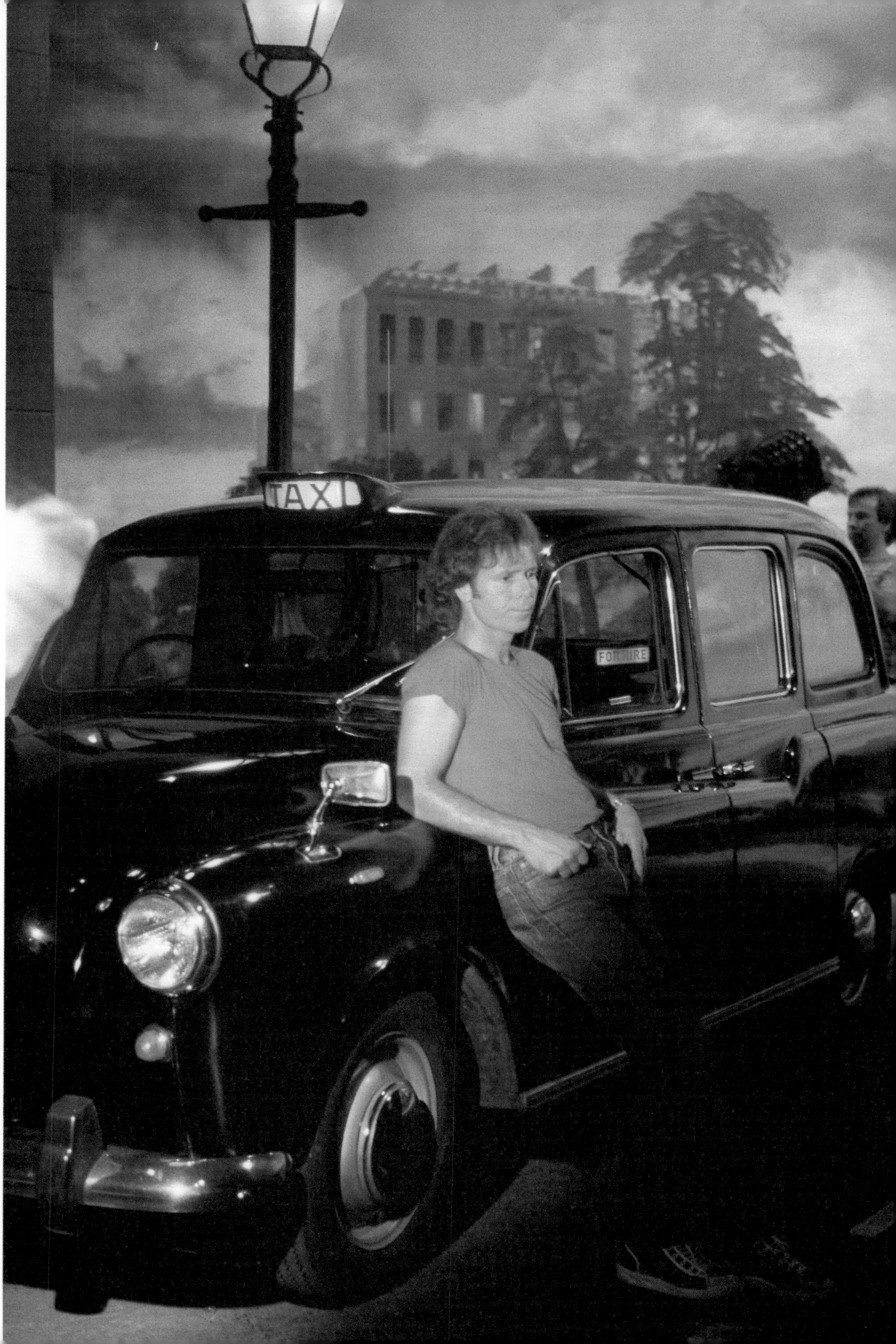
TAXI
FOR HIRE

13

9 In-between work at the video shoot.
10 'So you had no idea about my other job?'
11 'Never without my dancing shoes.'
12 'When the signals fail, they send for me.'
13 'With a girl like you . . .' making a video film for one of Cliff's singles.

14 Another bouquet for Cliff.
15 For once, no audience.
16 To think that once the only lighting was an on and off process.

for three years and had been accepted for the job as the film's nurse in residence. She remarked that she had not heard the Beatles and wondered what they were like – for 20 minutes she had been listening to the Shads performing Beatle favourites.

For Cliff there is also the fond recollection of making great use of the camera he had received from Sir Joseph Lockwood – chairman of EMI – as a 21st birthday present. He took thousands of photographs.

The decade would produce one other film – *Finders Keepers*, apart from *Two A Penny*, which he filmed with the Billy Graham organisation.

And then he was lost to filmland. Times had changed and he had much else in the offing. His Christian activities expanded and fought for space in an already crowded diary. In any case, he felt it was becoming increasingly difficult to find a good musical script, and this feeling gained momentum towards the end of the Sixties: 'I think of those films in the Sixties: *Finders Keepers* had the best music, but it wasn't the best film we had done. I didn't want to get into the rut of making films like Elvis did.'

The Shadows were not enamoured with the prospect of more filming. Cliff says, 'We had our own careers and they didn't interfere with mine and I didn't interfere with theirs. Brian and John were not happy doing films, and they don't enjoy it. So, at that time, it was on the cards that there may never be another Cliff Richard and The Shadows in film again.'

However, early in the Seventies surprise was in the air, for it was suddenly announced that he would star in a film entitled *Take Me High*. In the film he would fall in love with 25-year-old Debbie Watling, daughter of Jack, then one of Britain's best-known film faces. It was an event of sheer delight for the press who, long denied a real-life Cliff romance at least had a film 'simulation' on their hands. The 1973 film had one particularly passionate clinch that came the way of the 33-year-old bachelor. Said one headline:

CLIFF MAKES THE FIRST KISS LAST SO LONG

They believed the kiss was like no other – it might have been the world's finest. And Cliff increased media temperature by remarking about Debbie, 'She's fantastic. We exchange kisses all the time, but we treat that love scene rather beautifully.' But he denied it could be called 'erotic' and instead saw it as 'an old-fashioned falling in love.'

And that, alas is it, when it comes to films, save for documentary material with a religious tinge.

But there is theatre, and the stage has the honour of claiming Cliff's allegiance before the world of film. He had trodden the way of most beginners, at school. And during early times he talked a great deal about acting, as well as trying to compensate in practical ways for an obvious lack of real training. In early days, he suggested that the drama school course could teach him a lot, but added, 'but they can't give you talent'. He believed its value was reduced in the case of youthful students. 'The schools teach voice, speech, fencing and dancing, and those sort of things are good, but you have to live a little and mature a little before you can give real expression to the talent inside you.'

On feelings he was to say, 'Acting arouses feelings inside you, then you have to tell yourself how much of those feelings you need to express in each part of the performance.'

Early in his career he was much affected by advice he received from Robert Morley. He passed on this advice of Morley's: 'No one should avoid mistakes if it is in their nature to make certain mistakes. They should make them and discover what the cost of the mistake is, rather than constantly avoid it, and never really know the lesson to be learned from it. Making mistakes isn't that bad, as long as your mistakes are not destructive.'

Not all would agree with some of the young Cliff's remarks, but most actors and drama students would agree that they too would 'hope to profit from my mistakes,' like the early Cliff. But, of course, film and stage are not the same, and Cliff's professional experience came from the former.

In February 1968 he appeared in the ATV play *A Matter Of Diamonds* but it was not one of his successes. He received a cool reception for his performance although, as he remarked, 'Because this was my first dramatic role, I relied heavily on the director. Fortunately, he was pleased with my performance. I had to play a part that said things I didn't believe in, but I did it because this is all part of filming. There were no light moments, so I had to constantly concentrate on what was going on.'

He found television a slow medium 'unless you get a good script. One has to do these things and it is unfortunate that one can't always pick a winner.' He still wanted to work in this area, but he would want to ensure that the script was right for him on another occasion.

It would not be until 1970 that Cliff would appear in an actual theatre play as opposed to pantomime. This was Peter Shaeffer's *Five Finger Exercise*, which was followed a year later by Graham Greene's *The Potting Shed*. The latter was scheduled for Bromley New Theatre but, when the premises were demolished by fire, it was transferred to Sadler's Wells. In a sense, the new location was good for Cliff and fans, since Bromley, for all its merits, is a little off the main theatre map. In *The Potting Shed* Cliff took the part of James Calliger, a 30-year-old who is denied family love and attempts to find out why.

We all know that Cliff is a great and endearing singer. What many do not know is that he is also a fine actor and could have reached the summit in the theatres. I saw his performance some years ago in a play called 'Five Finger Exercise' and it was rivetting. But I suppose we must not be greedy. To have Cliff as a National Theatre star and a top singer would perhaps be asking too much. I am delighted that he has continued to grace the world of popular music, giving delight to millions. Long may it be so.

Lord Ted Willis

Cliff Richard was a very important part of my teen years. I still remember his first appearance (in glorious black & white) on SIX FIVE SPECIAL. I knew the words of all his songs & did my early courting with Cliff in the background. In the back row of the Embassy, Harpenden, I spent the whole of SUMMER HOLIDAY struggling (like a good student) to understand the intricacies of my first girlfriend's bra-clip. & I remember solving the problem just as Cliff got to the Acropolis. Keep it up, Cliff!

Bill Homewood

Jonathan Miller writes and directs for theatre. He came to the fore with the revue
Beyond The Fringe. He is one of the major names in his field.

Herb Ross produced *The Young Ones* and *Summer Holiday*, two of Cliff's most
successful films.

The original production had taken place 15 years previously, with Sir John Gielgud
playing Calliger. The reviews were favourable for both plays. For Shaffer's play, Cliff
grew a beard: 'I grew the beard to try and convince the audience I was not just another
pop star trying to act.' Producer Patrick Tucker did not approve; he thought it made
Cliff look too old and the offending hair was shaved off.

An unexpected happening was his decision to join with past and present pupils of his
old school in a production of Shakespeare's *A Midsummer Night's Dream*, in which he
played Bottom. This was produced by his old English teacher, Mrs Jay Norris. It opened
at Riversmead School, College Road, Cheshunt, on 3 July, 1974.

All this was pretty much small fry compared to his films. But it did provide inner
satisfaction, for this was something he wanted to do – and why not?

At this moment, the 'big' theatre event was still lying a decade away. This, of course,
was *Time*, eventually staged at London's Dominion Theatre in 1985. Here was an event
in the heart of London's West End; a major production that cost a great deal to stage
and that would receive full critical coverage. *Time* was the brainchild of one-time pop
star, Dave Clark. Clark was the drummer with the Dave Clark Five, a group from the
Sixties, protagonists of the 'Tottenham' sound from North London. The group, at different
times, found success both in Britain and the USA. In the late Sixties, Clark launched
into the world of film production without too much success; curiously, considering the
success of his film and theatrical expeditions in the next decade and the Eighties. Clark
said he had envisaged *Time* over a period of five years and promised that his show would

Lord Ted Willis is a well-known playwright and media personality.

Bill Homewood found TV fame for being The Backwards Man, has worldwide
acclaim for credits with the Royal Shakespeare Company and his celebrated
production featuring Estelle Kohler as Fanny. He is Dean of Studies at the new
much heralded British and American Drama Academy.

be the most complex and expensive seen in London stage circles. He promised to gather stars for his cast, with Lord Olivier being one of the first names announced. Cliff was asked if he would undertake the leading role.

Dave Clark told me, 'I didn't bully Cliff into taking a major role in *Time*. I wanted to use a rock star for the part and Cliff was my first choice. I played him some songs and he wanted to hear everything. Then he said he would be delighted to take the part.'

Clark was well aware that a year out of Cliff's life and existing busy schedule would mean a deeply thought-out commitment. He knew of old that Cliff was someone who would be totally involved, once the initial decision had been made. Clark's request more or less coincided with Cliff's own feelings that he wanted a return to theatreland. 'I realised he thought it was the right move for him and I must say he was as I thought: someone never bored; who always came in early; who was enthusiastic. Cliff is a prime example of someone who never holds back; he always gives a full performance. He fitted in well with everyone.'

Some of Cliff's friends thought the necessary commitment would prove stifling. Perhaps they would have been less worried in the Sixties, when he was used to giving up huge chunks of time to film and pantomime. Yet, of course, Cliff had made plain for some time that he had an urge to return once more to the land of theatre. He calls the worried supporters 'Job's comforters', now that the whole thing has been part of his life. The pragmatic Cliff felt at the time that, even if it was a disaster, it would release him with little to do and bags of time for tennis. Of course, he agreed, and said he would stay in the show for 12 months, and in so doing more or less ruled most other things out of his life. 'I did want to star in a West End musical and I could act, dance and sing, the three things I loved. And this show was quite something.'

As it was, he went through the whole year without missing a performance – quite a feat in itself. And he actually enjoyed theatre life. For once, he could hide away, there in his dressing room, which over the weeks he carefully furnished to make another home. Of course, his residency was not without problems. There was the August Bank Holiday when he wrote off his VW Golf on the M4; several bad evenings when he had sinus trouble and it hurt to reach the top notes, and, of course, there was the great blow when his long-time friend and second mother Mamie Latham died. He was, however, able to visit her as she reached the end of her life, for on the particular evening in question the

From the *Cats* lady and a million other shows.

here's to, working with you ong day
love Stephanie [signature] x

MARIA CALLAS
MEMORIAL EXHIBITION
DIRECTOR: ALAN SIEVEWRIGHT

Dear Cliff

When I was asked to contribute something to this book, my mind went back to 1961 when I worked with you as design consultant on 'The Young Ones', a film that has become a classic of its kind. In 'Expresso Bongo' you had really played yourself, a Top of the Pops star. But for 'The Young Ones' you had to make yourself into a screen actor.

I am tickled pink that you are still at the top after all these years, thanks to your abilities and hard work – above all, that you have never lost the affection of a huge public over all these decades.

Best wishes

Alan Sievewright,

Alan Sievewright has countless major TV, film and theatre credits and in recent has
been particularly known for his work in commemorating the world of the late Maria Callas.

stage computer system failed to function and the show was cancelled. It was something to say thank you for.

In January 1986 Cliff began rehearsals, with the overall cast boosted by the basic team of John Napier. He had won acclaim for his designs and creations on both sides of the Atlantic for his work in Cats, the Royal Shakespeare Company's productions of *Equus* and *Nicholas Nickleby*, and the stunning *Starlight Express*. Also boosting the team was top American director and choreographer Larry Fuller, with credits in *Funny Girl*, starring Barbra Streisand, *Evita, Sweeney Todd* and *On The Twentieth Century*.

The world premiere of *Time* was announced for London's Dominion theatre on 9 April 1986. The show took listeners and viewers away into another world and time – some 2,300,065 light years away – a mind-boggling concept. Life on Earth has been observed and found wanting. The people of Earth are threatened with extermination because they have been a cruel race, and their behaviour threatens the peace of the universe. Cliff

Best wishes from the Blackadder man and much more.

85

plays Chris Wilder and, mostly through song, he has to plead for Earth's future. Earth's main plus is seen in rock music. Chris eventually returns to Earth and pleads that it is up to all its inhabitants to be wise and make the Earth a better place to live.

During Cliff's residency, some 650,000 people saw the show. There was an 85 per cent capacity throughout the 12 months before Cliff's role was taken over – by David Cassidy, though both Freddie Mercury of Queen and John Travolta were strongly rumoured to have been chosen to take his place.

The stage set was sensational; full of exciting and extravagent effects. Some of the scenes gained audience applause, particularly the spaceship landing on stage and the Ascension scene, where lasers, lights and sounds often produced gasps of amazement.

At first, the show suffered from computer problems, but all soon fell into place, with only a few upsets ahead, one of which was when three technicians fell 15ft through a stage trapdoor as they tried to repair the hydraulic platform. The show met enthusiastic ovations and comment, with Cliff fan magazines full of letters of praise. But, while there were many commendations for the show, there were some harsh words from the critics. The esteemed Milton Shulman of the *London Evening Standard* doubted if anyone over the age of 25 would enjoy the proceedings unless equipped with dark glasses and cotton wool for the ears. He concluded 'If parents are prepared to sit through a gruelling event, I suspect that an audience of eight to fourteen year olds, too young to recognise the naivety of it all could keep it going.'

Another well-known critic, Sheridan Morley, writing in an illustrated history of the first 100 years of British musicals, saw it as one of the worst musicals of the century. He was baffled that an actor as great as Olivier should have become involved, even though it was only his recorded voice that was heard. In the *Sunday Times*, critic John Peter hoped there would never be anything like *Time* again; 'an apocalyptic rave-in for affluent zombies: an expense of spirit in a waste of electronics and high-tech engineering.' Whereas many critics disliked the show but said little of Cliff, Peter was most blunt: 'I don't think Cliff Richard could act his way into a deserted railway station.'

Michael Ratcliffe in the *Observer* must have made everyone happy when, in the first paragraph of his review, he wrote: 'The show looks absolutely sensational', but joy was shortlived, for the crunch followed. 'It needs to; the gap between the sophistication of what you see and the modesty of what you hear has rarely been so great.' However, he thought it the greatest light show in town, with effects even down to the 'most astonishing of all, the elephant hide walls of this usually duff theatre appear to come alive and dissolve before your very eyes as mirrored shutters revolve at lightning speed in one of the most enfolding and alarming effects that I have ever seen.'

Cliff's disappointment with the reviews was considerable, indeed he professed himself hurt. 'To my dying days I don't think I'll ever understand why the show didn't receive at least a couple of accolades.'

He also felt that some people saw the whole thing as an exploit by a group of people who had intruded improperly into the West End theatre's hallowed ground. In his opinion, the world of British theatre does not take kindly to nonconformists.

But, as he has said, team spirit and morale was always high, and they got on with the job and had the satisfaction of seeing high attendances. Cliff found Dave Clark 'very,

Poshed up for the end of *Time* party.

Freddie Mercury on the left, Dave Clarke in the centre and
... a cake in front of Dave.

very encouraging' and both agreed that, generally speaking, the people whose opinions mattered most were the ones who had paid for their tickets. Apart from critics, reviews and his overall relationship with theatreland, Cliff himself found the experience rewarding, and he has ambitions to play in another stage musical, should the right one come along, though it might not be a musical in the accepted sense.

On the last evening on which Cliff appeared, Dave Clark told the audience how they had known each other since the early 1960s:

> It has been an experience to work with Cliff. It is an amazing feat in our business to find a star that has never missed a single performance, who has given 100 per cent of himself every night. Cliff always arrives at the theatre two hours before a performance, he is always on stage 5 minutes before the curtain goes up, and for that alone you are a credit to our profession.

He presented Cliff with a lovely photograph of the Dominion all lit up at night . . . with *Time*.

Cliff answered, saying he thought he might have been bored after a matter of weeks, but it was not so. He hadn't had one boring moment. He also gave vent to his hostility with the press: 'If there are any press in here, I want you to hear this, you should write now, that this is the greatest thing that has ever hit the theatre.'

The final send-off was a very emotional affair, with even a Scottish piper coming on stage to pipe Auld Lang Syne. The cast sang the end of 'It's In Everyone Of Us' as they left the stage, and the curtain came down. The fans cried 'We want Cliff' – but sadly Cliff had gone, until the next time!

" As a dance-hall manager in the 60's who actually knew + worked with Cliff (I doubled as my own D.J.,) my ratio of girl-friends, out of ten, was — one, who liked me and, nine who stood for me because that was as near as they would ever get to the great Cliff. I wasn't at all put-out. "

They were great days.

Jimmy

Jimmy is **Jimmy Savile**, arguably 'the' pop presenter and much, much more!

6 ON THE ROAD

Big Country and *perestroika* may have combined to create a new climate for rock in the Soviet Union, as music competed with the Olympics for attention in the autumn of 1988, but 12 years before Cliff Richard had played to 91,000 Russians with eight concerts in Moscow and twelve in Leningrad. Cliff's visit in 1976 was the icing on the cake of a world tour, also including Rumania, Poland and Czechoslovakia. Cliff's manager, Peter Gormley, for one, was thrilled with the reception that came the way of his artist. Doubtless, these days, Cliff would not have had 'Love Train' deleted from his programme; although since the song mentions Israel there might have been questions. But why should the Russians have wanted Cliff? 'It's only because I don't smash up hotel rooms,' was Cliff's explanation!

Eddie Jarret, at Savile Artists, was the man who handled the delicate negotiations. The first hint that there was something in the air came from the contents of a letter penned by the British ambassador in Moscow. He had been told by the gentleman at the Russian state booking agency that the Russians might welcome someone who would have a wider appeal to youth than the usual visitors, the London Symphony Orchestra. 'So our ambassador got worried, I think, because he thought the man was going to ask for the Rolling Stones.'

A year or so passed, during which the Russian agent had enquired after Paul McCartney, Englebert Humperdinck and Cliff. Eddie was insisting the show there would be the same show as here, no diminution, the whole lot soundwise, or nothing. Eddie told the trade paper *Record Business* that he was not worried over whether a Russian acceptance would still not mean that all the conditions had been accepted. 'I asked six questions. They replied to two, but ignored the other four – and then denied having received my letter!'

It would be fascinating to know how the Russians viewed Cliff's music, but they must have been moved by his overall tidiness and good spirits. At this time, pop music in the USSR ran considerably behind that produced by other countries of the Soviet bloc. Russian music was an odd hybrid of traditional folk songs to which a western-style rhythm was added, aided and abetted by plenty of volume. Russian young people picked

Cliff's musicians and backing singers of 1988-89.

up some western music from a weekly Russian radio 30-minute show 'On All Latitudes' which had even been known to play The Rolling Stones.

The concerts went ahead, and Cliff found himself with some new fans, as he sauntered onto the stage in a white suit, set off against a sun tan he had acquired some weeks previously in Barbados. His albums, *I'm Nearly Famous* and *The Best Of Cliff Richard*, were released, and for a time there was talk that he might be the first UK pop artist to record in Russia, with a deal under discussion between EMI and a Russian record company. Paul Braithwaite of EMI said, 'Of all our EMI artists, he is the one we get the most enquiries from Russians about.' As it happened, nothing came from the discussions, but at least Cliff hit the road in Russia and commented 'All in all it was *fun.*'

They keep using the word 'fun' – the people who are involved in Cliff's career. It's a word he likes as well. Time and time again, in many interviews, those connected with him in a myriad of capacities speak of having had a great experience, and talk of finding pleasure.

The sentiments expressed to me at the end of the Eighties are very much like those that can be found in other sources over 25 years ago. Take the year 1961, the time of Cliff's 21st birthday, when Shadows man Hank Marvin was quoted as saying: 'The past three years have been the happiest in my life – and all credit to Cliff for making this so. He's a great guy to work with . . .'

Bruce Welch says. 'It's impossible to select any one incident from all the happy times we've had together – simply because it's all been one big ball!'

Arthur Howes, who promoted the majority of Cliff's early tours:

I suppose I am only echoing the sentiments of everyone else when I say that he's one of the nicest boys, if not the nicest, I've ever worked with. But that's invariably my reply whenever I'm asked about Cliff, and now I pass it on . . . Every night seems to be a highlight when you're with him. It's always hectic, it's always exhausting – but it's always a lot of fun.

At first it could hardly be anything other than fun. Everything was new, fresh and appealing. And before he was 20, after less than 18 months as a pop person, Cliff could say, 'One thing's for sure, more has happened to me during my 19 years on this earth than happen to most people by the time they're 100. I've done more; I've been to more places in the world than most people.'

He was expressing in varying journals of the time sentiments such as 'I didn't know so much could happen in five months,' and 'I have come to realise that each day is different from the last,' or again, 'Time goes by so quickly.' All of which goes to show that there was no lull, even in the earliest days. Cliff was not sitting around wondering if his debut single would make the charts, for he was busy at Butlin's earning some shekels. Soon he would see 'Move It' make the charts, and he would be touring the length and breadth of Britain and then heading for Europe.

Right from the start of his professional career, he was busy. 'It meant that I could not say to myself, next Monday I'll do this and next Friday I'll do that, because there were a great number of things to be considered before my personal pleasure.' He was soon telling *Hit Parade* magazine of his theme for a dream: he would make his diary simple – he would undertake two major one-nighter tours, probably of three weeks each. He would spend four weeks playing variety. He would make one film a year. There would be a summer season of six to eight weeks at a seaside resort or in a big provincial theatre. Another six weeks would be spent on the road in some new country and he would set several weeks aside for planning albums and singles.

The article concluded with Cliff saying:

> I don't know how many weeks I have taken up in my imaginary year, but it's bound to be more than 52 – which brings me back to real life, because there are definitely not enough weeks in the year for me! Even in my dream world, you see, I don't leave myself any time for a holiday. Don't feel sorry for me, though, because life is so marvellous that I never feel I need a holiday anyway!

He would find time for a holiday and he would fall in love with Portugal, where he bought himself a house, as did others associated with him. That said, he would still pack other days, weeks and months with endless activities, and being on the road would claim a goodly percentage of that time, especially in those early years, when everyone wanted this new British singer, and even America showed interest. The demand for Cliff 'live' has never slackened and he could easily fill his diary for five years ahead. 'Should I retire,' he told me on one occasion, 'It would take me five years to tour all the countries where I have a following.'

Just because people use the word 'fun', and Cliff himself is hardly averse to this sentiment, it should not be assumed that even a young Cliff relished the slog and grind. At first, it was fun without qualification. There was a genuine buzz in arriving and finding a venue ringed with chanting fans; in hearing screams and yelps and thunderous applause, and making the fast get-away. They were all things that he had once dreamed of, and the reality was not to be despised.

However, as he says, 'Believe me, racing from one town to another in a coach isn't always fun.' He remembers a time when he played the London Palladium and that seemed good. 'For the first time I was able to eat, sleep and live at home with my parents in their new house at Winchmore Hill, London, and it was a wonderful feeling.' However, a series of dates were arranged for him in Blackpool on the Sunday, and so, once that show was over, it was a fast car ride – 'a free-for-all race' – to catch the all-night train to London. And money wasn't so plentiful in those days for a good hotel and limousine.

Even a boy in his late teens could find life on the road a hard slog and 'pretty exhausting', but there were compensations and plenty of awards coming his way to make Cliff feel it was all worthwhile. Right from the outset, there were always new faces; some stayed only for a time, but others lasted. At Butlin's, there was Stan Edwards, renowned for fast, racy and amusing scripts. He 'did a great miming act to Danny Kaye records. He even looked like Danny Kaye.' It was Edwards who could claim to be the first person to introduce Cliff Richard and The Drifters. 'When I first met Cliff he was very nervous, and uncertain about his future possibilities. I found him a very likeable, sincere person and we became friends quite easily.' Even then, Edwards observed, 'he devotes a lot of time to rehearsing and doesn't think it very clever to have folks think he doesn't take a serious interest in his career.'

During those early times, Cliff had a flat in Marylebone High Street. It seemed a good idea, for it was a central base to which he could escape and relax from the rigours of being on the road, and ideal when gigs were in London or the surrounding area. Jan Vane became the first official fan club secretary. She became fascinated by this new singer.

> I remember it was really late on in the evening that I was there at the 2 I's and the group were packing away and talking to one another about last buses and trains. They reckoned they'd missed them all. I asked this lead singer if he'd made a record and he said, 'Me, no, we just play down here for fun.' We got chatting and I asked if we (I was there with my fella) could give them a lift home, which they gratefully accepted. We only had a Morris Minor (a very small car) and it wasn't until we were all packed in – Cliff, Sammy (Samwell), Tony, John Foster, myself and Eddie (my man) – that I thought to ask where they lived. I was so excited at having a real live group in the car. We then discovered they lived in the opposite direction to us. Well, with all of us and all the gear the car was somewhat overcrowded, so we had to take it in turns trying to duck down every time we passed a policeman. It was quite easy to get your nose stuck between guitar strings or crushed up against a drum. Anyway we got them all home safely and I exchanged addresses with Cliff and that was the start of it all.

It was Jan, Cliff's sister Donna and friends who often had the Marylebone flat ready for weary visitors. Jan remembers numerous occasions when they were 'out' of things at the flat but fortunately, in those days of trust and comparative freedom from rifling and stealing, there 'was a food machine – called the Iron Can – that actually dispensed sausages, bacon and milk. Can you imagine that now?' No, but it would be so useful! She remembers at Butlin's, during those early months, how Cliff and the others would write out requests from imagined visitors for his record.

Cliff's parents were extremely influential in the early years. Mum had understandable fears that being on the road and the instant success would change her boy. 'I used to worry that travelling around as Cliff does, seeing new places and faces, the simple home life which has always been ours would cease to appeal to him. It was wonderful to see him soar to the upper brackets of show business, but I knew that his stays at home would become increasingly infrequent.' As she admitted back in 1960, her fears proved groundless. Cliff was still warm-hearted and affectionate, with no airs and graces.

Cliff's early 'on the road' adventures saw him very much sought after by young girls, but at least he could remember his own fun-mania a year or so back when Bill Haley came to Britain. Cliff and friends skipped morning school to queue for tickets: 'Well, we began queueing at five o'clock in the morning. We felt a bit guilty, for two of us were prefects. The tickets were five bob ones – more than I really could afford, but we got them and, clutching them triumphantly, we got back to my home for lunch.' Cliff remembers the evening particularly for the way the audience responded. 'I'd never heard such a noise in my life – and there were his saxes and the beat of his rhythm section and the feet and hands beating in time – it was thrilling.' Years later, his father was to tell Cliff that when he came up on stage the noise was such that it sounded like an earthquake!

'Why do they keep writing that I'm joining Bros?'

Dave Clark was one of those who caught the early 'live' Cliff. He told me, 'I used to see him at Finsbury Park, really rockin'. He had this pink jacket and socks and was rather Presleyish. The place used to erupt.' Clark's meeting with Cliff came in unexpected fashion. Two girls had got to know him and began running his fan club. Those girls turned out to be Joan and Jackie Webb. 'I didn't know they had a brother. I lived in Tottenham and they lived in Enfield. In those days that was a distance!' So, one day, Dave received a telegram inviting him to the house. It was there, to his surprise, that he realised the truth, met Cliff and realised that his fan club was being run by Cliff's sisters! 'Cliff, even then, could take a great record and translate it onto stage. He's a rocker at heart.'

Often they would hit the road in a light blue 22-seater coach that began its calls at Cliff's flat in Marylebone High Street. The driver, who was simply called Joe, was given to humour and apparently quite happy to load the 'gear'. He was fond of his bus novelty motor siren, which emitted a sound not unlike a wolf-whistle and, from all accounts, caused many a head to turn. There were always some who recognised Cliff, and on the roads some drivers would draw alongside to give their passengers a closer view, drop back, and overtake again, as if unconvinced they were really seeing the new boy of

British pop. Should they decide to overtake once again to satisfy their curiosity, Joe would give them a further blast of his siren. Cliff invariably chose the front seat and, if it was a Sunday, he spread the Sunday papers out and looked for articles on himself, or pored through fan club letters. At stops, Cliff went foraging for the fruit machines and, once satisfied with the jackpot, or accepting that it was not his day, he would order pie and chips and wash everything down with some strong tea. Even in restaurants, Joe kept up his comedy routine, and would produce a very large rubber imitation hand which he would fit over his own and then proceed to scare the wits out of café owners.

By the time they left a theatre their bus would be covered with lots of loving inscriptions from fans, who would leave messages written in lipstick and greasepaint. On the way back, there would be another stop at a transport café, preferably one having 'Move It' on its jukebox.

Cliff's first British travels were not always peaceful affairs. As Pat Doncaster, co-author with me of *Cliff*, recalled at the time that the book was written, Cliff often found himself on the receiving end of an uncooked omelette of eggs and tomatoes, bottles, and missiles of all kinds. Louts would storm the stage. Indeed, there was a 'bother boy' contingent that lay in wait at some of his concerts. As Pat recalls, on one occasion in 1959 at the Lyceum Ballroom in London's Strand, the management closed the act after the third number, such was the ferocity of the hooligan element. Naturally, the press latched on to this and even the music weekly the *New Musical Express* questioned his act, especially his appearance on 'Oh Boy!' and its influence on young minds, but that article by Maurice Kihn was relatively mild compared to another in the *Daily Sketch*. Cliff has never forgotten these pieces and indeed made reference to them at a 25th anniversary party that was organised by the EMI record company, pointing out that he had lasted despite these predictions of his imminent demise.

Maurice Kihn, a major figure in pop magazine-newspaper publishing, had written:

His violent hip-swinging during an obvious attempt to copy Elvis Presley was revolting – hardly the kind of performance any parent could wish their children to see . . . While firmly believing Cliff Richard can emerge into a top star and enjoy a lengthy musical career, it will only be accomplished by dispensing with short-sighted vulgar tactics.

Cliff insisted that he never consciously set out to be either vulgar or 'sexy' and felt that he had nothing to be ashamed of in his performance. The upset caused him to lose his voice. His other bookings at the Lyceum were cancelled. Sadly, there were other journalistic repercussions. A saddened, unwell Cliff made his way back to Marylebone. His mum came to stay with him. A reporter called, had innumerable cups of tea, buns and biscuits, and chatted away, with the eventual conclusion coming later, when the particular newspaper for which he wrote ran the line 'Cliff is running back to mum', 'Cliff frightened of rioters', 'the sexy Cliff', and so on, leaving both Cliff and his mother sickened.

Eventually the flat had to be vacated, partly because Cliff didn't like living on his own, even though there was often boisterous company around, and also because fans found out the address.

If London gave him problems, then his fast-moving popularity led to times when 'I would have to hide or stay in the theatre'. He tells of how on one occasion when he was playing in Stockton the police had told him to remain in the theatre but 'I was darn hungry and I knew there was a hot meal waiting for us'. He peered through a crack in the stage door and, apart from two girls, it seemed quiet. Then he heard one of them discussing how they would lie in wait, covering both exits. 'I thought, right, I'll fool you. I borrowed a cap from one of the stagehands and my road manager's mac, that was about two sizes too big for me. I put on a pair of steel-rimmed spectacles and out I sneaked, convinced that not even my mother would recognise me.' Alas, he had walked a mere three steps when someone recognised him. How? Cliff says, 'It's my nose that gives me away. I'm convinced about that.'

It was in 1960 that Cliff went on the road in America for the very first time. His courtship of the States has never really been successful, but at that time, as later, all seemed possible; and, of course, Cliff has had a number of big US chart singles.

He went full of enthusiasm, flushed with his own success here and filled with excitement at being in the country that had spawned his heroes Elvis and Frank Sinatra. In the States, he travelled by coach and sometimes found that there was a 500-mile distance between one night's show and the next, often with two houses on one night. He was part of the Frankie Avalon Show. Along with Frankie and Cliff went other US pop heroes of the time – Freddy Cannon, with whom he became good friends, Conway Twitty and Johnny Preston. Reaction was good, and the stronger it was 'the less the rest of the cast liked us'. For Cliff and The Shadows it became a battle – bringing British pop into the American stronghold. 'Living Doll' charted briefly, from late 1959 into the early part of 1960, but went no further than number 40.

On his return to Britain, Cliff reminisced about the lovely silver, streamlined coaches that bore on their side 'The Biggest Show of 1960'. Each seat had its own heater and could tip back until it almost formed a bed. 'Mostly we travelled at night. We would leave about 12.40 at night after the show, and arrive in the next town early morning.' Venues varied from vast halls and arenas to ice-hockey stadiums. He told *Hit Parade* how, at one Pennsylvanian location, they performed in the open air on a stage made up of three big lorries. They were placed 'side by side, with their backs facing the audience. The stage was laid over the open backs of the lorries, and the drapes were laid over the backs of the drivers' cabins. Then Paul Williams' orchestra took their places at the back of the stage, and we went on and gave our performances.'

Cliff's only TV appearance was on the Pat Boone show. Boone was a major US and UK hit artist of the time, and his appearance here gave Cliff a welcome push. Also, he met various disc-jockeys and attended an ABC-Paramount record conference, where he talked to the assembled staff. He left, and returned optimistic, while aware of the difficulties of making an impact in such a vast country without living there. He said, 'I certainly hope I'll be invited again some time in the future.'

Save for a brief charting of his rather good version of 'It's All in the Game' in 1974, that reached 25 in the *Billboard* listing, there was little in prospect for Cliff until the results of his rejuvenated mid-1970s British recording career spread across the Atlantic.

As a fellow artiste can't help but admire his achievements in show business over the last thirty years.

People talk to me about the music of the sixties and how it always seems to be being revived. In Cliff's case, he's never needed to be revived, he's never been out of the scene.

Sincerely,

Freddie Garrity

FRANKIE VAUGHAN O.B.E.

We all know how proud we are of this great entertainer and all the thoroughly deserved things that have been said about him, but I have one special tribute to Cliff and that was when our mutual friend was tragically killed in a car accident, the late, and much loved Dickie Valentine.

I travelled back from a holiday in Majorca to be involved with a Benefit being staged at the London Palladium for Dickie's wife and dependants and when I was told that I was sharing a dressing room with Cliff Richard it made me realise what a warm person Cliff was. He had also dropped everything to be at that Benefit and from then on I was also a fan of his.

The expression "he's a nice guy" is thrown about very easily, but in Cliff's case it fits like a glove.

Frank.

Frankie Vaughan

Freddie Garrity fronted the enormously successful 1960s group Freddie and The Dreamers. He remains much wanted on the show-business circuit.

Frankie Vaughan was one of Britain's most successful pop stars of the 1950s and early 1960s and is now a major person in show business and theatre.

He found Top 10 success with 'Devil Woman' in 1976 but was unable to follow this with other vital hits. However, he still had ambitions across the Atlantic and he set out on the road to America again. He received much support in the States from Elton John, a megastar at the time, whose Rocket Records put muscle behind Cliff's undoubted claims to popularity. Initially, he went for a nine-day promotional trip and, full of dreams still, he told the *Daily Mail*'s Douglas Thompson in Los Angeles, 'I have waited 18 years to make some sort of name for myself in America. If it doesn't happen now, I won't be suicidal.' But he felt the time was right, for he saw a greater acceptance of people as singers regardless of whether or not they delivered the youthful image goods. The respect and awe which he felt for America were evident: 'It's huge. The largest record market in the world. It's got to be the most discerning rock and roll market, too. This is where it all came from. This is the fatherland of rock.' No, the desire was not for money – 'I don't need it' – it was the desire that has permeated the bloodstream of every prominent rock star I've met: to be a major name in the land where rock had its birth. Naturally, Cliff was not unaware that huge sums of money would flow his way if US success came, but as he said to Thompson, 'it will be English taxed, you can be sure of that'.

But the small mark made by Cliff on the American rock map soon disappeared. All was not lost, however, for pop has an arresting facet to it; it is possible to find the right sound all of a sudden and fortunes can change drastically. So it proved for Cliff, who had six US record successes between 'We Don't Talk Anymore' toward the end of 1979 and 'Daddy's Home' in the summer of 1982. His success led to a North American tour, early in the 1980s, which was repeated again in the late summer of 1982.

Cliff's North American Tour was an outstanding success. There were standing ovations in Seattle and New York, terrific audience response in Philadelphia and Cleveland, and it was reported that there was standing room only in some centres. The whole tour reached its crescendo, with 3,000 ardent fans supporting him in the Santa Monica Civic Auditorium on 18 April 1981. Dixie Gonzales, President of the Cliff Richard Movement, USA, was there: 'He didn't just walk out on stage . . . he literally exploded onto the stage in a whirl of smoke and colour with "Son of Thunder", and the feeling that swept through the audience was like a jolt of electricity!'

n a Summer Show at the Queens Theatre,
ool with Dora Bryan and Les Dawson.
essingroom was immediately next to the tele-
, and between shows I answered a call. The voice at
ther end said politely "May I speak to Miss Dora Bryan
se?" and I enquired "May I ask who's calling please?"
voice said "It's Cliff Richard" and I answered "Hallo
ff, it's Ronnie Hilton"..... he laughed and said "Oh,
Ron, are you doubling as a doorman then?" I laughed and
id "Cheeky sod" and called Dora.
e is a very worthy credit to our business.

Ronnie Hilton.

You would not think, to look at me, an elderly actor, a solo performer, Bible story teller to the Nation—and Jewish yet, that for six months in 1960 I sang and danced with Cliff Richard at The Palladium! We closed the show; we were the big finish.

On the fourth night I forgot the words of our song. It did not matter. The screaming in the audience drowned any sound we were making!

DK

Ronnie Hilton was one of 'the' voices of the 1950s pop world and he continues to thrive in general entertainment fields.

David Kossof is one of Britain's best loved performers, mainly through his one-man show where he updates biblical stories. He accompanied Cliff on some of his first concerts.

Part way through his set, Cliff said he assumed that none of his audience would remember his early days. Perhaps because of the age of the audience, or because of the feeling that many American rock fans have for music history, his remark was greeted with cries of 'Move It, Move It,' and that is what he sang. He also paid tribute to Elvis and sang 'Heartbreak Hotel'. During the concert, fans streamed to the front and offered an assortment of goodies, ranging from flowers to gold jewellery to stuffed animals.

Later, he said the most important gift was the love that pulsed through the auditorium. Gonzales says, 'This concert symbolised the total impact of the tour; America had been slow to wake up, painfully so to many of us who had been waiting patiently all these years.' He felt America had fallen that little more in love with Cliff. It was about time too! Cliff's mother had flown over for some of his tour and, along with Olivia and Bill Latham, she was spotted at the New York booking. Fans had also travelled the Atlantic. At Denver 40 fans flew in, courtesy of the *Daily Mirror* Pop Club in Britain, as Cliff played in the new Rainbow Music Hall on 14 April, in front of 1,400 people. None of the seating was further than 70ft away from the stage, so there was an unusually good view for everyone. The 40 British fans remained in the auditorium after the show and met Cliff, who shook each by the hand, signed autographs and chatted with them.

The American press is quite different from the British. There are famous newspapers, but they serve cities or areas and in the music publishing world in America, unlike Britain, there is no national weekly music press. In some major dailies Cliff did attract notice. The rock critic of the *Los Angeles Herald Examiner* noticed that Cliff on the road attracted 'a comfortably middle-class, all-age audience' and on the musical front he observed, 'his pop songs are simply too modest, too tidy and too reticent to render him a star in America with, well, the staying power, of Olivia Newton-John, with whom he sang the duet last year. Richard's latest album is called *I'm No Hero*, and his self-deprecation is as accurate as it is charming.' He admitted that Cliff's string of hits had removed him out of a purely cult following and indeed found him quite capable of satisfying an audience. In looks he found Cliff 'looking blown-dry and almost teenage' and earning a standing ovation even if that seemed 'improbable'. These days Paul Grein is an ace charts commentator for *Billboard*; in 1981, he was reporting for the *Los Angeles Times*. He found Cliff in 'peak form', though he found this unsurprising when set against the simple fact that 'Richard had 23 years to rehearse'. He found the uptempo tunes the highlight of Cliff's set, but shining through was what he termed the 'unbridled joy of the music, which was the real message'. He saw Cliff exhibiting dramatic moves, poses and gestures that gave a theatrical edge to songs in the English Music Hall tradition. 'His show was a reminder of what pleasure it is to watch a real pro in action'.

The British press, too, went along for the ride. Monica Gillham, writing for pop weekly, *Record Mirror*, paid Cliff various compliments; she said that he was 'admirably professional', 'high gloss', 'skilful', 'polished', though she added that she also felt things

were 'thoroughly bland', even if 'unquestionably there is something fascinating in watching a well-trained creature go through his paces', but 'the thrill is gone' and if 'he plays his audience with all the finesse of the veteran he is', and 'doesn't miss a single intricate light cue, doesn't miff a single gesture', she still thought 'it was an oddly dissatisfying show. All the pieces were there but they didn't add up to anything'.

Ricky Sky now works for the *Sun*, but at this time he worked for the then relatively new tabloid the *Star*. He remarked 'American audiences are convinced he is a newcomer. They can't believe he is 40!' Sky quoted Cliff as saying 'Cracking America has always been my one remaining ambition, but I didn't want to desert Britain so I've had to do it slowly. Even now I'm worried that it's going to take up too much of my time – and I don't want that.'

From the vantage point of 1988, *Billboard* writer Steve Gett suggests that the only way Cliff can arguably take America is by spending at barest minimum six months there, working his backside off with endless PA's, concerts and perhaps recording in America with American writers and producers. His *Billboard* compatriot Paul Grein is, with Gett, a Cliff admirer, and both genuinely feel that Cliff has deserved transatlantic success, but are not too optimistic for Cliff's future chances. 'At the moment America is heading for another youth phase and he is a trifle old. Yes, he has given some wonderful shows and he is well received here in Los Angeles on his visits but that doesn't add up to national penetration,' said Grein who, with all his expertise in the American market, sees it all as a little too late. However, the record market is volatile and it always promises hope. Other commentators would suggest that Cliff should settle for what he has, which, after all, is most of the world, something few others have ever known. But Cliff returned to America in 1982 with Dixie Gonzales reporting that two advertised concerts for Los Angeles had nearly sold out before even advertisements could be placed.

America should not, of course, be allowed to dominate any coverage of Cliff 'on the road' for the rest of the world has greeted him with enthusiasm – a reaction that has come from countless countries across Europe, behind the Iron Curtain, into South-East Asia, Japan, Australasia, and South Africa, always rich grounds for records and 'live' visits.

Invariably a greater proportion of Cliff's time has been spent in Britain than in any other place. Since his Christian days began, from 1966 onward, fans have often had two visits from Cliff to their town, the 'secular' and 'religious', although both have become more intertwined as the years have progressed, with the second characterised more by the proceeds being for charity than by the nature of the music and light show.

It's not surprising that some of the most extravagant moments in Cliff's 'live' career have occurred on his birthday, for it seems that he is rarely off the road for this occasion. Peter Gormley remembers a delightful event that occured in 1961.

I remember having the greatest feeling of warmth and satisfaction when Cliff was playing a concert at the Birmingham Hippodrome. Cliff was introducing one of his numbers, 'My Blue Heaven', and he happened to mention that it was included on his new LP – and with a chuckle, he added that the album would be released on October 14. Immediately the audience recognised the significance of that date and, practically with one voice, burst into a roof-lifting chorus of 'Happy Birthday To You'. Cliff just stood there completely stupified by this demonstration of affection, while Bruce and Hank – who were quick to assess the warmth of the fans' sentiments – stepped forward to conduct the audience from the footlights. Cliff was absolutely knocked out by this.

EMI had its own party to celebrate Cliff's 21st and for this they invited press and celebrities to a party, printing invitations on silver cards shaped like keys. The previous year, they had had a greater 'family' affair – a few days late as Cliff had not been available on the actual day. Cliff had assumed he was visiting EMI on a business matter. Ron White, who was the Executive responsible for the A & R Department at EMI and was also General Manager of the Company, says that when Cliff approached the room that was full of guests an appropriate signal was given, so that when Cliff entered, the Shads broke into Happy Birthday.

14 October 1980 saw his birthday celebrated in front of an enthusiastic audience at Manchester's Apollo. Apart from opening the show in the manner in which he had finished his 1979 concerts, appearing with just an acoustic guitar to sing 'Living Doll', there was an extra-special reception, with cheering that lasted for almost five minutes. The audience sang the traditional song of the day, to which Cliff responded with a few lines of 'I'm 21 Today', though he was heard to say there had been 30 odd birthdays plus '10 even ones'. Naturally, there were presents. Someone had remembered a remark he had made on the radio – to the effect that he didn't use stage make-up and gave him some Polyfilla. In 1986 Cliff arrived at Helsinki on 14 October. The fans gathered at the airport broke into the familiar song.

February 14 has been another 'love' day for fans: 1988 saw Cliff in New Zealand on the final night of his tour. On this occasion, following a rendering of 'One Night', he was given a huge red heart made of 90 fresh carnation flower-heads, which eight fans of the New Zealand Cliff Richard Movement had spent three hours assembling. Other fans brought flowers, wine and chocolate to the stage.

Obviously, there have been some poignant moments when Cliff has been on the road, if only because Cliff takes time off to visit the less fortunate. In Brisbane, Australia, for instance, he met a young girl called Rachel Scriven who learnt she was fast becoming blind, apparently with no hope of a medical cure. It was her great wish to see Cliff before going blind. During another tour, he gave a charity evening in aid of an unemployment project run in Birmingham, England, by the local branch of Youth For Christ.

There were also awkward times. One of the most unexpected, was on the last Friday of May 1963. He had been booked as part of Leslie Grade's colourful Holiday Carnival Show at Blackpool's latest and most comfortable ABC theatre. It was a race against time for everybody, and given Cliff's passion for detail, he was inevitably exhausted even before the concert. Andy Gray, editor of the *New Musical Express* during those heady days of high circulation, reported that Cliff and the Shads made the first of many stage entrances in a little sports car that circled on the revolving stage. Cliff's opening number was 'Summer Holiday'. It was then he suddenly realised that he hadn't been forewarned of one vital fact: this was a stiff-shirt, specially invited audience, with barely a teenager to be seen. Here was an artist who had lived and thrived on screams and yells, even

CANVAS CHAIR
Purveyors of Fine Visual Images

How many 'hellos' and 'well dones' have we said? –
And will keep on saying!

BEV SAGE   STEVE FAIRNIE

Bev Sage and **Steve Fernie** have been part of Writz, Famous Names and more recent together as The Techno Twins. They also run Canvas Chair.

insults, and who now found himself in a scenario where no one did anything but applaud politely. It required some very quick unconscious thinking and adaptation, even in vocal levels and gestures and, of course, without screams to contend with it seemed as if everything was passing by that little quicker. It was a night to remember and while initially Cliff saw it as a 'most frightening' occasion, it became a good story to tell later.

On one occasion in America, he had found problems with his voice and was amused when his support act Sheila Walsh walked up to him and gave him a little bottle of throat spray. The wit of Cliff broke through with the remark, 'This has been going on all day. beautiful women come up to me and give me these sprays.' He confessed his voice sounded strange, 'stranger and stranger', but promised that, if he could not sing, he would recite his words. This was greeted by the audience with considerable approval.

In West Germany, at one evening concert, Cliff suddenly yelled 'Crackerjack', at least proving he knew the name of a popular British television show! He tried to explain what this show was but it became the 'in' word of the evening and every time he mentioned it, or was about to do so, his audience yelled out 'Crackerjack'. He proceeded to ask the audience what 'that' word might be in German: British folk in the audience, wishing to save him embarrassment, tried to tell him the word was the same, and simply screamed 'THAT'. In his confusion, Cliff took the sensible route away from the growing melee and said that he would be singing 'Now You See Me Now You Don't', but the audience shouted out 'No, you've done that one.' So he had talks with the band and finally swung into 'Has To Be You'.

At least constant touring can help Cliff to recover lost ground, even if of a minor kind. During his Silver Tour, he told his London audience that, at the time he had recorded his first album, he had been suffering from laryngitis and had made a mess of the song 'Donna' adding that he had always hoped that he would have the opportunity to do it again. That night, his sister Donna was in the audience and the time was right.

One evening in the late Seventies, Cliff was playing to 1,000 guests at a dinner at the Lakeside Country Club at Frimley Green, Surrey, in aid of the International Year of The Child. Cliff appeared at a quarter to midnight and was soon in his stride but suddenly, quite unexpectedly, there came a crashing sound as some electrical cables for the sound system fell down from the ceiling in front of the keyboards. 'What was that?' asked Cliff. To which, with some humour, group member Adrian answered, 'that is a lead-ing question.'

MY HOW TIME FLIES!! 30 YEARS IN SHOW BUSINESS. DOES IT SEEM THAT LONG? FROM PICTURES YOU'VE HARDLY CHANGED AT ALL.

I AM WITH THE GOLDEN NUGGET HOTEL IN LAS VEGAS,

WOULD LOVE TO HEAR FROM YOU......AND ALL YOUR NEWS. SAY HELLO TO EVERYONE FOR ME. TAKE CARE.

LOVE.

CHERRY WAINER

Cherry Wainer appeared frequently with Cliff during the early days and in his first effort as a songwriter was for her – 'Happy Like A Bell', written in 1960.

Sometimes quick measures have had to be taken when the planned moment appears on the verge of backfiring. Although this happening did not, in fact, occur when Cliff was on the road, it's worth mentioning a story told by Michael Hurll, who was filming Cliff in Scandinavia. They had heard that Bergen had a reputation for being one of the wettest places in the world, with rainfall 300 days a year. 'We thought we'd have Cliff singing "Raindrops Keep Falling On My Head" but when we arrived the temperature was 79 degrees, the skies were clear, and we had to hire the Bergen Fire Brigade to provide the rain!'

Cliff is no stranger to the effects of rain, real or induced. His Australian visit in 1988 was hit by elements raging in apparent dislike of him. His show in Rockhampton, Queensland, suffered in this manner and the one in Darwin almost went the same way. However, the crowd stayed put and Cliff said he would stay and sing to backing tapes – in the event, he 'just sang in the rain for two hours' and described the event as a 'World first "concert in torrential rain".'

Fans have been mentioned in passing, but they need some special words in this chapter, for obviously Cliff would have no career if, out there on the road, there had been no response! On stage, Cliff and fans have always enjoyed a camaraderie, and they've often joined in the general chat between Cliff and group, especially during Cliff's time with The Shadows.

Apart from paying money, fans can become part of the act. During a concert at the Queen Elizabeth Stadium in Hong Kong, Cliff sang 'Summer Rain'. During his last concert ICRM members opened paper umbrellas as he started to sing this song and then put them on the stage, creating an unexpected and powerful visual effect. At Cliff's December 1987 concert at Birmingham's NEC, Cliff encouraged photographers in the audience to take part in a special effect with him. As he posed, on the count of three, one of his backing singers took a picture from the back of the stage as thousands of flashbulbs glittered in the auditorium.

Cliff has a way of flattering fans. Nicoline Broderson writes of his concert in Copenhagen in May 1988: 'He welcomed us to his show and said he was very glad to be back in Copenhagen. When the mini-tour was first suggested, Cliff only agreed on the condition that he should return to Copenhagen. We really enjoyed all this flattery, especially when Cliff told us that the Danish concerts had been among the highlights on the last tour.'

Rob Witchell, President of the South African Cliff Richard Movement, extols the way Cliff treats those who work with him and notes no egotistical desire to prove himself or add lustre to his own standing by reducing other people. Those fans who have made it back-stage during Cliff's tours often speak in this manner. Joy Reading of Stourport-on-Severn says, 'how calm and relaxed he was, not a bit big-headed, he was really great.' William Hooper, President of the Gloucester-Oxford area Fan Club, has never found a Cliff concert audience that did not ask for more. He remembers queueing for hours to obtain tickets as a schoolboy. Hooper still attends every Cliff concert and runs to the front to lead fans in chanting 'We Want Cliff, We Want Cliff.' Sometimes, he says, 'there are a lot of males in the audience, but I'm usually the one nearest the stage and standing. The others are still in their seats and I'm surrounded by females. Can't be bad, can it?'

Cliff rarely gets angry, but there have been a few occasions when he has. Joan Batten caught him rehearsing in Durban, South Africa, in 1980. She remembers that he didn't have his regular band, and was finding that the make-shift unit couldn't get a number the way he wanted. After five or so efforts, one of 'the band turned to Cliff and said "it'll be all right tonight", to which person Cliff gave a withering look and said, "I want it right now, and you're not going until you get it right." It's this sort of attitude, of dedication to perfection, that has got Cliff where he is now.'

Some fans admire his energy. Ann Cherchian writes, 'I don't know of any performer who gives one hundred per cent of himself to his audience the way Cliff does. On stage he is electrifying! The way he jumps up and down during a rock 'n' roll number, his every movement timed to the beat of the song, his trim figure never tiring, never showing any sign of fatigue.' She recalls an occasion during *Time* when a man dressed in yellow trousers and jacket jumped on stage and confronted Cliff, but Cliff kept his cool and carried on with his lines. 'For a few seconds I thought this had been added on the script (she saw *Time* on 132 occasions) because he never faltered; he just carried on as usual, like the true professional he is, until the security guards came over and the man jumped off the stage. Cliff was very lucky that night; he could have been hurt.'

Jennifer Chatten, president of the Yorkshire Fan Club, is among those who, having got backstage, have found Cliff charming and concerned. She first met Cliff when he and The Drifters were in concert at York Rialto. She arrived at the theatre early and hoped to catch a glimpse of him. To her surprise and joy, Cliff suddenly came into sight 'strolling casually along the street. My mum, who had left me to go shopping, passed Cliff and said that he looked like the Pied Piper with a string of girls following him. Behind Cliff were Hank and Bruce wearing cowboy hats they got from the fair being held near where their coach was parked.' Jennifer persuaded theatre staff to let her into the theatre and, during a rehearsal break, he came down from the stage and autographed some things for her, including his first album.

When Cliff returned to Harrogate after 26 years it was a particularly moving experience for Jennifer. In 1959, as a 14 year old, she had sat on the front row of the Royal Hall to watch him in concert.

> Even in my wildest dreams I could never have imagined that, next time Cliff was in Harrogate, I would be president of one of his fan clubs. To make sure he got my 'Welcome back to Harrogate' message, I took a table decoration of fresh flowers for Cliff's room (it included some white roses) and a little basket of Yorkie bars for Cliff and his band. Cliff's nickname for us is The Yorkies!

Doug Pickett from Grimsby remembers the first time he was persuaded to attend a Cliff concert. 'You could hardly hear him or The Shadows because so many girls were screaming in the aisles.' Away from the hysteria, he and a small group became fans and, as a result, he founded a local branch of the fan club. Its 400 members cover the wide age spectrum of 14 to 86! Pickett is one of those who finds 'Cliff really is genuinely nice. When working at the Mecca, I dealt with so many pop singers and some just couldn't have cared less about their fans. But with Cliff it is so different.' Pickett admires Cliff for the religious stance he took in 1966 and says, 'it was quite a thing to do in those swinging days of the Sixties.'

Lynne Kitt, president of the Cliff Richard Movement in New Zealand, first became aware of Cliff's 'magic' when she saw *The Young Ones* at the age of 12. She missed his New Zealand tour, but she did see *The Young Ones* again and then 'the name Cliff Richard became etched on my mind'. Since then she has seen him on his six visits to the country and has even met him. 'In 1973 I discovered the human being Cliff is, and observed something of his personality . . . there was a total naturalness to the man which dispelled my nerves.' In concert she has found him 'dynamic' and says 'his concerts reflect his unique flair and easy rapport with his widely age-ranging audience (how many pop/rock concerts can whole family groups enjoy?).' In general terms, she says he projects a naturalness and even a slight shyness which is endearing: 'I've not always agreed with his opinions, but I admire his honesty and sincerity, the sensitive and caring spirit he displays.'

West German Grete Bieler is another person who has found that Cliff has time on tour to meet genuine people. She and some friends met Cliff and Bill Latham in a Hanover hotel. 'When Cliff came along he was so kind and friendly and there was no embarrassing silence . . . Although he must have been in a hurry he didn't show any haste or restlessness. He radiated such a peace and quiet that I've never known with any other person.' She also recalls a concert of Cliff's at Wembley. She came over from Germany with a friend of hers who is handicapped and confined to a wheelchair. They asked if they could see Cliff backstage and, with their wish granted, had an enjoyable conversation. She met Cliff again in Osnabruck during his Autumn tour in 1987. He wrote some kind words on a card she had bought for Val, who by then was in very bad health. 'She received the card two weeks before she went to be with our Lord forever. So Cliff gave her a very special joy in the very latest days of her life.'

Lakeword, California, is the home of Janet Rainey, a fan of Cliff's since his *I'm Nearly Famous* album. Being a Cliff fan has given Janet a chance to meet other like-minded people, sometimes from other countries, 'I keep in touch with a lovely Dutch couple I met.' Fans from Germany have been guests in Lakeword, while Janet has stayed with them in Hamburg. She detects Cliff's love for his work as he performs and realises that he is enjoying himself as much as the audience. She is one who appreciates his willingness to share his faith, even during so-called general rather than gospel concerts.

Bo Larsson from Sweden remembers vividly the beginning of his affection for Cliff's music. 'It began at Stockholm Tivoli Garden in 1961. Cliff and The Shadows were in concert, and I was 16.' Now 43, Bo says his flat is a 'Cliff Museum'. Through the years, he has met Cliff many times. The first time Bo Larsson caught Cliff on the road was in Aarhus, Denmark. Since then he has journeyed afar and received hospitality from Cliff fans in other countries. When Cliff played his Stockholm concert on 13 October 1985, Bo and others anticipated Cliff's birthday of the following day and brought on stage a huge birthday cake in the form of a guitar.

Mrs Rose Nesbit of Blaydon, Tyne and Wear, writes that Cliff makes her feel that much younger when she sees him perform on stage, and she is far from being alone in such a view, since many marvel at how young Cliff looks and how agelessly he moves during his long and emotionally tiring set. Cliff concert tours always spawn new fans for the various local Cliff groups and these organisations vary in number from four to several hundred. One of the most successful has been the Waterlooville Meeting House, Portsmouth. They meet locally in the Scout Hall, have regular discos, and celebrate the various highlights and anniversaries in Cliff's career. Around 150 people come and dance to Cliff's music and there is always a raffle in aid of Tear Fund. Its organiser, Ruth Wylie, says, 'We travel to concerts together by coach, playing Cliff cassettes there and back and we all wear our Meeting House T-shirts – Cliff calls us the Blue T-Shirt Brigade.' On an occasion such as Cliff's show-biz anniversary, they hire a local restaurant and the manager obliges by playing only Cliff's music.

One of Cliff's closest media friends and trusted persons is a German girl, Hanne Jordan. She has worked in Britain for many years and is the important British correspon-

106

dent, feature writer and photographer for *Pop Rocky*. Her first contact with Cliff was in 1973 when she attended a press conference at the Inter-Continental, Hamburg, at the time Cliff was on the road pushing hard with 'Power To All Our Friends'. Her own career has since flourished, but at that time she was involved with the business rather than the journalistic-writing area, and she has been an avid follower of Cliff, talking and photographing him through many tours.

Her first major assignments centred around Cliff and outside of her own meetings she has observed him in action at the press conferences that always precede or accompany his tours. 'Sometimes he is like a gun, he shoots words out so fast. He is a quick thinker and journalists have to move fast. He is someone who always wants to please and is easy to talk with.'

For long-time fans it is, of course, the one-time association of Cliff and The Shadows that brings to the fore so many precious memories, not least for the stage camaraderie that they had with each other, which produced and stimulated a humour that was much enjoyed by the huge audiences that greeted them wherever they played those many years ago.

Cliff-Shads tours offered people two starring acts for the price of one. And the Shads had their own followers who did not always think as much of Cliff. Invariably, when they hit the road, there were those who wondered if there was any disagreement over who should get the attention. On one occasion, Cliff was asked if he and The Shadows had too many record releases. He agreed over-exposure can be harmful but said, 'Generally, The Shadows come out about three months after me; so that, if I am lucky enough to have a number one hit, we don't clash. People say "Ah, The Shadows have knocked Cliff out of the number one spot", but that is planned, and with any luck they are still in the Top 10 when my next record is released, which means we are always in the public eye.'

During spring 1963, frequent questions revolved around whether Cliff and The Shadows were still friends with the departed Jet Harris and Tony Meehan. 'You just don't end a friendship like that. They didn't leave us in the lurch and there were no bad feelings. When they went, we wished them the best of luck. We were the first to send them a telegram on their success, though we didn't think they'd make it like they have.'

Their many times together combine to make a story that has been told elsewhere – a story that could not have been imagined in their wildest dreams. It had all begun in that amusingly innocent fashion when Hank was asked 'Would you like to join Cliff Richard?' Hank remembers his reply, 'Who's Cliff Richard?'

They would hit the road, on tour, with little money. Hank says, 'The very first tour we did, Cliff just split the money with the group – five ways. I think we got 12 quid each. And then in 1959, when he was big, we were getting 25 quid a week. But, in those days, for 25 quid a week I had a flat in the West End. I was married and I still had money left at the end of the week.' They all travelled together, mostly by coach, sometimes by train, or even by car. It was on these coach journeys that the guitars came out and the songs came. 'The songs came from that kind of atmosphere.' Cliff often found himself given a room apart from The Shadows but he used to find his way into theirs, and there was a period when he simply said he could be 'put up' with the Shads. He didn't like the solitude of his own room where nothing much was happening, quite unlike the bustle and noise of The Shad's quarters. Sometimes there were arguments and disagreements – and they could be fierce – but these were simply disputes and upsets among friends.

Cliff gradually saw the entourage that accompanied him on the road increase, as his presentations grew more ambitious and, at times, spectacular. Here, his present business manager, David Bryce, has been a veritable tower of strength; a man respected, even feared by some, who dislikes second best as much as Cliff. Bryce, the brother of the late and much loved and missed Dickie Valentine, first worked for Lew and Leslie Grade. He handled numerous tours for rock 'n' roll stars of the time, including Bill Haley. The Grades became Cliff's agents and so David came into contact with Cliff's manager Peter Gormley and, of course, with Cliff himself. His first tour with Cliff was the artist's second. Cliff's equipment was meagre: 'We just carried three Vox AC30s and a drum kit, and we did all the security ourselves.' The simplicity of those early times is well illustrated by a much repeated joke of Hank's. When asked about the light show, he would say 'on and off', and the story never fails to raise a smile.

The days of three Vox AC30s and a drum kit are far, far away. A look at Cliff's tour programme shows a team including a Production and Design Manager, Lighting Design and Operation, Sound Engineer, Monitor Engineer, Stage Equipment, Lighting, Starlight and Rigging, Trucking, Catering, Merchandising, Printing and Brochure concerns, without mentioning press and publicity – both here in Britain and in all the territories to be visited – with perhaps a general promotions concern to cover various territories and, finally, a tour manager and stage manager. The tour arrangements will have been made by Savile Artists, the in-house agency and promotion organisation that, until recently, was headed by Eddie Jarret. Indeed it was he who established the company in 1967 to handle all Cliff's live dates, with the exception of Gospel bookings, which are handled by Bill Latham.

Stage designer John Seymour told me, 'The sets get more dramatic as time goes on. It's a world that seems to have grown so much and acts vie for the best sets and Cliff has had a taste of the real big-time with *Time* but that was a static set; it didn't have to be moved from place to place.' The size and scope of his current stage sets have been a contributory reason for Cliff's practice of playing a large number of concerts at one venue – it would be impractical both to move and assemble such a stage set within short spaces of time, and someone like John Seymour is limited by the kind of theatres and halls available.

We have to keep realistic and not go over the top. I have 120 people in the crew, and even then we do not have one man for every job and there is some doubling and so forth. I do the stage designs myself and I follow everything right through. At first I will come up with an idea and then build a small model, in scale and in cut-out form. I have to ensure, apart from the splendour, that Cliff has plenty of room to move, for as you know he is given to athletic movement!

John has been involved with Cliff ever since the Gospel tour of 1975, and was part of the 'pop' team that went to Russia in the following year. Band members and back-up have undergone changes over the years, but they all talk of Cliff being easy to work with. That said, they are conscious of his exacting standards. He is seen as a happy man, permeated with an inner peace, though one member thought it worth stressing that he's been free of marriage commitments and so able to further his career and direct some of his emotions in that direction. So long as there is a genuine 'work' ethic, then all is fine. Along the roads and paths there have been plenty of fun moments.

The boys told me:

We went one night in search of a fish and chip shop and Cliff came along too. The chippie's owner seemed transfixed and kept saying 'can't be, can't be' but then it was. There was some bloke who came up and demanded Cliff's autograph and then uttered the immortal words 'Sign it. I don't like you, it's for my mum'. Rarely have we seen him lose his temper. There was a time in Yugoslavia when some English football hooligans were causing a fracas and general nuisance. I think they were stunned to see him, and he told them in no uncertain way to 'shut up' for he felt they were an embarrassment to our country.

Cliff on the road has brought joy and pleasure to so many people, but reviews have always been mixed. A review by Mick Brown in *The Guardian* on Cliff's Wembley concert started caustically by saying, 'Cliff was middle-aged at 21, his most damning contribution to swiftly transform the adolescent petulance evident in his first record into the suffocating cosiness which has characterised his career ever since.'

Brown moved on, however, to say that the show proved enormously enjoyable as Cliff appeared to recall that 'momentary fling' and interprets Cliff and the past with flourish.

Its principal attraction, of course, is nostalgic. Some, like 'Lucky Lips' and 'Bachelor Boy', seemed like the bizarre fruits of a full-frontal lobotomy operation the first time around, and they have hardly improved with age; it takes a perverse sort of talent to invest them with any sort of enthusiasm and conviction, yet Richard pulls off the feat with staggering aplomb.

Not quite the praise that Cliff's fans would approve of, but praise nevertheless.

Mirror Group Newspapers

The Daily Mirror was the first British national Newspaper to write about unknown young Cliff Richard 30 years ago.

We have something in common neither he nor this newspaper ever get any older !

And we are delighted still to be covering Cliff's extraordinary career.

With all best wishes,

Yours sincerely,

HILARY BONNER
SHOWBUSINESS EDITOR.

DAILY EXPRESS

Like one of the seven wonders of the rock world, Cliff Richard remains indestructable.

In a somewhat destructive industry, swamped with debauchery, drugtaking and other excesses, he remains so throughly nice and clean-living.

His extraordinary appeal is hard to analyse.

I onced asked Cliff how he would like to be remembered. The answer was in his dressing room - a framed inscription sent to him by a fan, saying; "Rock 'n' Roll and God work together in the hands of someone who loves them both."

As Paul Simon wrote, 'Every generation throws a hero up the pop charts.' Cliff has succeeded in conquering the pop charts for several generations and no doubt, more to come.

7 IN INTERVIEW

To most people, it may not be the question of all questions, yet, to a pop star, it could well be the one that marks a decisive growth in popularity and media interest. It is this: what is the colour of your eyes? It is a question Cliff Richard has been answering with an unswerving assurance ever since he first appeared in his pink drape jacket, pink day-glo socks and grey suede shoes.

Admittedly Cliff has had other questions flung his way. He has been asked 'What is the colour of your hair?' and 'How tall are you?' and once the physical tantalisers have been exhausted, then enquiry has moved to 'Do you like curry?' and 'What do you do in your spare time?' In the early days he was asked whether he had always intended to choose the pop world, or what professional career he might have chosen if he was not a pop singer and, inevitably, as in the sternly titled Cross Examination of *Record Pictorial* in 1963: 'You are the pin-up boy of thousands of girls. Do you want to marry a girl in show business?'

Two years into his career, Cliff was saying, 'questions, questions, questions.' What would he like a son of his to be? How are his songs written? Where does he like to spend his holidays? Sometimes he appeased the fans' and press's appetite for trivia. 'I like things with lots of cream,' he told the *Daily Mirror* in 1964, while Ann Leslie of the *Daily Express* learnt, during the same year, that 24-year-old Cliff had no less than 40 pairs of cuff links, 150 ties, bought six suits a year, had a weekly allowance of £10 that he spent on records and, to top it all, 'literally hundreds' of shoes. At other times he filled in some family background, as when he revealed an early love for kite flying and said how important it was to Indian kids. He talked to *Jackie* and said 'I often tried to eat lizards – yes, it's true! When I was a little kid, I would eat anything I could lay my fingers on. Flowers. Grass. Twigs. Anything. And I've been told that my Dad often used to dive across the floor just in time to stop me putting a lizard in my mouth.' Was he serious? It was Fergus Cashin in the *Daily Sketch* who pinned Cliff down on the apparent smallness of his consumer spending. 'Well that's a silly lie. I allow myself ten quid tax free pocket money . . . I have two cars (one's a £4,000 Thunderbird) and I don't even buy the petrol out of my pocket money. I sign for everything. Meals, clothes – the lot.' as they say, even £10 can go a long way, sometimes.

By 1970 he was unhappy on £1,000 a week but, as *Reveille*'s Dennis Holman was to realise, this was during a period when Cliff was uncertain how he should respond to the claims of Christianity.

David Wigg is the Executive Showbusiness/TV editor of The *Daily Express* and is one of Britain's foremost music writers.

It was pimples and not prospects that sometimes worried him. 'When I was 14 I used to think how marvellous it would be to be 20 and shave every day. Now I shave every day and I wish I didn't.' It must have gained him many male fans, and doubtless he had in mind an earlier traumatic experience of shaving: 'My first TV show, when I was told to remove my sideburns and stop being a little Elvis. I had to throw away my guitar and that taught me to use my hands without having a lump of wood to hold.'

Enquiries about his leisure activities revealed that he was a keen supporter of Leyton Orient and had sometimes gone to matches muffed up and 'disguised' with dark glasses, and his present-day craze for aerobics had its roots in the 23-year-old who swam for an hour or so a day, played badminton and said 'believe me, you've got to keep up with the pace'. Twisting and jiving kept him happy, but not ballroom dancing: 'That sort of stuff is not for me.' In the early days he travelled with a portable battery television set, cine filming was a must and, when time and weather permitted, there was sunbathing. Apart from learning that Cliff enjoyed curries, reporters over the years have revealed by astute questioning that he takes honey and not sugar in coffee, avoids sweet and fatty foods, and has at times had passions for Chinese and Polynesian foods, but the most arresting Cliff food information was contained in an article that appeared in the *News of the World*, 30 October 1960. In this feature Cliff expanded on his early love for Elvis Presley, 'he's the greatest as far as I'm concerned'. Presley admiration led Cliff into trying the culinary habits of the King of Rock 'n' Roll.

> I tried sauerkraut. I took just one mouthful and – ugh! – it was ghastly. From now on Elvis is welcome to my share of that stuff. One of his favourite dishes, I hear, is peanut butter and bananas on toast. Sounds pretty awful, doesn't it? But I've tried it and that's one of his recipes I intend to keep. Try it.

An outsider to show-biz and pop might well wonder what it matters what Cliff, or anyone come to that, likes and dislikes, wears, does, and so forth. I have no wish to indulge in some kind of quasi-psychological enquiry into the demands of twentieth century Western culture for trivia but such tit-bits do seem to be the spice of life, whether they are to be found in the more sedate quarters of *Harpers and Queen* or the frenzy of a teen pop journal. And for a record and entertainment industry starved of sufficient radio stations

Malcolm Muggeridge once edited *Punch*. He has countless journalistic and radio credits and many years ago astonished many when he professed he had been converted to Christianity.

Sue Lawley is a household name in British television and radio worlds, as a presenter and interviewer.

Sheridan Morley edits *Punch*, is a major theatre and literary reviewer and is the son of the famous actor Robert Morley.

Gordon Honeycombe is one of Britain's foremost television presenters and personalities.

112

I am very pleased to join others in a tribute to Cliff
at this time.
I remember his magnificent support for The Festival of
Light at the Hyde Park Rally and the great meeting at
Central Hall Westminster.
Very best wishes to him.

Yours sincerely,

Malcolm Muggeridge.

[signature]

PUNCH
PUBLICATIONS LTD

CLIFF RICHARD

As Robert, my father, once played Cliff's father
in a film called THE YOUNG ONES I vaguely feel that
we must be the same generation: in that case, how
come he (Cliff) now looks young enough to be not
only Robert's son but also mine ?

[signature]

...wley

...I was a teenager at school in the Midlands, I had
...f's name scratched on my tin pencil box (a free
...t from Cadbury's of Bournville). Had I been told
...en that I would one day sit in a television studio
...d interview him in front of ten million people, I
...uspect I would have turned quietly crimson and
...ainted. When that moment finally arrived - in his
...thirtieth year in showbusiness - he was as charming as
...the thirteen year old Lawley might have hoped. The
...then forty two year old Lawley was employing a nanny
...half her age who could speak of little else but
..."Cliff". And my small daughter, has long been convinced
...that "Summer Holiday" is the"most grooviest" film she's
...ever seen. A string of examples which possibly sum up
...the appeal of an extremely nice man.

[signature] Sue Lawley

TV-am

I have now left TV-am and am concentrating on my own writing career
- although I shall continue to appear here and there on the box.
I feel diffident about providing any tribute to Cliff as I have never
met him, and I think it woud be a presumption to commend anyone
I didn't know.

One question for him, however. When is he going to team up with Diana
Rigg and play Viola and Sebastian in Shakespeare's Twelfth Night? Has
anyone ever commented on how alike they look, as brother and sister?

Best wishes,

Yours sincerely

[signature] Gordon Honeycombe

GORDON HONEYCOMBE

to play an artist's music, such tit-bits here and there provide useful reminders of an artist's existence, especially if the writer begins with something like 'Cliff Richard, whose new record "Visions" is released this week, says . . .' On a teen level it seems that a successful recipe must comprise general gossip and so-called 'human' details. Certainly this was the staple fare of the early British music weekly press and well represented in a paper like the *New Musical Express* and the monthly *Rave*. In the 1980s, after a period when everything seemed so very precious and suffocating, when the choice was between pretentious intellectual analysis or overt rudeness to artists, there arose, in the midst of declining sales, excellent magazines such as *ID*, *The Face*, *Q* and *Arena*. Best of all, in terms of pop star gossip style interviewing, was *Smash Hits*, a magazine that exceeded in sales the circulations of all music weeklies put together. *Smash Hits* brought something of the old days, though not necessarily so attractive to artists, who can grow rather weary of being asked yet again the colour of their eyes, hair, legs and armpits.

Of course, Cliff, and a relatively small number of artists of some standing and length of pop service such as Bryan Ferry, Paul McCartney, Mick Jagger and David Bowie, do find their interviewers concerned with matters other than food fads and details of their favourite videos. Cliff's eligibility in the marriage stakes has been a particularly popular subject for interviewers, closely followed by his religious convictions, whether he is gay and when he will retire. It might be noticed at this point that no mention has been made of his musical output – the strangeness of this will be discussed later in this chapter.

Cliff's role as Britain's most wanted bachelor was well established, almost from the start. He was called the 'golden boy', and if rotten eggs were thrown by the Teds, there were kisses from the girls. Cliff told reporters, 'I don't have any hang-ups. I don't have a great urge to be married. I'm not pursuing anyone and feel very fulfilled.' Now, there was a challenge both to girls and reporters and it's not one that they have relinquished through the years. The matter has still been thought relevant enough for leading women's weekly *Woman's Own* to serialise his thoughts on the subject from *Single-Minded*, published by Hodder and Stoughton in 1988.

More teen-oriented magazines soon found out that Cliff had a corner in his heart for blondes but he wisely added a remark to make everyone happy, 'in the end I couldn't care if the girl was blonde, redhead or brunette.' Cliff's ideal would possess a sense of humour, certainly laugh at his jokes, have a love for music, ability to get on with other people, have a tidiness about herself and her surroundings. But who was he dating?

Here, when interviewing techniques wore thin they were replaced by direct observation, and Carol Grey and Carole Lynley, both seen as happy girls without a trace of 'actressy' temperaments, were soon reported to be dating Cliff. Anyone Cliff was seen with was viewed as a possible, and the lad himself faced probing questions, as did the lady, if the media could persuade her to speak on such a delicate matter. Both Susan Hampshire and Debbie Watling, Cliff's costars from the 1960s *Wonderful Life* and the following decade's *Take Me High*, were to be hounded. But then, as one reporter wrote after witnessing *Wonderful Life*, 'he still makes every girl in the audience feel deliciously cosy. He makes every middle-aged woman wish he were her very own son.' Cliff often told reporters in answer to their girl promptings that he had had a few near misses. With whom? Not an unreasonable question. And in 1964 Cliff names a 21-year-old dancer by the name of Jackie Irving. Friends or more? Cliff was to say 'She and I know that marriage is out of the question,' and Jackie, admitting she has more or less a regular boy friend, said, 'I realise it wouldn't do Cliff's career any good at all if he got married. It would only annoy his fans.'

Later Cliff would tell reporters, 'Jackie is the only girl I have ever contemplated marrying . . . I'm glad I'm not in love with a woman who is going to make me want to come home all the time. My lifestyle would have to change.' Pressed by reporters, Cliff would often name the right age for marriage. In time, 23 became 25 and then 27 and later 32.

At some point he ceased making predictions. Olivia Newton-John and Cindy Kent would soon be romantically linked with Cliff and plagued with questions. Once he said of Olivia, 'We are great friends, but I haven't asked her to marry me.' And there were others, including a dark-haired 18-year-old called Louanne Richards, a dancer from Devon, who stepped out with Cliff for the premiere of *Wonderful Life*, blunting current rumours that Susan Hampshire was the one. By 1980, Cliff was telling *Daily Mirror* writer Pauline McLeod that he had three ambitions: one was to be in a stage version of a rock 'n' roll musical, another was to be a hit in America and the third was to have a wife and children, with the added rider, 'But it has to be the right girl. It has to be for good.' He told the *Daily Express* that 'it would be fatal to search desperately for a bride.'

The more seasoned journalists had by now come to the conclusion that Cliff might be more career minded than anything else, and certainly a check through the newspaper files would have unearthed a remark from 1960 when he said, 'If I had to choose between marriage and my career, I'm afraid I would put my career first. You see so many people depend on me.' But by the early Eighties the real romantic wedding seemed possible. The press was agog and hardly able to contain its excitement. The *Sun* quoted Cliff as saying, 'Yes, I do love Sue Barker, I can't deny that and I wouldn't want to. We've talked about marriage, certainly, but neither of us think there is any rush. Yes, I'd like to marry and have children at the right time. I have realised I do need to be in love and that no man is an island.' The more cynical checked to see if Sue had made a record or was in need of some publicity after another of her 'almost' famous tennis victories. It seemed not. Naturally reporters wondered about their relationship before they were married, given the conflict between modern sexual morality and Cliff's Christian principles. Sue told *Woman* magazine, 'All he's saying is he doesn't believe in sex outside marriage, that marriage is sacred and if, in God's eyes, you choose a partner for life, then that's your partner sexually, too. But if celibate is what Cliff is, then I am as well.' The Cliff fan club magazines printed pictures of a happy Cliff and Sue, and there must have been many tearful girls all over the country. No doubt dedicated fans preferred the front cover of *Cliff United*, in December 1982, showing Cliff with his Mum, rather than those pictures of Cliff and Sue.

The *Mail on Sunday* had it all under control. They observed Cliff out to dinner with Sue in 1982, seen together at the prestigious Variety Club Lunch of '83 and together, though not smiling quite so rapturously, at Wimbledon a year later. The Sunday magazine of the *News of the World* revealed the duo had long telephone chats and that Sue turns to Cliff for comfort when she's having trouble with her game. And Cliff did say, 'All right, I miss Sue every time we're apart because we have been seeing a lot of each other lately and I think, oh drat, when I sit down to dinner on my own . . . I'm just going to wait a decent amount of time . . .' Sue felt the same. Asked about her feelings toward Cliff and future commitment, she told the *Daily Mail*, 'It is not Cliff I am not sure about, it is myself. I want to slow down and not rush into anything. It is silly to say we are just good friends. Anyone can see it is much more than that.' Yet the big question was: could she give up her career or Cliff his? 'Tennis and the need to win is still in my blood', said Sue, and Cliff could not disown his continuing hunger for music. But did they really have to give up their careers? Couldn't they manage time together without it being total time? The questions flew but at least they were serious ones and not always just fodder for sensationalist headlines. Not all mentions of Cliff and Sue were on the subject of their romance. In March 1984, on the BBC 'Wogan Show', Terry coaxed Cliff into admitting the role Sue had played in introducing him to 'weights and things', and remarked that Sue had told him of her ability to defeat Cliff at arm wrestling. But Wogan did not use the moment to tread the well-worn path of Sue and Cliff's on-or-off romance.

The *Dorking Advertiser* was gripped by a startling new angle when they heard that Cliff might be in the process of buying a mansion at Abinger Hammer and decided, since Cliff was a born-again Christian, that they might ask the local born-again rector the Rev. John Bryn Thommas if he had any foreknowledge. He was quoted as replying, 'I have heard it from several sources. They say he has built the tennis courts for a well-known tennis player.' Well-known tennis player – it must be Sue Barker! Alternatively, though perhaps not as interesting, this possible buyer might actually have a passion for tennis.

So there would be headlines like 'The Look of Love', 'Sue's Look of Love', 'Love Match for Cliff and Sue', 'Cliff Courts His No. 1. Sue', 'Cliff and Sue are a Smash Hit' and, inevitably, 'Love - All! Cliff's in a Clincher'. In the end, of course, it was all to no avail. 1985 saw Cliff on the Simon Bates BBC Radio One show saying 'Two years ago we talked very deeply about the possibility of getting married and decided against it.' Cliff seemed more than a little weary with some of the pressure that stemmed from apparent press snooping and questioning. 'You can tell the press that we are extremely good friends but that's not enough for them. They want to know if you're shacked up together or if a baby is on the way.'

Away from endless questioning on love and marriage, the years have seen many press speculations as to whether Cliff is gay. In show-biz you cannot be Mr Clean. At first the question did not arise for early media attention made the normal assumptions of the time – it was presumed that Cliff would marry and the matter was reduced to the question of who the girl would be.

It was when nothing seemed to be happening on the marriage front that suspicions arose. There were interviewers who wheedled from Cliff the admission that he had felt worried at times when friends of his gradually left the single ranks and he seemed the only one left. Media pressure to find a soulmate hadn't helped his peace of mind, which had not been helped either by pressures from friends and Christians who thought marriage might be a good idea. Fans, while having some concern for his happiness, were often preoccupied with their own, and a desire that he should remain their fantasy idol. Said the man at the centre of all this: 'I used to get upset over people who suggested unless you were married you were not a complete person and couldn't possibly be happy. But I don't believe that any more.' Unfortunately, of course, such a statement flies in the face of generally accepted notions that there is something all-fulfilling in marriage, and especially contradicts some Christians who have rewritten the New Testament in their own terms to denigrate the single state in comparison with marriage and the family, a view that can cause much distress to the childless.

The press and other media have never seen Cliff as the leader of the 'singles' or congratulated him on choosing the single state. Occasionally, though, someone has displayed sensitivity, for example, Simon Bates, in an interview with Cliff on BBC Radio One, January 1985. Bates said, 'I wonder underneath, if you are an impatient person, who needs to be on his own sometimes?' Cliff replied:

I have found it therapeutic to get away. When I go to Wales, it is beautiful, right on the edge of Snowdonia that I can, I know it sounds silly, but I do my best praying, when I am on my own, because there is nothing to get in the way . . . I go completely on my own. I take two dogs and a guitar. I do my own cooking, which is fairly bare, you know you get your lamb chop and stick it in the oven, whatever it is, that sounds dreadful, but it is fairly basic, but I just eat every day and walk a lot. I don't know, if I could live like that, live a hermit existence.

It was John Blake's now famous article of 12 June 1978 in the London *Evening News*, which brought the 'is he or isn't he gay?' question into the public forum. The article had a stirring headline – MY TEN YEARS WITHOUT SEX – and contained one of Cliff's particularly memorable statements: 'I don't believe in sleeping around and I'm damned if I'll marry just to prove I'm not gay'.

Blake asked him how he felt when people suggested he is probably gay. 'It's untrue but I have given up even talking about it because I think nothing I say will change anything.' Cliff expressed displeasure that people should make criticism and judgments of his sexual preferences. He also said, 'It's just a fortunate thing in my personality that I maybe don't need marriage.' Wogan once asked him if celibacy appealed and received the reply, 'It's not a matter of whether it appeals to me or not. It's just the lifestyle I choose, or rather the lifestyle that chose me.' None of this though should be seen as Cliff's inability to live with others. He has never expressed a desire to live on his own and throughout most of his career he has lived with and shared his home with others.

For many years Cliff has lived with his manager of Christian and charitable matters, Bill Latham, and with Bill's mother Mamie. 'Over the years Mamie became a second mum to me and shared so much of what I did. She was also gracious and elegant.' In April 1986 she became very ill and was taken to hospital. 'On the evening of 24 April I was able to visit the hospital and kiss Mamie goodbye for the last time. She was 84.' In an interview with James Ashwood in *Woman's Day* Bill responded to a remark that his close relationship with Cliff has caused some speculation. The genial Latham, always gracious, merely responded with 'I suppose the homosexual innuendos are inevitable. I can understand that people put two and two together and make five.'

There was another bout of gay gossip in 1980. The *Sunday Mirror* headlined: 'Give the Gays a Chance' Says Gospelling Cliff. Cliff had said in response to Robert Edison's questioning, 'I'm not saying that people of the same sex can't have perfectly good relationships, but I don't see how the Church can actually embrace it, or imply that homosexuality is all right. On the other hand, that doesn't mean the Church shouldn't understand it and maybe accept it more.'

The *Star* newspaper writer Rick Sky said there is one question the people always want to ask Cliff Richard. And here is his blunt answer: 'I'm NOT homosexual.' And in February 1980, he more or less repeated the remark he had made to John Blake two years before, 'But certainly I'm not going to get married just to justify myself to other people.' Later, in the article, after saying women were attracted to him, he said 'But if there are girls who want to sleep with me because it is a challenge, that's their problem. I know that people find my lifestyle hard to accept but I think it is sad that we live in such a mixed-up society that assumes that any adult who is single and over 20 is gay.'

Cliff has never expressed intolerance towards gay people although at times he has been outspoken over the antics and tactics employed by some gay movements. He was particularly annoyed when Gay Liberation Front members picketed the inaugural meeting in London of Mary Whitehouse's anti-porn movement. He found distasteful their dressing as nuns and 'screaming like banshees'. But he was extremely well-disposed toward Boy George on one of his Wogan appearances, even remarking that the Boy had some rather lovely dresses. Doubtless the question will remain and, as he said to Don Short in the *Daily Mirror* in 1969, 'Of course, I've heard stories that I must be homosexual because I've never married. That's terrible, but there's nothing I can do about it.'

Arguably more hurtful has been a continuing suggestion in some areas of the media that Cliff's Christian convictions are related more to a desire to remain a star and sell records than any real heartfelt experience. Such a view is plainly ridiculous. There must be easier ways of maintaining a career than taking a vast array of mixed religious luggage on board. Admittedly the supposition might have gained some credence in early years, although even then it depended upon an ignorance of the fact that, while he was making hit records, touring around the world and starring on television and radio, Cliff was also attending Bible class at a North London church with other young people, and without any provision made for this star status.

At first, the main thrust of media interviewing was directed to the basic question as to whether Cliff would remain in show business or find a role within a specifically religious area. In this, it was Cliff's understandable indecision, as much as anything, that created the situation. Obviously, there were many voices competing for his attention and ultimate commitment. Wisely, he decided he would stay in show business.

Initially there was a reaction of amazement and incredulity on the part of the media toward his major public declaration of faith. This was made in June 1966, at Earl's Court, on stage with the American evangelist Billy Graham. Neither Cliff nor Billy could complain about the degree of coverage or the subsequent demand from seemingly every

'I'm for serious – lots of times'

118

newspaper, journal and radio station for interview. It was a demand that was to continue for several years, and indeed the religious element would feature in almost every interview from June 1966 onwards. The main difference between Cliff's answers of the 1960s and the first half of the 1970s, compared with his responses over the next 10 years, reflect Cliff's own greater grasp of media opportunity, and his growing confidence in pushing his faith. Yet for all that, he has maintained a forceful declaration of his faith that has rarely seemed heavy or overdone. He has never come across either as patronising or boring in the countless interviews that have filled pages for over 20 years.

He was asked how he felt now he was a Christian. He replied 'I've never been so happy in my life.' Was it all a stunt? 'Not for me.' Which individuals had helped him toward his decision? Obviously one was Bill Latham; another was his old English teacher Jay Norris; then there was David Winter, at that time an influential Christian journalist and eventually to be ordained while he was head of BBC religious broadcasting. A surprise answer was Susan Hampshire, with whom he had worked on the film *Wonderful Life*. 'She had gone to work with Albert Schweitzer. While we were sitting around the film set waiting to work on different scenes, we talked a lot together. I owe a lot to her. She helped me come closer to the Church.' So how would he marry pop activities with

his Christian affairs? 'I will simply tell the office that I am not available for show business offers during such and such a period.' Initially, Cliff spoke at countless churches and commended his faith. It was ideal ground to experience close contact with record fans and pleased Christian young people. At the same time it gave room for media people from smallish towns to ask their questions rather than being left with syndicated copy or press releases.

His small-time activities in the religious world left many media people at a loss for words. It was so unusual that it was often reported with great seriousness in quarters that normally concentrate on the sensational. So it was that *Reveille* for 1 July 1970, simply said

> He involves himself seriously in Church activities, in particular the Crusader Union, a Christian youth organisation which promotes Bible study for young people between eight and eighteen. Part of the work is social, and Cliff, who is leader of the Finchley Class, helps organise holidays and excursions. He has recently returned from the Norfolk Broads where, for two weeks, he cruised with four boatloads of boys.

The questions flowed. How can a Christian mix in the 'nasty' world of pop? 'There doesn't have to be sex and drugs in rock and roll – although there usually are.' How do you see yourself as a Christian in the pop world? 'I just make the most of my career to do Christian things. I'm not just a pop singer. I'm a Christian pop singer.' Would Cliff be talking to people if they are moved by what he says? 'It's unfair to say this, but I don't trust that everybody would come for the right reasons if I stayed behind. I think there might be an element of people who would come back just to be close to a pop singer.' Wasn't there a contradiction in doing a Gospel tour and then following it by a rock 'n' roll tour?

Harry de Louw with Anton Hussman has been responsible for the running of the International Cliff Richard Movement that brings together most of Cliff's fan clubs.

Richard Barber edits the high selling British independent television magazine *TV Times*.

HARRY DE LOUW INT'L°
pop music consultants

I met Cliff for the first time in 1962 and after that first meeting over 50 times. I am glad I choose him, as he is still around and I learned a lot about the show business. And for me he did not change since the first meeting on April 6th, 1962.

Yours as ever,

Harry

"Awards come and awards go but when the readers of Britain's most widely read, paid for magazine vote Cliff Richard their favourite singer not once, not twice but four times in a row, you have to sit up and take notice.

When Cliff accepted his latest award, he seemed a bit puzzled as to why he consistently beat off challenges from the likes of Bros, Madonna and Kylie Minogue. I don't think there is any mystery at all – and, clearly, nor do the readers of TVTimes."

Best wishes,

Yours sincerely,

Richard Barber

RICHARD BARBER
Editor

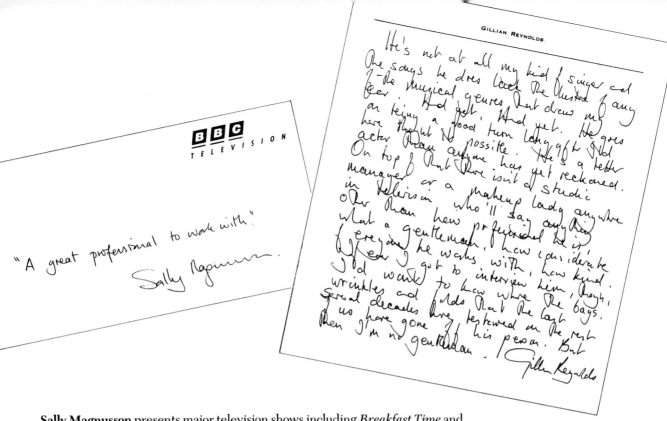

"A great professional to work with".

Sally Magnusson

Sally Magnusson presents major television shows including *Breakfast Time* and *Songs of Praise* for the BBC.

Gillian Reynolds is a well known television presenter and journalist.

Not really. The reason I separate them is that there are people who don't necessarily want to go and hear Gospel music so, by advertising a Gospel concert, anybody that comes knows they're going to hear Gospel music, so therefore I'm being legitimate. I'm not misusing my platform. I still have a responsibility to those who don't want to come so I do a secular tour, and I still do a smattering of Gospel stuff in that, but I choose material that I think is valid musically, so nobody minds that.

How had his faith changed some of his basic attitudes? 'I know there are a lot of humanists in the world, but sometimes that's *not* enough! I was *always* a humanist, I cared (in a way) about people, but *now* it's far deeper in that I care about them not only *physically* but *spiritually* as well. So I want to be involved with every aspect of their lives.' Is it a hard struggle to live up to a standard? 'I fight evil. If I think rotten things I hate myself. I try to be fair to people. Sometimes it is hard.' How did he keep spiritually fit on the road? 'It not difficult really. A Bible doesn't take up much room in my suitcase.' Is entertainment the most important thing in your life? 'It needs a lot of prayer and a lot of grace to keep it in its proper perspective.' Has your decision to become a born-again Christian helped you to be fulfilled?

I got to the point where I had all the fame I could handle and more money than I could spend. I have everything I could want thrown at me – fame, money, girls . . . I should have been hysterically happy. I was happy enough, but I certainly wasn't

121

hysterically happy. I thought: 'Well, is this it? Surely there's got to be something else?' And there was. There was God.

You are happy? 'I'm doing the things I believe I should be doing. The main thing I believe I'm loved by God and I think that is the answer to everything.' Not everybody digs your Christian stance. 'The thing that Christianity teaches above all things is that you must have an adherence to morality and people hate this: they can't bear it.'

Radio and television presenters, especially those at national level, have extracted rather more details and considered statements from Cliff about his faith and future, particularly in interviews held in the 1980s. There have been a number of positive times in which general chatter about Cliff's music and records have been blended with talk of faith and belief, always completely unassuming and natural.

It was in conversation with Terry Wogan that Cliff expanded on the general theme of why he had not given up show-biz after his declared Christian conversion.

I nearly did give it all up but the very fact that I have the power of rock 'n' roll behind me gives me a platform . . . I've spoken to so many ministers, friends of mine who are ministers, and I've said, you know, what do you think about all this and every one of them without – well, with very few exceptions – has said 'If you give up the platform, in a few years you'll be forgotten as a name and you won't be a draw' . . . we want to try and attract people and make Christianity look attractive. Why should it be that people look at a dowdy old closed-up church and assume it is Christianity. Christianity's what we make it and . . . you know, I'm not the only one . . . look, you happen to be talking to me tonight but there's a lot of hip people around – younger than me, too! – and who find it very relevant and live their lives by it and their lives are successful. I don't mean successful financially or fame-wise but because they're satisfied people.

On another occasion, a lengthy interview for local radio, he was asked by Nigel Cutteridge whether he went out for converts during his Gospel tours.

Converts? It's a funny, loaded word, really, because what I go out there to do is try and raise question-marks and grey areas in people's minds: maybe they've not had a specific thought about a particular subject . . . and, if I can raise a question-mark which makes them think about it, which might ultimately lead to their conversion, then that would be fantastic. Ultimately, though, I can't be after conversions, because God is the only one who can convert somebody; I might be instrumental in persuading somebody that there may be something but ultimately it's between that person and God.

While Cliff's religious views have either been solicited or somewhat ingeniously introduced by Cliff himself into a conversation, he has not over the years been reticent in speaking on other subjects.

On a number of occasions he has attacked drug taking and particularly when it has involved pop stars. Right from the early days, and unswervingly so since, he has stressed, in answer to questions, that music personalities should exercise 'responsibility for the young people coming up'. Pop stars 'need to be more careful because of the image they create and because of the people following them.' More recently, he has expressed pleasure at the increased concern by pop stars for world poverty, best illustrated by events such as Live Aid.

During the Live Aid campaign he remarked with some humour to a journalist, 'It's great to find Bob Geldof is a goody-goody now. I used to be called that in a detrimental way.' Way back in 1982 he told a journalist, 'If someone thinks I'm goody-goody then I'm winning.'

Cliff's media path has been relatively free of unpleasantness. While some have poked fun with mild malice and a few have forecast his demise at regular intervals, by and large, he has attracted sympathetic coverage of his activities. He may not have been covered in the way he would like at times, but spite and hostility have been absent, save for one piece in the *New Musical Express* that resulted in a rare bout of lasting anger and a subsequent libel case which he won with damages.

Cliff's views on South Africa have been questioned with some severity by the media. He has made numerous trips to South Africa and, from early times, has condemned apartheid, although that has not always been noticed. His reaction to press criticism in 1963 was a trifle unfortunate for, perhaps thoughtlessly, he told the press, 'The coloured people seem happy. They're treated well'. During the same period he was asked by writer Fergus Cashin, 'How about the colour problem?' 'We were too busy to notice. I saw coloured servants, of course. But they are well paid and seemed quite happy. I mean to say you get white people who are servants.' He was asked if he played before coloured audiences in South Africa. To this he said, 'Yes . . . Indians and Africans. They don't applaud. They just scream at the end.' How did he feel about coloured singers? He answered, 'Just the greatest. Take Ray Charles. No one, but no one, can get that kind of feeling into a number. He's fabulous.' Over the years Cliff's visits to South Africa continued, with adverse comment, while he has pointed out that he has always stipulated that he shall play to mixed audiences. However, in 1985 he found himself on the 'black list' of entertainers who have been breaking embargoes on playing in South Africa. He spoke of this on Swedish radio in 1985 when he was asked 'What has it meant to you to be on the black list?'

> I have been against apartheid for many years. I stopped making commercial concerts five years ago, you know, before it became popular, so I couldn't understand why people were choosing to make life so difficult for me when I have spoken openly against apartheid for many, many years. So I told them that I don't make concerts there; I make no commercial concerts in South Africa. But I am a Christian and so my beliefs will, therefore, take me there sometimes. So they took me off the black list.

When he was asked if he would be going back he stressed a desire to meet some of the Christian leaders and that he might be part of a 'wonderful evangelistic event'.

In his book *Single Minded* he comments further:

> I know the condemnation that South Africa and its people have received, and it has

123

hurt and disappointed me – not because I feel that the condemnation was unjust but because it has been delivered so often without love and without compassion for all segments of the community.

A little while back there was a cruel song on Spitting Image which had the refrain . . . 'But I've never met a nice South African'. Well, I have – many of them, of all races – and I feel really offended when the world tars every one of them with the same apartheid brush.

One matter remains for this chapter – the media and Cliff's music. It's always been a complaint of his that so few reporters, journalists and reviewers give real time to the music he makes, rather than his image and personal life. In more recent years he feels he has been recording albums with considerable depth, noticeable for good sound construction, better-than-average lyrics and, as his supporters would add, coming with a vocal drive and delivery that shows greater maturity and skill. Too often, he has been interviewed briefly about his latest single or album, then been taken through the familiar path of marriage, homosexuality, faith and age. Certainly, those lengthy radio programmes with DJs such as Simon Bates, Richard Skinner, Roger Scott, Roger Day and Mike Smith have been full of fascinating music dialogues. But, after pouring through endless cuttings and radio-television transcripts, I agree with Cliff that not enough attention has been paid to his music and, if it had, then arguably his music stature would be that much higher in more progressive music circles.

Cliff says, 'I think I do more interviews than anyone else I know.' Or, for that matter, than I know.

Quotes, culled from here and there and some in person.

Sir Laurence Olivier on Cliff in the musical *Time*:
My congratulations to Cliff Richard. He has been a delight to work with.

Jet Harris, once a member of The Shadows:
All the best for 30 years graft.

John Friesen, worldwide music specialist and supplier of Cliff memorabilia.
All the best on 30 years.

Richard Skinner, Radio One DJ, BBC.
Cliff Richard has a remarkable capacity to remain credible and contemporary on the rock scene.

Tim Rice, major media personality and lyricist:
Happy 1989 and many more. I am lucky enough to have remained in close contact with Cliff since my Norrie Paramor days.

Elton John: foremost world rock star.
He is always in what's happening music and for me that is the key ingredient for his continued success.

Olivia Newton-John, once closely associated with Cliff, still a great friend, and world famous music star in her own right:

He gets better and better as the years go on. Cliff has class and he has kept up with the trends so far as his music goes. It is difficult to imagine showbusiness without him.

John Blake, major press and one-time top pop writer:

Rock is gut music. It is about rebellion and being young and fast and sexy. However glossy his hair, however spirited his Pinocchio dancing, therefore Richard is altogether too well scrubbed and asexually wholesome to be a real star.

Tony Meehan, record producer, drummer, associated with Jet Harris, and the original drummer with The Shadows.

There are colossal problems in the music business. Cliff is the exception rather than the rule. You have to have that something special which Cliff has, or you are just an ordinary person who has talent and you get rocketed into this life.

Russell Davies, media personality, one-time television reviewer for *The Sunday Times:*

Today, the Cliff Richard stage performance is a sort of lively professional demonstration of past styles, and very well done. Having acquired the versatility of a session-singer, he can manage most sorts of material.

Shakin' Stevens, leading British solo pop star:

His track record speaks for itself and every true professional in the business should admire him for being around for so long.

Peter Powell, once a leading DJ, now someone who manages artists:

He is part of our musical heritage, a stalwart.

Thereza Bazar, hit artist both solo and one-half of Dollar with David Van Day:

I've met him, and I think he looked incredible. He must have very, very special qualities.

David Van Day, one-half of the hit group Dollar with Thereza Bazar:

Cliff is uniquely professional to have sustained such a long career in this business and yet be nice about it.

Pat Boone, famous pop star of the 1950s, 1960s, US TV presenter.

Britain's most important singing and recording star.

Alistair Pirrie, television and radio presenter, former producer of major UK music show *The Roxy:*

He has always chosen such good material. The most annoying thing is that he looks so good.

Lambeth Palace London SE1 7JU

I am conscious of the many good things which Cliff has
contributed to Christian life in this country and pay tribute to his
consistent witness to the centrality of faith in everyday life. I wish
this publication well.

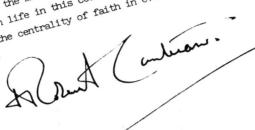

 EVANGELISTIC ASSOCIATION

I have scores of recollections of Cliff Richard

My mind goes back to the occasion in the Earls Court Arena
during the Greater London Crusade of 1966. We heard of this
young pop singer who was a sort of pop idol to young fans. We
were told that he had become a Christian and that he would be
willing to give his testimony at one of the meetings.

His singing, to me, was different--but impressive! He gave
a marvelous testimony about his Christian faith. Much more
important was the fact that, by speaking at this meeting, he
nailed his colors to the mast. It was interesting to read in the
Daily Telegraph in August 1988 that his witness today is "still
inspired by unfudged Christian moral values" and that "scandal
has never been attached to his name." This is a wonderful
tribute to someone who treads such a knife-edge path as he has to
do as a well-known performer.

I recall with great joy the news we received in 1980
that Cliff Richard had been honored by Her Majesty the Queen by
being given an OBE. We Americans are a little overawed by these
special honors--but we do realize that they mark a tribute being
paid by the nation to an individual. Cliff was well deserving of
this honor, and he never allowed it to "go to his head." He has
remained the same likeable, humble, and God-centered person.

I count it a privilege to have him associated with that
forthcoming mission, and I am glad to have this opportunity of
paying my tribute to a true Christian entertainer--all-time box
office star--leader, author, and loyal friend.

Billy Graham

8 FAITH AND ITS EFFECT

It took Cliff a long time to pluck up enough courage to tell the world 'I'm a Christian'. There was no reason why he shouldn't keep his beliefs private. After all, he looks on sexuality as an area that is personal and private, and one he will not share. But he chose to make public what he believed. His Christian 'coming out' at a Billy Graham campaign meeting at Earl's Court on 16 June 1966 was headline news in the press and on radio and television.

That evening Earl's Court saw a seasoned entertainer, experienced in stage presentation, become as awkward as a gawping kid with his first girlfriend. He had terrible pins and needles, he tried to raise his arms for emphasis but could not, and he walked off with his arms so positioned that some wondered if they were tied to his sides. He was dead scared.

However, it did not seem that way to some of those who were there. Janet Stafford, then a student nurse, now married to a Methodist minister, remembers:

It was all quite a shock. I had no idea he would be there. I don't think it was his message that counted, more his courage. He seemed quite fluent. I had no idea he was going through such inner turmoil. It was so unusual for a pop star to get up and say he was a Christian. To say he was for LSD, yes, but not for Jesus. I remember at the time I wasn't prepared to say I was a Christian amongst my friends because it was very unfashionable, but I thought, if he can do this in front of so many people, then I can do the same with my friends. I was a Beatles fan and this moment made me a fan of Cliff. This event was so good for our generation, for everything seemed to be saying it was fine to take drugs, pot, and we needed some sanity and some leadership from our idols. I regretted that my hero, Lennon, seemed so mixed up. As a musician he was great but neither from him nor from others did we get honesty. I was training then and at 18 I laid out my first body and I couldn't make sense of it. What did Lennon offer? Cliff pointed me towards Jesus. It was a great evening and it has stayed with me ever since, so I am grateful to Cliff.

Cliff was aware that many people did not approve of the Graham revival method. 'I know people criticise the Billy Graham kind of conversion, but if it doesn't last, then it wasn't for real in the first place. After all, Judas's conversion didn't last, did it?' He felt his life had changed. He told Vic Ramsey, an evangelist of the time, 'Many young people think it's only for the old fuddy-duddies but it's for young people as well, and that's what I mean by being relevant. Yes, sir! It works!'

Billy Graham is the foremost Christian evangelist in today's religious scene.

Cliff Richard has raised over £500,000 through his gospel concerts. But more. He has visited our projects and programmes in Africa, Asia and Latin America. Largely unheralded and unannounced, his rapport with children and adults in some of the poorest countries of the world has to be seen to be believed.

Having accompanied him on all these overseas tours I would like to pay tribute to a unique "Christian Ambassador" for his genuine love and concern for the people who benefit directly from the remarkable amount of money that he has raised, not only through his concerts but through films, videos and a variety of audio-visual aids.

On behalf of Tear Fund and those on the receiving end of your loving concern Cliff, thank you — so very much.

George Hoffman
Founder Director of Tear Fund

'Cliff is one of these amazing and gifted personalities that remains, it seems, forever young — in spirit, in heart, in enthusiasm and commitment.

His continued popularity and acceptance with both the Christian community and secular world and media for such an extended period of time attests to the unique and enduring qualities and gifts that God has given him, and his commitment to them. So, from this Cliff to "the Cliff" congratulations, and God bless you.'

Sincerely,
Cliff Barrows

Richard Bewes

We are sometimes asked whether Britain has any effective 'evangelists.' We ha one, but no one in this country is better at communicating the Christian messa ordinary people than Cliff Richard. He is Christianity's best spokesman around t parts.

George Hoffman was for many years the much loved Director of Tear Fund, the major Christian based relief charity that is much favoured by Cliff.

Cliff Barrows is a household name for his long-time involvement in the Billy Graham Association.

Richard Bewes has worked closely with Cliff in many of his religious activities. He is Vicar of the famous All Souls Church, London.

His Billy Graham adventure was the culmination of a long soul search, and in fact he had already appeared at a number of Christian gatherings without the press being aware. As David Winter says:

Bill Latham had been painstaking in keeping it quiet up to the Graham meeting. I think some people have wrongly assumed that it all happened that night in June. However, it was a very public declaration and Cliff knew he was burning bridges that evening. And really the repercussions have never died down, it's always been hard for him as a pop star to mingle freely, and in some Christian circles you will find people adulating him or treating him in a way that makes it hard for him. I think he has coped with it sensibly.

The eventual decision would mean some alienation from the mother he adored. For hours, day, and months he had argued in dressing rooms with friends like Hank Marvin and Liquorice Locking, for Liquorice especially was into the Good Book, and its interpretation by the Jehovah's Witnesses sect.

There were friends of Cliff's who worried, not so much that he was looking for inner meaning and satisfaction, but that his direction appeared to be towards the Witnesses. Three schoolteachers came to his rescue, his old English teacher Jay Norris, an RE

18

19

20

21   22   23

17 The famous three: left to right – Bruce (Welch), Brian (Bennett), Hank (Marvin).
18 People said Radio 1 DJ Mike looked a trifle like . . .
19 A failure here spells disaster for M. Read Esq.
20 Trying out their next party piece.
21 'No, it *was* out!'
22 It went somewhere.
23 'Sometimes, I don't know how I do it.'
24 No time here for thinking about the next hit.
25 I support young stars of the future.
26 'All my world's a stage'
27 The great double!
28 'Mistletoe and Wine' – the number one selling single of 1988.
29 Signing his *Single Minded*, another number one, in the book charts.

26

28

SINGLES

75

TITLES A-Z (WRITERS)

1-2-3 (Estefan/Garcia) 72
9 a.m. (The Comfort Zone)
(Henshall/Helms/Chandler) 19
Chambers
Air That I Breathe 60
(Hammond/Hazlewood)
Angel Of Harlem (U2) 12
As Long As You Follow 66
(McVie/Quintela)

Loco in Acapulco 9
(Collins/Dozier)
Love Like A River 58
(Climie/Fisher/Morgan)
Love Never Dies 63
(Caffey/Caffey/Nowels)
Megamix/Mary's Boy Child
(Remix) (A)
Fanan Reydim/Various-AA) 52
Hairston

Back and Better than Ever...

CROSBY, STILLS, NASH & YOUNG
★ **AMERICAN DREAM** ★

31 DECEMBER 1988

TOP 100 ALBUMS

1 1 7 PRIVATE COLLECTION ★★★
Cliff Richard (Various)
EMI/Virgin/PolyGram
C:TCNOW 13/CD:

2 2 5 NOW 13! ★★★
Various (Various)
Warner Brother
C:WX 221/C

3 5 5 GREATEST HITS ★★
Fleetwood Mac (Various)
Really Useful/Polyd
C:ALWTC

4 3 8 THE PREMIERE COLLECTION ★★★
Various (Various)

5 4 25 KYLIE ★★★★
Kylie Minogue (Stock/Aitken/Waterman)
CBS/WEA
C:H

6 6 3 THE HITS ALBUM
Various (Various)

7 11 10 THE LEGENDARY ROY ORBISON ●

51 44 9 RAGE
T'Pau (Roy Thomas Baker)
Siren/Virgin SRNLP
C:SRNMC 20/CD:CDSRN
Telstar STAR 2352 (B
C:STAC 2352/CD:TCD

52 NEW CLASSIC LOVE SONGS
Various (Various)
Tabu 46315:
C:463152-4/CD:463

MY GIFT TO YOU
Alexander O'Neal (Jimmy Jam/Terry Lewis)
4th + B'way/Island BRLP
C:BRCA 519/CD:BR

...k (Chris Blackwell)
Vertigo/Phonogram VEl
C:VERHC 62/CD:8

Epic MO
...DC 45

29 27 9 The...

30 26 6 Br...

31 33 11 ...
Pasadenas (V...

32 35 74 HEARSAY ★★★
Alexander O'Neal (Jimmy Jam...
Precious Org/Phon...

33 30 3 THE GREATEST HITS OF HOUSE ●
Various (Various)

34 31 7 THE MEMPHIS SESSIONS ★
Wet Wet Wet (Willie Mitchell)
CBS 4629431 (C)
C:4629434/CD:4629432

35 41 5 TILL I LOVED YOU ●
Barbra Streisand (Various)
Telstar STAR 2316(BMG)
C:STAC 2316/CD:TCD 2316

36 34 39 THE GREATEST LOVE ★
Various (Various)
Telstar STAR 2347 (BMG)
C:STAC 2347/TCD 2347

37 39 7 BEST OF HOUSE '88 ●
Various (Various)
Stylus SMR 861(STY)
C:SMC 861/CD:SMD 861

38 42 14 THE WORLDS OF FOSTER & ALLEN ●
Foster & Allen (Eamonn Campbell)
Elektra EKT 44(W)
C:EKT 44C/CD:960774-2

39 40 33 TRACY CHAPMAN ●
Tracy Chapman (David Kershenbaum)
Dover/Chrysalis ADD 5(C)
C:ZDD 5/CD:CCD 5

88

89 99 2 THE BEIDERBECKE COLLECTION
Various (Brian Hainsworth/Keith F...

90 80 6 RAPPIN' UP THE HOUSE ●
Various (Various)

91 RENAISSANCE
Aswad (Aswad)

92 87 7 REMOTE
Hue And Cry (Goldberg/Bionde...

STATISTICS (Wk)   This Week   Year To Date
New Chart Entries 1   710
Panel Sales Percentage ...... +44%

30

31 33

32

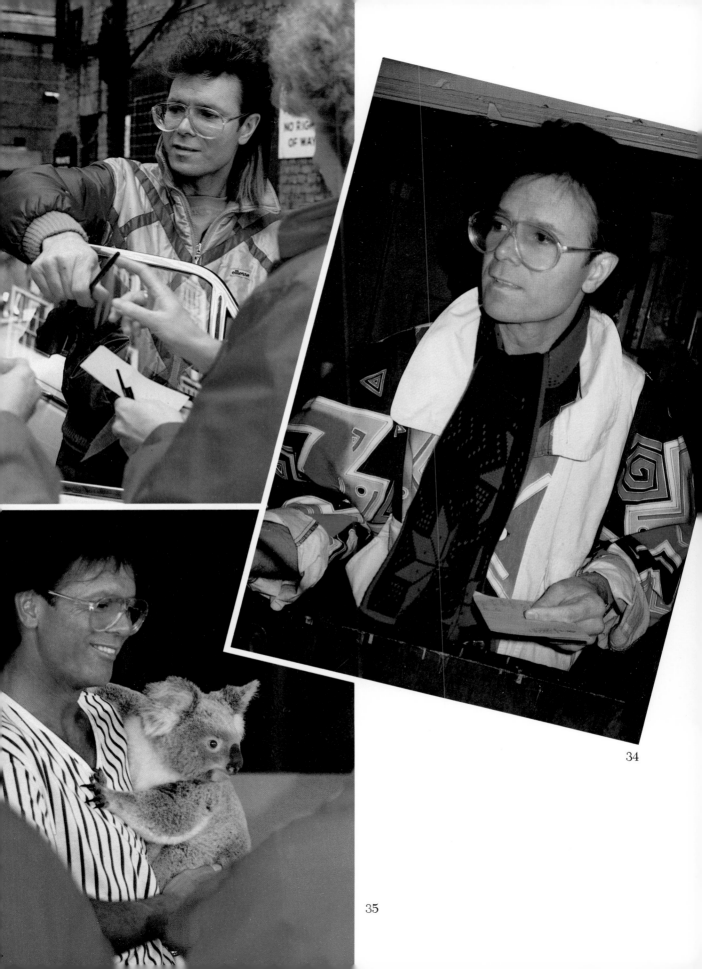

34

35

30 With Bill Latham, who runs his Christian and charity diary, and 'personal' side.
31 The number one man, David Bryce on the right.
32 Cliff and Mum – quite a couple!
33 'You've got the right bloke?'
34 'Not another hundred to sign!'
35 'Yes, he did help me end 1988 with number one single, album, compact disc and video, plus the number one book.'
36 Just Cliff.

teacher by the name of Bill Latham and his friend Graham Disbrey. There was another influential person – David Winter, then a journalist, now ordained and head of the religious broadcasting service of the BBC. Astonishingly, Cliff started attending Bible classes, a Crusaders group and, when he could, he was in church. Mainstream faith won the day and he claimed his allegiance. Cliff's mother and sisters, however, had accepted the Witness faith, as of course had Hank Marvin. To this day, his mother has not given up hope that Cliff might join the Witnesses. However, it seems unlikely, for his faith has broadened and deepened, and rarely wavers. His long standing friend Bill Latham comments:

> I think when Cliff became involved in mainstream Christian expression, he recognised a dimension of faith he hadn't seen before and it appealed to him. I think he found the Witnesses somewhat legalistic. His decision wasn't easy because of the family's move towards the Witnesses. They still argue, Cliff and his Mum, but they do so out of mutual respect for each other's beliefs. To take an obvious illustration, with the Witnesses not recognising Christmas in the same way that mainstream Christians do, it means some distance at a time of year when certainly most Christians are waiting to greet and recall the Saviour's birth.

Bill dealt with Cliff's spiritual questions, while at school he had Cliff's younger sister, Joan, in his class. Cliff had achieved more than most British pop stars, yet he was searching for meaning behind it all. 'I was human as the next person,' is Cliff's general remark to those who think it strange that he should have contemplated a religious answer to his wanderings of the early 1960s:

> I remember going through a period of thinking: I may be rich and famous but I didn't feel that necessarily meant that I was absolutely fulfilled. The more I thought about it, the less fulfilled I felt. Therefore, I wanted something more than show business could offer me. I asked a lot of questions and it naturally led around to spiritual things. I found Christianity had been on my doorstep for so long, that when I came to talk to people about it, I realised I knew nothing about it all.

Outwardly, of course, all had seemed well. There were Cliff's luxuries – clothes and a black Cadillac. He sported neatly-cut suits and was often voted the best-dressed man in the country. Cliff to many epitomised the kind and considerate Englishman. People described him as friendly, affable, not priggish, given to modest behaviour off-stage. He was a good boy, the sort every mother would like as a son or son-in-law. But Cliff felt there was something missing:

> I found I wasn't satisfied with my life. I still enjoyed singing, but I didn't want to go on tours. I discovered I was too concerned with wanting to be liked. I started seeing people I'd been at school with. Some of them were a year or two older than me and they'd gone on to be teachers. Well, we had a few talks and they did me a lot of good. I got this feeling that I could be much closer to God if I made the effort. So I did.

And yes, in his customary manner, he was single-minded.

Religious leaders became interested in his spiritual journey. After all, he was an unexpected catch and he might conceivably be an important witness among young people. His willingness to stand with Billy Graham was a pointer, but then not all religious onlookers would be persuaded that he had been genuinely converted until he gave up his career and so removed himself from this musical outpost of Satan. Some still wait.

He said contradictory things to the press only in so far as he kept changing his mind. It was far from an easy situation: should he stay in show-business or not?

The press and pop journals of the time devoted oceans of copy to Cliff's religious dilemma. They produced a motley collection of headlines: 'Holy man from outer space – Some fans have odd ideas about me – Cliff'; 'The Gospel according to Cliff'; 'My faith and the cynics'; 'Cliff quits talking about religion'; 'Cliff's retirement depends on his O-level'. The latter headline prefaced an article in the *New Musical Express* in January 1967, in which writer Alan Smith told how Cliff was testing a possible teaching vocation by ensuring he had minimum requirements to train as an RE teacher. 'I just want to be an ordinary teacher in an ordinary secondary school. I don't care if some people think I'm a phoney: they're entitled to their opinions and if that's the way they feel, okay.' He said he would resit the examination if he failed, but as it happens he passed.

Cliff's growing uncertainty about his future in music and a widening of his interests beyond records and record tours caused friction with The Shadows. Bruce was one who always spoke his mind and certainly he and Cliff had many a tussle. At first he was pretty jocular when asked whether there was any difference in their relationship. 'Well, he's lost two stone in weight for a start,' but he felt that Cliff's commitment to music was wavering, and was affecting the Cliff-Shadows partnership. At least Cliff never introduced religion into the recording studio, unless he was recording one of his religious albums at the EMI studios in Abbey Road. Engineer Peter Vince says it was quite different with Hank and there came a point when Hank was told forcibly to curb his religious practices.

Cliff never allowed his religious faith to interfere with his professional commitments, whereas Hank would on occasions say he couldn't attend a session. At lunch-time he would get out his Bible and in the evenings he would go out and knock on doors around about. EMI people who lived in the area would say 'Hello Hank,' and then say 'no thanks' and close the door. I believe it is something you have to do as a Jehovah's Witness.

Maurice Rowlandson, an associate of the Billy Graham Evangelistic Association base in London, told me:

Having nailed his colours to the mast, Cliff went on from strength to strength. It became his own desire to leave show business and possibly become a teacher. Many of his friends, especially those in the Billy Graham team, advised him against doing this and pointed out the value of carrying a witness for Christ in the show-business world. In this, Cliff had counselling from David Winter, John Stott and others.

Rowlandson believes that his eventual decision to remain in show business proved to be the right one. On a personal level he remembers the time when Cliff came and sang at a party which his son Gary had organised for 120 people in the Rowlandson's home in Stanmore, North London.

> Cliff sang for about 40 minutes and then spent another 40 answering questions. Amongst them came a question from a sophisticated son of our local estate agent who asked, 'If I become a Christian, do I need to go to church?' Cliff replied, 'No! You don't need to go to church. That's not necessary at all. But I will say this: *if* you become a Christian, you may find Christians more in church than anywhere else. It might just happen that you would come to *want* to go to church!' Later another question was asked by the same young person, 'If I wanted to become a Christian, how should I go about it?' Cliff replied, 'Read the Epistle to the Romans followed by John's Gospel.' This young man went away and did that, and six weeks later telephoned my home at 7.00 in the morning to talk to my son and to say that, as a result of what Cliff had said, he had become a Christian.

Bill Latham rejects any suggestion that Cliff's conversion, which heightened his media profile at this time, was a clever publicity ruse. 'It certainly wasn't to support a flagging career. Why did he need that?' Yet some suggested it. It would be interesting to round up the cynics and, from the vantage point of Cliff's 20-year Christian commitment, ask them how they feel now about their earlier remarks.

Certainly there was this unique position of a major pop star taking on board a belief that was more than just an assertion of basic human values such as kindness, love, generosity, sympathy and support for one's fellow creatures. He was assenting to actual facts centred on Jesus. And even more unusual was the public nature of this assent, for no other major pop stars had ever let their beliefs lead them into such diverse avenues. Cliff mixed with north London teenagers and learnt from them. He went into schools, stood on platforms and withstood often biting ridicule from those who never saw beyond the demands of getting a story.

Cliff would make new friends, sometimes lesser-known artists within the music world. One was Cindy Kent, lead vocalist with The Settlers: 'I met Cliff at Potters Bar, in a church vestry. The vicar said something like, "Here's someone from show-biz," as he introduced me to Cliff. I remember asking Cliff if he could suggest a church I might attend. He said I should find my way to St Paul's, Finchley.' A few weeks later The Settlers were billed at London's Royal Festival Hall. 'It was our first big solo concert and he came with a church party and he liked us and he was to ask us if we would like to support him through Europe. We gladly accepted.'

Later Cliff and The Settlers would star in a religious television programme *Life With Johnny*. Cindy, looking back from the late 1980s says,

> He's moved along a path and grown so much. I don't think he's someone who looks back much. I think he's a wonderful person and I am unreservedly a great fan. What you see is what you get, with Cliff. There is no ulterior side to him, no deep undercurrents. He's a very talented performer, very straight and honest. I have been fed up watching some people get at him, including some Christians. He has stood the test of time and, yes, he has been surrounded by great people . . . It took some time to find himself as a Christian but see what has come out.

131

During the late Sixties Cliff filmed *Two a Penny* for the Billy Graham Evangelistic Association. His appearance in the film produced dramatic newspaper headlines for he did not want a fee and Equity was annoyed, and demanded he should be paid. Dora Bryan was cast in the film, and she had met Cliff briefly on another occasion, 'Well, it seemed a novelty acting role to me. Jim Collier had rung my agent and the suggestion was that we should all meet for lunch, and I remember Nigel Goodwin was there. I recall Cliff was very shy, unused to this kind of company, perhaps. Anyway, he behaved very decently.' When the film was completed all went their own ways, but Cliff did not forget Dora. 'I was appearing in *Hello Dolly* in Liverpool and Cliff phoned me and said I had to meet a friend of his, Max Wigley. Max and I became friends and he was instrumental in my becoming a Christian. He's now a canon; at that time he was a curate, one of those nice outdoor, ruddy-faced young men.'

The actor, Nigel Goodwin, mentioned by Dora was another early show-biz friend who was influential in Cliff's Christian life. Goodwin had met Cliff before his Graham explosion, and had done so at St Paul's. Later Goodwin, Cliff and others gathered often at David Winter's house. Goodwin shared Cliff's vision for a centre in London where artists could come together for mutual support, encouragement and strengthening in the Christian faith.

Goodwin says

In those days the evangelical wing of the Church was very suspicious of the arts and anyone pursuing a career in an arts discipline. The group met for six years to pray together and share faith and from this there came what is known as the Arts Centre Group.

I remember taking part with Cliff and James Fox in the Amsterdam Congress on Evangelism sponsored by the Billy Graham organisation. We presented, along with Dave Foster of Euroevangelism, a dramatic piece on the dilemma of modern youth, who saw the Church as irrelevant and out of touch with their generation. I well recall an awful happening.

The dramatic and sad event Goodwin refers to was when the Norwegian contingent walked out in protest as Cliff rose to sing. The following day, Goodwin observes, these people 'were among the first to ask Cliff for his autograph . . . for their daughters, of course.'

Goodwin married Gillian Duncan, a daughter of the renowned preacher of the time, George B. Duncan. Cliff and many other friends preceded the Goodwin wedding in Glasgow by playing a charity concert in a large, packed cinema. The interest raised by this meant there was not only the thousand invited guests inside the church, but two thousand outside, completely blocking the centre of the city, leaving buses and cars stranded in a sea of people.

Goodwin says, 'The centre for which we had prayed and planned, the Arts Centre Group, opened in London in July 1971. Artists came for lectures, debates, discussions, counsel and advice. Cliff was involved from the beginning, giving his time and wisdom unselfishly.'

Genesis Arts

I know of no-one who so clearly loves what he does - his music - and who loves who he does it for - his public. Long may the light of Christ in him shine brightly into our fearful and fragmented world.

Thanks for you brother

In His grip Nigel

The Arts Centre Group exists to encourage Christians in the arts, the media and entertainment. One of our greatest encouragers is Cliff Richard. Cliff was a founder member and has consistently identified with us and given his loyalty and support for over seventeen years. It's mutual!

Helen Morton
Helen Morton
General Administrator

We all know that Cliff is a devoted Christian and one can clearly see this being reflected in every part of his life.

Rob Witchell
President, S.A. Cliff Richard Movement

Nigel Goodwin appeared in the film *Two A Penny*, with others and Cliff he founded the Arts Centre Group.

Helen Morton is Administrator of the Arts Centre Group, a body that has had much support from Cliff.

Rob Witchell is associated with the Cliff Richard South African fan club.

Late-night supper parties were held, to which well-known music performers and the casts of West End shows came, and talk went on into the early hours of the morning.

Around this time Cliff purchased Battailes in Essex, a large country house with extensive grounds and an ideal place to retreat and be spiritually recharged. 'Retreats and weekend courses were held for artists run by Jack and Pauline Philby. We helped at weekends and an annual Arts Festival was held.' Battailes proved financially impossible and was sold. But the Arts Centre Group thrives, now situated in Short Street, within yards of the Old and Young Vic, encompassing a mass of arts activities, prayer and counselling services, a restaurant and administrative aid. Cliff still holds supper parties to which media figures may find themselves invited. Goodwin recalls a supper party event during which 80 artists heard the Reverend David Watson, 'only a few weeks before his early death,' and Cliff was said to be 'thrilled to see friends and artists eagerly listening'.

Goodwin, looking back over some exciting years, sees Cliff very much as someone 'who has maintained a strong and faithful testimony that it is possible to be thoroughly Christian and thoroughly professional in today's world. To think that once Cliff had been seriously considering whether it was possible for him to continue his career as a singer with his new-found faith!' Yet, of course, not without flak from many quarters. Cindy Kent told me, 'I think I would be fed up with some of the criticism and certainly I've felt that way for Cliff, but he's had this dedicated, single-mindedness, and marvellously has not been blown away.'

Along the way Cliff has found time to encourage other artists and singers with a religious commitment: some whose talent either as singers or songwriters is confined to the relatively sheltered world of religious record companies and religious television; some who aim to bring their music to a wider public. Cliff has produced artists, lent them his backing vocals, aired their songs in concerts and included them on his albums.

It would be wrong to think of any of these artists as Cliff clones, or in some way extensions of Cliff's ministry, and certainly he has never adopted that attitude. He has always known when to drop away quietly, while maintaining an overall interest.

Arguably the best-known artist associated with Cliff is Sheila Walsh. She rides high in the religious music world, yet, in spite of a number of British television outlets she has made only very minor ripples on the more general music world. For a time she was managed by Bill Latham, and she supported Cliff on his 1982 and 1984 British Gospel tours. She enjoyed a brief British chart placing with a song entitled 'Drifting' with Cliff supplying some vocals and, as with the album of which this is the title track, coproducing. Cliff's contribution was seen in some quarters as a ploy to launch Sheila onto a wider market, though quite why critics chose to sharpen their pencils on this is not easy to understand, since numerous pop acts have been produced or had contributions from fellow professionals without provoking the slightest raised eyebrow, and, in any case, why shouldn't Cliff help promote someone.

Amy Grant is the foremost artist in the current Jesus music world and has successfully crossed over into the general music scene in America.

Ray Goudie is lead singer of Heartbeat, a professing Christian group who have enjoyed UK pop chart placing.

George Hamilton IV, a Christian, is one of best known American country and western singers.

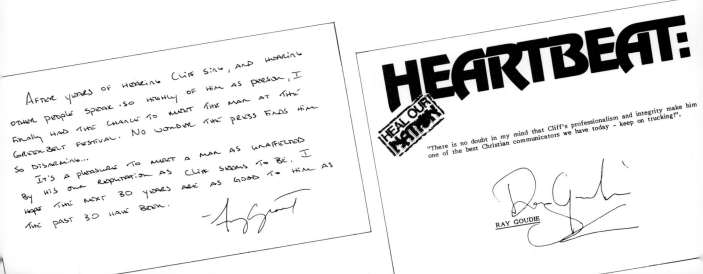

After years of hearing Cliff sing, and hearing other people speak so highly of him as person, I finally had the chance to meet the man at the Greenbelt festival. No wonder the press finds him so disarming...
It's a pleasure to meet a man as unaffected by his own reputation as Cliff seems to be. I hope the next 30 years are as good to him as the past 30 have been.

— Amy Grant

HEARTBEAT:

HEAL OUR NATION

"There is no doubt in my mind that Cliff's professionalism and integrity make him one of the best Christian communicators we have today - keep on trucking!".

RAY GOUDIE

'Yes, Sheila Walsh has agreed to spend four weeks, ... no, four years
listening to all my recorded songs.'

Sheila told me, 'Some of the DJs have told me they didn't play the record because
they felt I was just trying to climb on Cliff's back and preach the gospel.' Undoubtedly
there has been a definite prejudice among some DJs and producers against Christian
things, for the same objectivity is not employed against a myriad of artists who are far
more voluble in their beliefs and allegiances, whether it be in advocating that drug use
is normal and permissible, or in extreme left or right wing political stances.

Cliff and Sheila did get interviewed on the popular BBC Radio One's *Newsbeat* and,
after giving the background to their initial meeting and subsequent association, Cliff said,
'Well, the single is because we are what we are. We will choose the kind of single that
will not bring any dishonour to the faith that we hold, but in fact the single itself is just
a lovely love song.'

George Hamilton IV

Cliff Richard has been a tremendous
"Witness" to all of us - I'm grateful
for that & I respect him for his
talent and his forthright stand for
our Lord and saviour!

Warmest regards -

Geo. IV

It is reading of his faith in Jesus Christ and <u>seeing it in action</u> around the world which gains my support.

Because of Cliff's witness, I am encouraged to be more bold in my own personal worship. After all, if one can pay homage to a rock star, how much more so to one's Lord and Savior who was crucified for unworthy you and me and LIVED to tell about it!

Judy Donofrio

Judy Donofrio
Cliff Richard Good News Meeting House of Los Angeles

Judy Donofrio runs the Cliff Richard Good News Meeting House in Los Angeles.

Cliff may have a global reputation far ahead of Sheila Walsh's but there are those for whom Cliff is unknown and Sheila more prominent. At the Greenbelt Festival in 1987, in the artists's arena, an American girl was making enquiries about a very promising male back-up singer on a Sheila Walsh record. She ventured the brave opinion that he had a definite future!

At least there could be no confusion when Sheila brought Cliff on stage at an American concert in Eestes Park, Colorado, in August 1985. She told the audience,

You know it's kind of intimidating really when the person in your backing vocal group has sold over a hundred million records in his 25 year career in gospel music – not gospel music, 25 year career in rock music. He has been in the charts all these years. He recorded a song with me, he's one of my best friends in the world. I love him with all my heart.

For Cliff the concert came during a period when he had contracted viral laryngitis and he had to cancel five shows. He told the audience, 'I know that I can at least croak something at you.' He talked of his record successes, of gold discs achieved with The Shadows, but this was a lead into his describing how Christian faith has made such a difference to his life. Eventually, after more chatter and joking with the audience about his vocal problems, he sang 'Lord I Love You.' He told the audience, 'You know, some of my best praying is done when I walk my dogs, I live in a really beautiful area right by the golf course, and it's so fantastic I feel somehow, when you're actually close to nature, like when you look up in the mountains here, you're far more aware of God's presence. I know when I'm walking I pray a lot.' Cliff appeared several times on Sheila's major British BBC television series *Rock Gospel*, where she shared presentation credits with Alvin Stardust. It was on this programme that Cliff popularised the word 'Rockspell' which, he said:

Conjures up what we want to say. We, as Christians, want to say, we don't know how to do anything else, except rock and roll. It is all I have ever known and loved all my musical life, and to combine your message, which is a Christian one, with the music that you make turns it into Rockspell, but it is no different from any other

136

kind of music. It is just that we are far more positive about our approach to life, and therefore our messages are more positive.

Sheila, speaking about the involvement of Alvin Stardust, a successful British pop star, says:

Cliff and I have worked with Alvin a lot. We knew that Alvin didn't know God, but that in his heart he was searching. We thought it was right to befriend him, and be with him, and share the things of the Kingdom of God with him. I was on tour in America and Cliff phoned me and said, 'I think I would like Alvin to come along to our church next Sunday. What do you think?' I said, 'I think that would be great.' So we invited Alvin and his wife, Lisa, along to our church. And Gerald Coates was speaking and at the end he said, 'I really believe that there are people here tonight who need to know God for themselves, and that is why I want you to have the opportunity now.' And as he looked up, he saw that Alvin had stood to his feet, and that night Alvin gave his life to the Lord.

Gerald Coates has become one of the major figures on the British House Church scene and he was partly responsible for bringing Cliff and Sheila together. Cliff sometimes attends his Cobham Fellowship. He has his views on Cliff's ability to withstand criticism:

Ian Hamilton is MD of the British end of the American gospel music record corporation Word Records. The company issues various religious based albums of Cliff.

Luis Palau is one of the world's foremost Christian evangelists.

CASSETTES RECORDS PUBLISHING

We're privileged to have been part of your message of "relevant Christianity". I believe you've conveyed this more effectively than anybody else of our generation, and I sincerely respect and thank you for it.

Yours sincerely,

Ian Hamilton
Managing Director

Luis Palau
EVANGELISTIC ASSOCIATION

I was privileged to work with Cliff Richard for the first time in August 1977. Cliff gave a tremendous boost to my team's first U.K. mission by sharing his Christian testimony and singing on a youth night during that mission.

Besides singing, Cliff gave an astonishing testimony to his belief in the resurrection of Jesus Christ.

The next time Cliff and I were together, for Mission to London, he joined us at least three times, including the closing night.

The most memorable night with Cliff during Mission to London was the time he invited 100 acquaintances in the arts and entertainment field to come out to Queen's Park Rangers football stadium.

Still, many of Cliff's friends came, heard the Gospel, and then joined us afterwards for dinner at a London restaurant. Cliff and I spoke on how to come to peace with God, and the seed of the Gospel was planted in many hearts.

The next year, Cliff joined us for a major youth rally in Amsterdam. The venue was jam packed. Cliff was at his best (though he's always excellent!).

Among those who came to Christ that night was an Uruguayan woman who had worked in the red-light districts of Holland for some 17 years.

What else could I say about Cliff? I think it's significant the way he opened the doors for Sheila Walsh, then a relatively unknown Scottish singer, to later go nationwide on BBC.

I look forward to the next time Cliff ministers with our team,

--Luis Palau, international evangelist
Portland, Oregon, U.S.A.

He's easily hit by it. It's not unusual after a bad press, particularly if it's about his
Christian faith or behaviour, for him to have sleepless nights, even if the reports are
untrue, which invariably is the case. I think he examines himself far too thoroughly to
see if there's a grain of truth in what has been written. He is, in my opinion, over-
alert to the fact that he has to set an example of what a Christian really is.

Coates sees Cliff as a sensitive person. 'When I set up a meeting between Cliff and a
musician who has a severe drink problem (which I had completely forgotten), it was Cliff
who reminded me that it might be best not to take a drink until our guest had left. 'But
although he is a sensitive man, he also has very strong convictions and very high
standards.' Coates disputes popular views that Cliff is a lonely man and speaks admiringly
of the endless programme of activities that often means 'he has hardly got a moment to
breathe'.

John Perry, singer-songwriter and sometime member of Cliff's backing group on tour
and record, is another person much influenced by Cliff. On one occasion he toured the
world as part of Cliff's gospel package and, as he says, 'Sometimes it meant churches and
not platforms and we had to sit through everything, including the sermon, before we
got to Cliff's bit. I saw people actually enjoying themselves. I must be honest. I was
trying to find what they were all on about . . . all these kids banging guitars and leaping
about and having a good time.' He remembers one particular occasion when he heard a
'heavy-duty preacher and basically he told me my life story, that one had my name on
it, and I sat there, and thought how does he know all that?'

He remembers that the preacher asked people to take the step and accept Jesus into
their lives. 'The thing was, I was sitting next to all my mates. Tony Rivers was there,
and all the chaps, I mean this was embarrassing, and, although I kind of wanted to, I
was a bit embarrassed. Well, he said, people should put their hands up and the hand
went up, and I looked at it and said "Get down!" It was almost like that.' The indecision
continued until, 'the next thing I knew I was up and walking down the aisle. There were
tears streaming down my face. I was totally wiped out, embarrassment forgotten, a weight
off my back . . . I had not known anything like it. Top to bottom totally cleansed. Brand
new. Absolutely beautiful.' He says that Cliff and Bill Latham couldn't believe it but
later when they got together they shared their joy.

Garth Hewitt is the best-known male artist from the religious music world with whom
Cliff has had strong association. Hewitt has recorded several albums and has performed
around the world with his own songs, as part of the Amos Trust, and also extensively for
Tear Fund. Increasingly, his passions have been devoted to the social and political

'I've just told Luis Palau that he can sing and I'll preach.' 'You can't help
reflecting and reflecting on amazing times.'

138

implications of the Christian faith that should go hand in hand with Christian commitment. Hewitt is not given to producing friendly religious ditties or writing vapid tunes. His own love and understanding of rock 'n' roll means he composes from a contemporary background.

> We've worked on a variety of things, from Tear Fund to social celebration events and, of course, his Gospel tours, like one in which I toured Europe. That must have been 1984. Very enjoyable. Cliff also produced an album of mine and a few singles. He's someone without side and he's always said to me 'share my dressing room' and I've found him basically very relaxed and easy to get on with.

Hewitt, like so many others, has been impressed by Cliff's professionalism and determination that, whatever the event, it must be as good as it possibly can. He also speaks of Cliff's influence as remarkable. 'More than anyone he has made faith acceptable, made it OK to talk about faith, and we must remember that he talked about God when it was not fashionable. It's been anything but a flash in the pan with Cliff.'

Garth has doubts about Cliff's attitude towards South Africa. It is not the question of whether or not Cliff supports apartheid, because he patently does not; rather it is on the question of what kind of contact, if any, should be maintained, even at gospel-concert level. Hewitt says;

> I think black Christians are saying 'don't go' and they feel betrayed, even if he goes to perform in the gospel area. I know some black religious leaders would love to talk with Cliff. In the past I have been to South Africa with Cliff and now I think we were used and we were naive. I couldn't do it again, playing at Sun City was a betrayal, not that it was intended as such.

Cliff has furthered the career of a Yugoslavian singer-songwriter, Alexander John, and in recent time has been willing to lend time, support and his name to John's heart-felt desire to further Slavonic-Western relations. John has had hit albums in Slavenia where he is one of the few musicians working in a pop-rock form. He first met Cliff at Zagreb after the 1968 Eurovision Song Contest. At the time he was involved in general publicity work and he remembers he was putting up some posters for one of Cliff's Gospel concerts with The Settlers. Cliff was around and, 'I asked him for his autograph, and I got to know Cindy Kent of The Settlers.' He was able to share his Christian faith with them. Cliff was very much the major Western musician. 'I remember it was either the Beatles or Cliff. He played an important role in the development of European and Eastern music.'

The upshot of this and another meeting was an invitation from Cliff to make contact should he come to the West. John proved to be a very talented singer-songwriter and Cliff's awareness of this led to John supporting Cliff on some gospel dates. 'I had songs I wanted Cliff to record, but I didn't like to push them. Cindy (Kent) seemed the way "in" but when Cliff was aware he rather typically said "what's the hurry?" and I realised I had lots to learn.'

Eventually Cliff would sing some of John's songs and help him in recording his own. He has never wavered in applauding Cliff's efforts:

140

as a person, as a professional, as a craftsman, as a Christian – well, the combination of all these in one person is quite something. I don't know what my life would have been if I had not met him. And it should never be forgotten, whether we are talking about gospel or secular, that Cliff has been one of the few Western artists to spend a great deal of time in Eastern Europe. He has given so much hope to Eastern young people and the general Christian cause.

The last in this selection of people whom Cliff has influenced is Dave Berry, who is much associated with the Arts Centre Group, has managed the group Go West, and has a ministry that offers counselling to musicians. He has particular memories of Cliff at the 1978 Help, Hope and Hallelujah event held in London's Royal Albert Hall for Tear Fund. He also recalls him at the same venue for a special memorial event celebrating the work of David Watson, the British Anglican clergyman whose life was prematurely ended by cancer, terminating an inspiring Christian ministry. Berry has also been with Cliff on many less prominent occasions. 'He is always so cheerful, a nice bloke to be with. I think Cliff has paved so many ways, opened so many doors for other artists.' Berry says he is acutely conscious of the heavy burden that lies upon the shoulders of someone like Cliff. 'I mean, he only has to make the smallest mistake, and the whole world will point the finger. I think it's been marvellous to see a close protective circle around Cliff and here someone like Bill Latham has been terrific.'

Outside of encouraging fellow artists, broadly speaking Cliff's Christian ministry has fallen into a number of areas, some more weighty and time-consuming than others. The two most prominent have been his regular Gospel concert tours and his association with Tear Fund. Then he has participated in various one-off events and been responsible for best-selling religious books, records, concerts, videos and Bible-reading tapes.

Initially, Cliff's Gospel tour concept was guided by his desire to 'say thank-you to God' with the money raised for a variety of causes. Cliff would be interviewed by Bill Latham, and he would sing songs, often accompanying himself on guitar. These were rather intimate affairs and even when performed in large halls they were an extension of the kind of thing Cliff did in schools, colleges and churches. Cliff was near to the audience, and indeed many of his pop fans, who were not particularly into his religious beliefs, would still go because it meant they were close to their star. Gradually, the shape changed and, save for a larger number of overtly Christian songs, Cliff's Gospel concerts have been as professional as any he might perform. But for all that, they've been Cliff stringing a lot of songs together and chatting at varying lengths in between.

Nowadays there is more use of large venues. Bill Latham says, 'It's all down to cost factors. Year by year, like everything else, the cost of putting on tours increases. We've taken the view that these Gospel concerts should be every bit as exciting, as impressive as the commercial concerts, that Christian events should be just as good as, if not better than secular events.'

Some 30 to 32 people are involved with the Gospel tours. The tours have not been without criticism, mainly the view that, in creating this professionalism, people may be more impressed by the visual presentation than by hearing the communication of the message. 'It's certainly a dilemma. It would be nice to go back to some of the old places where the theatres are smaller.'

Cliff's Gospel concerts have spanned the globe and it's this world base, with the accompanying fund-raising by fans that is one of the most remarkable aspects of his work. It seems reasonable to state that no music star has such a network, or has helped raise so much money for the needy over such a long period of time. These tours often make room for the special event. During his visit to Australia in early 1983 Cliff played a special benefit concert in Adelaide to help victims of the devastating bush fires that had swept through southern states. Cliff explains it casually. 'When we tour we take so much out of the country – it is great for us that we are able to give something back.' In England he played a special concert for the 10th anniversary of the Arts Centre Group, and on 13 July 1985, he carried through a prior booking at the Odeon, Birmingham, in aid of Tear Fund, although he had been invited to be at the Live Aid event at Wembley. He decided not to disappoint people who had bought tickets for Birmingham, and he was after all raising money, like Live Aid, for the Third World.

Talking on one occasion about concerts – Cliff began calling them Rockspell events – he spoke of raising £130,000 in 1984 and in excess of £100,000 in 1985. He said, 'I'm combining my faith, my music and the fact that when we work together in this way we are able to change the lives of people around the world.' In Jersey he raised some £25,000 for starving refugees in the Sudan, besides monies for projects in the Channel Islands. He has played concerts in Belfast, with two concerts on one occasion specially planned so that money raised could finance the purchase of a four-wheel drive pick-up truck for missionary purposes in Argentina.

> I see these Gospel events as a 100 per cent opportunity to share what's deep inside me. Yes, it is allowing myself to be used. A lot of people say that in a detrimental way, but that is exactly what a Christian ought to be open for and I think I'm fairly intelligent and I know when people are using me. Christians have tried to make use of me and you can spot them a mile off.

Cliff's Gospel forays into Eastern Europe can mean crowds of over 4,000. In 1985, in Warsaw's Gwardia Sports Arena, his appearance drew from one pastor the remark, 'Before this we knew him only as a fine singer, but people I talked to were amazed and surprised that he presented the Gospel so clearly. Cliff appeared more as an evangelist than a singer!' Cliff was asked on this occasion why he was so articulate about his faith and he told them that the Bible tells Christians always to be ready to give a reason for the hope within them.

But the Gospel tours do leave some dissatisfied customers. During the summer of 1983, some Dutch fans believed they were paying for a general music concert, since various posters seemed to suggest he was presenting a Jubilee (his 25th year in the pop business) concert, whereas it was nothing of the kind. Bill Latham found himself on Dutch radio trying to calm things down, to introduce some perspective and point out Cliff's total innocence. Fans claimed they had been cheated and demanded the return of their money.

And it must be said that Cliff often lends his support to causes that are not directly

142

Christian-based although their ideals will be in accordance with his accepted faith. He took part in International Sport Aid Day, an offshoot of Band Aid and Live Aid, and masterminded by Bob Geldof. Cliff appeared in London's Hyde Park in black track-suit bottoms, a T-shirt in black and white bearing the words, 'World Workout' and along with other stars, such as Elaine Page, Lulu, Lisa Goddard, Alvin Stardust and Marti Caine, undertook a 15 minute workout. He supported EMI's release of 'Live-In World', the result of international stars getting together in an effort to raise money for drug rehabilitation programmes. The single took a mere seven weeks to record and in giving his services Cliff was joined by Nik Kershaw, Sinitta, Holly Johnson, Nick Heyward and numerous others. In April 1988 he was prominent in a special performance of *Time* for the Aids campaign, though he was no longer starring in the Dave Clark musical.

Over the years some of Cliff's appearances have been very low-profile, even if it's the large event that attracts media attention. On 5 June 1975 he headed a special charity concert at the Manchester Free Trade Hall where the proceeds went to the families of Sgt Williams and PC Rodgers, two officers who died while on duty during rioting in Manchester. And in September 1988 he could be found at Oakleigh School in North London. He arrived a little before two in the afternoon, dressed in a summery cream suit and was introduced to Judith Charlesworth, the school's headmistress, before finding his way to a small platform. Oakleigh is a school for handicapped children and the Cliff Richard Fan Club under Janet Johnson had raised £14,500 to purchase a special minibus for the school. In his speech Cliff expressed his pleasure at the event and remarked that the afternoon was doubly precious because his next call would be to the Finchley Crusaders who were celebrating their 80th anniversary. Cliff went on:

It's taken just 18 months to purchase the bus – I've always been thrilled that my fans have supported me in this way – I feel as though I'm supported even though I had very little, if anything, to do with the raising of the money . . . what you're involved with here at Oakleigh is something special . . . so I'm thrilled to say that my fans have made it possible for me to hand over a set of keys.

It is Tear Fund of all causes, that has been Cliff's great love affair. In a sense he chose the organisation rather than being courted by them. He was young in the faith and he wanted to see things happen. He didn't have too wide an appreciation of Third World suffering. It was more to satisfy an inner word that he said he ought to be doing something, and he admits he got a personal buzz in those days from his involvement. It was David Winter who pointed Cliff towards what was a fairly new relief agency. Winter, at this time in his career, was the lively editor of *Crusade*, a monthly evangelical magazine that had, among other things, a definite interest in the arts. The magazine's parent was the Evangelical Alliance, which had established The Evangelical Alliance Relief Fund. Fortunately the initials produced Tear Fund, a more 'hip' name for an age gradually becoming obsessed with communication. True to form, Cliff was not content just to involve himself in fund raising and encouraging a greater sense of awareness and consciousness amongst young Christian fans. He decided to verse himself thoroughly in the agency's work, and to his slight surprise he became an enthusiast. Tear Fund was going places, it had passion among its team, and soon Cliff would see his practical involvement (mainly raising money from his Gospel concerts but also playing some high-profile events) firmly stamp the organisation's name in public recognition and beyond church and religious circles.

The already mentioned Help, Hope And Hallelujah concert was the start. The concert raised £2,000 and an ambulance was dispatched to South America. Soon there would be another Cliff connection with Tear Fund, for his friend Bill Latham was persuaded by Tear Fund's director George Hoffman to take an administrative role with the organisation. Bill became its first education secretary and then deputy director. In 1969 Tear Fund's income was £50,000 and by 1982 it had grown to £5 million. Obviously, Cliff is only one of many advocating its work, but his profile has been such that, without his prominent public stance, at least in early times, it would not have grown to its present size. The original emphasis was on relief for the Third World but it soon widened to include

WENDY CRAIG

Cliff's energy, courage and steadfast faith have been an inspiration to Christians of all ages, and at all stages of their spiritual development. God bless him always with the health and vitality he needs both for his singing and for furthering God's message in his own, unique way

Wendy Craig.

I'm sure countless people, especially parents, are grateful for the uncompromising stand of Christian values that Cliff has made over the twenty? years. And I, personally, have been deeply appreciative of his willingness to identify himself with us at times when the media itself has been less than helpful. Though those times are changing as more and more young people are responding to the kind of challenge that Cliff presents.

We shall always remember the generous & amusing way he presented our Annual Award to the Blue Peckers team in 1985. His ability to combine fun with faith is something we could all learn from him.

Mary Whitehouse

Wendy Craig is a well-known British actress with numerous TV credits

Mary Whitehouse is one of Britain's best known names, particularly for her strident campaigns to improve moral standards in the media.

144

development grants, the sending of personnel overseas, individual sponsorship of children and students in developing countries, handicraft marketing and support for evangelism and Christian education.

In spite of Cliff's heavy media workload, his recordings and tours, his home-based activities, he has somehow found the time to visit poor areas of Asia and Africa.

At the beginning of 1989 Hoffman moved into a consultative capacity in Tear Fund. Hoffman has guided Cliff through his Christian commitment to this agency, making sure that he has had time to breathe and, above all, continue a pop career.

My meeting with Hoffman quickly established one thing – there is enormous love for Cliff.

> He's a remarkable person. There is always a freshness about what he does, an enthusiasm, an interest. His infectious spirit has enlivened many of the field trips on which went. It doesn't matter where you are, he'll find an orange box and the concert will begin! People loved him, even though some had no inkling of his pop stardom, so they weren't agog to think he was there with them. He had a gift of spontaneity that simply shines through.

His travels with Cliff have given him an insight into the problems of being a star. 'On flights, Cliff has unbelievable patience. Do you know that people even wake him up? We took him economy because of what we are, but that is something we had to really look at for, tired as he was, people still asked for his autograph, even stewardesses. He had no peace and he needs isolation to recharge.' It's also interesting to hear someone like George catch the same professionalism as others from the different vantage point of the rock world.

> He agreed to come and play at a church youth event. I got there and heard the sound of guitars and there he was with the youth group, playing away. And on another larger occasion here he was spending the afternoon working out his move-ments, his cues, and wanting to get things right and so busily chalking his move-ments. Next came song rehearsal! He could have just come on and people would have responded and thought it was great he was there.

So Cliff has given Gospel concerts for Tear Fund, narrated soundtrips, had involvement in numerous kinds of ways because

> Not only does Tear Fund offer material aid to those who need it, but also it is aware that those same people need the gospel of Jesus just as desperately. And it seems to me that this two-pronged attack sums up what the Christian's attitude to other people ought to be, and basically, more importantly, been the means of persuading people to give.

Cliff tells in his book *Which One's Cliff?* of an incident that almost changed his life. It happened in a Bihari refugee camp. 'Everyone in those camps, even the babies, was covered in sores and scabs,' and Cliff, mainly for the benefit of a photographer, had bent down near one of the children. Someone stood on the child's fingers, making him cry out with pain. 'And as a reflex, I grabbed hold of him, forgetting all about his dirt and sores. I remember now that warm little body clinging to me and the crying instantly stopped. In that moment I knew I had an enormous amount to learn about practical Christian loving but that at least I'd started.'

Cliff has never forgotten the incident; he has told the story many times but an important twist remains. George Hoffman tells me how, in discussing the moment, Cliff was driven to consider that his music career should end, and that here, in that situation, he should find his next role. Cliff says, 'It was illogical, I suppose. I'm not qualified in medical and other matters. I thought what I was doing a little easy. I could arrange my 20 concerts for Tear Fund, enjoy the event, and we'd raise a great deal of money.' To Cliff this seemed so puny when set against the work of those he had seen in Bangladesh. He was set right by a nurse, Liz Wilkinson, who told him, 'Without you and other Christians at home, we wouldn't be here! We need each other.'

I spoke to Liz, now living in Twickenham, Middlesex. She recalls the incident well. 'All worries vanished when he came. He was genuine, and he had time for everybody. He was very moved by what he saw.' She recalls how he found love from the children and remembers 'he was taken aback, at first anyway, by what he saw.' She says at times he was overcome by emotion, choked by what he was seeing. 'He had a profound effect upon us all.'

'Foreign visitors were always welcome: kids would simply follow the visitor around. Cliff, of course, sang, including at a local hospital, at a Salvation Army home, and yes, to us as well.' There was nothing Cliff could do medically but he could encourage the nurses. 'He would come over to where we were living, talk, and eat with us, and then sing.' Liz talks of visitors who brought very welcome soap, shampoo and talcum powder. 'Well, these came from some of the people with him; he brought his guitar, it was such a morale booster.'

Liz has been a district nurse and health visitor in England since those days of the early 1970s. She has a three-year-old son Stephen. 'We had another child but he died on Christmas Day in Great Ormond Street Hospital. That was our tragedy. And do you know Cliff wrote me a letter? I was so touched. It's the mark of who he is.'

Cliff has often met and talked with Tear Fund staff at the Teddington headquarters, attending special events including the annual carol service. On 21 December 1984 he went shopping in London's West End for handicrafts made by poor families. It was a media-conscious exercise to make people aware of the more than 330 craft products marketed by Tearcraft, the subsidiary of Tear Fund. The products were sold at St Peter's Church, only 100 yards away from busy Oxford Street. Cliff even walked the streets with a sandwich-board.

He has appeared at several press conferences intended to gain publicity for Tear Fund in the popular press. At these he has been interviewed by George Hoffman and spoken separately. Among Cliff's many comments at one major conference in the autumn of 1985 were, 'We want people to give helpfully of their time, of their prayers, and of their finances. The problems are going to go on for a long time. So we need to instil in people the need to be concerned long term.' He was asked, 'Do you see yourself drawn more and more into this sort of work?' In his reply Cliff said,

I am already drawn into it pretty well, as far as one can go really. Obviously the work together – the value of my being involved in things like this [...] a secular commercial career that makes it possible for people to [...]meone that they see on *Top Of The Pops*, and other things like that. But [...]ork really well together. It seems to me that one gives me the platform, from which I can then do these valuable things and do them over and over again.

During the press conference Cliff told of a family who lived on the tiny Haitian island of La Gonave. He found their poverty moved him to arrange financial help so they could be clothed, fed and educated.

Four years after his momentous Bangladesh visit, Cliff was once more visiting that country, and also India. This was the time when he met Mother Teresa and her Missionaries of Charity. 'I'm not sure whether she was more nervous of meeting me, or I of meeting her. What a fabulous person, totally wrapped up and involved with Jesus and, because of that, involved with people.' Just a stone's throw from the teeming crowds on Calcutta's pavements, he spent an hour singing carols with the sisters.

Besides his Tear Fund activities, Gospel concerts and overall support of numerous charitable concerns Cliff has appeared countless times on radio and television, from introducing hymn-based programmes on radio and television to those based entirely on his perception of faith. Arguably the most sensational of these was the 1967 appearance he made with Paul Jones, then a 24-year-old former university student and lead singer of the very popular Manfred Mann group, on the ABC show *Looking For An Answer*. The show began by showing clips from the controversial film *Privilege*. In this film Jones played a pop star cynically exploited by religion. The programme makers cut from *Privilege* to Cliff standing alongside Billy Graham. It was a cue for the programme's presenter and interviewer, Robert Kee, to ask, 'Is the Church exploiting Cliff Richard too?' Cliff was asked whether he felt embarrassed watching the show and it was mildly suggested he was 'using' his mass pop acceptance to persuade people they should be in church.

Both Cliff and Paul Jones seemed best when testifying to their own position. Certainly Cliff was better when testifying to his own faith than arguing the pros and cons of Billy Graham's evangelistic mission. Jones was cynical, not willing to let Cliff or Billy Graham get away from a central point that they were working in an area of mass hysteria. 'Right, so you, Cliff, are giving them Christ. Well, I say you're not, you're giving them a show.' Jones said there were many ludicrous statements made by Billy, not least the remark 'Let the bombs drop – we have joy inside.'

But the future would hold an unexpected sequel, in Paul Jones's own Christian conversion during the mid–1980s. He was 'an atheist of some 25 years standing,' but became interested in spiritual things. He met his future wife, Fiona, learnt she went to church, accompanied her, heard an address that talked of Jesus as 'the Way' and decided there and then 'that guy's either a liar, or he's telling the truth. There isn't any other alternative, no alternative explanation.' In 1967 it was a clash of pop stars with different ideas about ultimate reality. Today, they share a common faith.

Other important events have been Cliff's Greenbelt Festival appearances. 1979 coincided with his return to the top of the charts in the British hit parade. He was back in 1983 when the Festival was held at the première outdoor rock venue of Knebworth.

It was one year when Greenbelt Festival Radio was launched and w
at 11 a.m. the first song to be played was Cliff's 'The Only Way Out'.
Cliff also spoke on the station:

> I sometimes think that we forget not only have we to speak of our faith, and si
> our faith, but we have to be our faith. And how can we be a Christian banker or
> Christian artist, for that matter, and I want to show them that this is how I have
> .been performing as a Christian, because there is a group of people who say that
> rock 'n' roll is evil, and I am saying that this is not true, it is absolutely untrue.

Cliff was not without his worries, for he recalled 1979 when he was disturbed by people
who shouted at him on stage and cried for Larry Norman instead:

> I didn't come to Greenbelt to be shouted at, and Larry is a good friend of mine.
> So, I told them off from the stage. Do not try and put a rift between Larry and me,
> you will not succeed. We are not in competition, we both love Jesus, and we are
> here to perform our own types of music. If you prefer Larry, fine. I have got my
> fans, he has got his . . . here at the festival I am a Christian entertainer, and I want
> their support (the audience) whether they like it or not, because I am out there
> representing our Lord.

There have also been several major advertising promotions in which Cliff has been
prominent: his backing of a Children's Hospital Appeal sponsored by Weetabix, and a
nationwide campaign aimed at getting people to read the Bible. In the former campaign
the Weetabix company donated 2p for every special hospital token in an effort to raise
an appeal target of £250,000 with £10,000 being donated for 25 children's hospitals across
Britain. The latter saw an advert in the *Daily Telegraph* during the first week in February
1986. The headline was IS MUSIC THE MOST IMPORTANT THING IN CLIFF
RICHARD'S LIFE? The advert was masterminded by a wealthy American Trust, the
Arthur S. DeMoss Foundation. Also backing the project were Lord Tonypandy, former
speaker of the British House of Commons, a Christian, and former Vice-President of the
Methodist Conference; and the well-known BBC television tennis commentator, Gerald
Williams, also a Christian.

And Cliff has continued to support major evangelistic events. He supported the Rev.
Jack Filby when he organised a series of rock gospel concerts at St Paul's in 1973; and
he lent vocal talent to the Banquet events at London's Wembley Arena that were
organised by Gerald Coates. Besides his association with Billy Graham, there is his
attachment to a newer evangelist, the South American Luis Palau, who is hailed as Dr
Graham's natural successor on the world evangelistic stage. Cliff sang for the evangelist
on several occasions during his London campaign of 1986. To Palau it was something of
a surprise that his stage could be graced by a pop singer and that the person should sing
and speak of his faith so assuredly. Cliff invited 100 acquaintances in the arts and
entertainment field to come to the Queen's Park Rangers football stadium. Many of these
friends joined Luis and Cliff afterwards for dinner at a London restaurant.

It was not the first time they had worked together. Palau recalls that the first occasion
was .in August 1977 in conjunction with the Jubilee '77 Christian Festival at Cardiff

Taking the bows and claps, at a special *Time* performance for Aids victims.

Castle. Cliff's visit to Cardiff gave television coverage for the mission at a time when such coverage didn't come easily. Cliff was a special guest for the film *God Has No Grandchildren* that was made during Jubilee '77. Palau tells me,

> I remember another time. Cliff joined us for a major youth rally in Amsterdam. Cliff was at his best (though he's always excellent!). As I recall, he was in a flamboyant red outfit. He put out more energy than I'd ever seen him do before, singing some well-known clean love songs, then testifying about Christ. I again threw out my notes (not my usual style!) before getting up to speak.

But how does the future seem as a Christian for this elder statesman, not only of British pop, but of rockspell? He told me shortly before his 48th birthday that he still finds life exciting, with so many challenges. He saw himself fully occupied, given many marvellous opportunities to witness. His view of modern times was simple 'I reckon this is the most exciting age to be in' – a comment that comes from the background of a man who has used the world's media resources so well, and for so long. His faith stands sure, growing and widening; more tolerant of others who fail to see his way than perhaps five or ten years previously.

He despairs a little at being pop's major Christian statement, especially since there are quite a few figures in contemporary music with Christian allegiance, many of whom seem unwilling to make popular statement of their faith. His influence has been enormous, and not merely 'put there' in the public eye. Gill Snow of the Cliff Richard Organisation has told me,

> on file we have many letters from people for whom Cliff's ministry has meant so much. I don't think Cliff has ever liked the 'split' nature of secular and gospel and I think he prefers the style of recent albums where both nestle together. I think Cliff has enabled some people to pick up on the gospel. Sometimes he has been a link, for others much more.

When he announced his Christian commitment at a Billy Graham meeting people said it would not last. Yet, it has. In pop Cliff is a survivor; in religion he is a survivor.

9 THE FINAL WORD...
from Cliff

A view of the last thirty-odd years – how to be objective and even remember! Records, shows, tours, TV plays, stage, films, my specific Christian activities – which aspects of all these do I recall? Thankfully Tony Jasper has sorted some of them out.

In immediate terms I think of the great crowd which has stayed with me: Peter Gormley, David Bryce, The Shads and Jack Good. I'm conscious that whatever I've done has always had to be done again and twice as good the second time. You can never choose to stand still in this business. I have nothing to regret. There have been a few set-backs from time to time but nothing major. I've had my little attempt at everything going!

There is only one word to describe my thirtieth year in this business – *fantastic*. I thought that I could go out while I was at the top. I thought about announcing my retirement! What better way, in the thirtieth year when I had at one and the same time a number one single and album in the charts. I even suggested it to David. It seemed a natural thing surely, to consider saying farewell when it was all on one mighty high.

Well, I decided not to give it all up. I still have better albums to come. I still get excited when I hear good songs. I still want to perform and I still have lots and lots of ideas and things I want to do, so how can I call it a day? I still get excited and that's it, really. No, there is more to come!

When I step aside and look at the last thirty years and more then I think, yes, I am a survivor. I'm still on the road, in the clubs, although there have been some moments when I've held my breath, as for instance during 1974 and 1975 when I seemed to hit a low. But I can almost claim to have had three top ten hits for each and every of my years in the business. I remember at the end of each year saying to myself that I would be around the next year.

I've had the right people with me. I was talking the other day with David and Bill Latham and saying should I have more of a profile. This is an 'image' time when 'image' is important. Then, blow me down, I go on tour in my thirtieth year and tickets are sold out at theatres within 72 hours. Perhaps I needn't worry. My fans trust me. I think people who come to my concerts trust me that it will be good. Over 200,000 people came to that tour – that's a big fan club! I feel there are many more who would have been there if they could get tickets.

'You can't help reflecting and reflecting on amazing times'

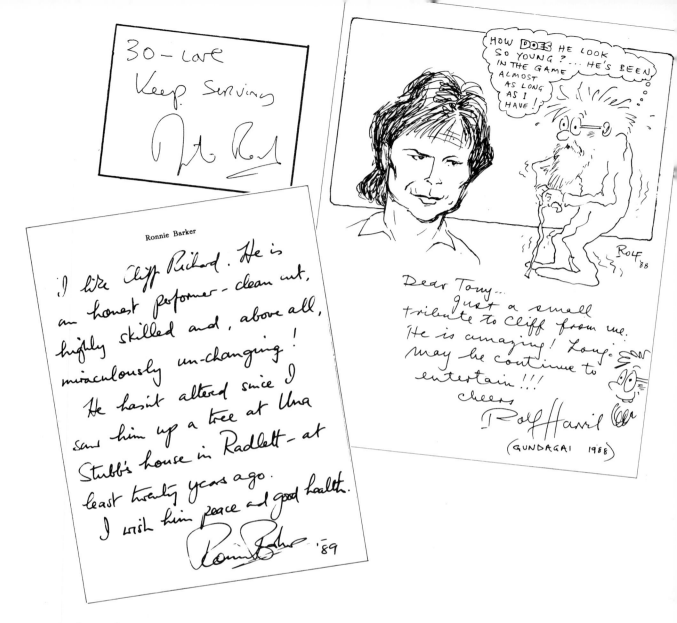

30 - Love
Keep Surviving

Ronnie Barker

'I like Cliff Richard. He is an honest performer - clean cut, highly skilled and, above all, miraculously un-changing!
He hasn't altered since I saw him up a tree at Una Stubb's house in Radlett - at least twenty years ago.
I wish him peace and good health.

'89

Dear Tony...
Just a small tribute to Cliff from me. He is amazing! Long may he continue to entertain!!!
Cheers
Rolf Harris
(GUNDAGAI 1988)

HOW DOES HE LOOK SO YOUNG? ... HE'S BEEN IN THE GAME ALMOST AS LONG AS I HAVE!

ROLF '88

Mike Reid is a great chum of Cliff's and is a leading British DJ. He has penned a number of pop books.

Rolf has had many hit singles, and as an artist adorned a number of BBC TV series.

Ronnie Barker is one of Britain's funniest and most perceptive comedians.

I feel I've survived the onslaught of new artists and critics and that I've done things my way. I don't know if I'd call myself unique but I know I've proved that rock 'n' roll is not just about sex and drugs or whatever else. Many mega-stars have dabbled in areas that I've not touched. I think I'm one of the few artists who have done justice to the

152

music. There have been others who have come across powerfully but they haven't lasted. Some performers get over indulgent, and they lose their enthusiasm, eventually getting sucked into a kind of boredom.

I've survived umpteen changes in culture, numerous youth explosions. I can relate to the word 'survivor'. I've always trusted my instincts and never more so than with 'Mistletoe and Wine'. I think it's a truth-filled song, even if it isn't a great composition. I just felt it would go places. Not everyone liked it but it caught the feelings of countless others.

Can I say more about the 'family' that has been around me? There have been some break-ups but I can honestly say that any splits have been amicable and I've remained on good terms with those who have departed for one reason or another. Some things

Kim Wilde has **Ricky** for a brother and producer, is the daughter of **Marty** and her mum was once a popular girl group singer. Kim is Britain's most successful girl singer with consistent hits from the early 1980s.

Frank Dunlop is Director of the world famous Edinburgh Festival.

Jan Harvey is an actress and found national fame for her acting in the popular television show *Howard's Way*.

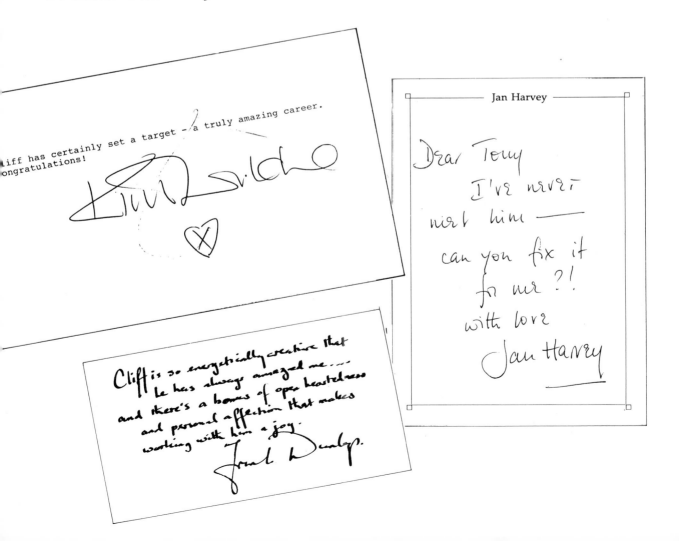

Hank Marvin, Bruce Welch and **Brian Bennett** form The Shadows – the legendary group that once backed Cliff and does so from time to time at special events.

just had to happen – that's best seen in my parting from The Shads. That relationship couldn't go on forever but we get together from time to time both socially and musically. Obviously I would single out some people, like Peter Gormley, who has now, as it were, retired, with David Bryce taking over. Both are fantastic people, but, I've said it many times, Peter has to be one of the 'greats'. He enjoyed such respect and was consistently straight and honest in a business not always known for such things. And I have never forgotten Norrie Paramor. I remember the time when he said he could go no further with me – no guile, no fake, never a cheat. Here I was with all my hits and he told me I should find another producer – we had gone as far as we could together. David has been my producer since 1961 isn't that terrific? My backing group has changed but only for creative reasons whenever I felt that I need to move on, or perhaps they have.

As a pop person I think there is a major difference than, say, being a painter. No-one sees that person perform, but when I record then it is important for me to be seen to perform well too. You have to get over what you are singing about and it's really important that I come across as someone who likes and enjoys what he does, and that the fans genuinely enjoy me, the band, the shows, whatever.

I think it's valid for me to think of myself as a survivor. I've often said to Peter, 'When will it end? How do I recognise the time to stop?' There are so many things I would like to do, I see lying before me more opportunities and challenges than ever before. I thought this before my double topping of both the British single and album charts at the end of 1988.

Let me say why the future seems so exciting – first, my album sales have gone up and up. My 1987 album *Always Guaranteed* was my most successful ever studio recording

'Fortunately they found me – you could get lost on the St George's Estate.'

Cliff,
From the Victoria Hall,
Hanley in '58, to Wembley Stadium
in '89, we've had some great
times. We are proud to have
been with you for some of
the journey. Long may we
both continue. Don't forget,
its been nice trying to work
with you!
 Seriously many congrats'
 Love
 Bruce Welch

HANK MARVIN · BRUCE WELCH · BRIAN

Dear Cliff,
 don't listen to Bruce & Brian,
it was easy working with you, well
not that bad anyway.
 Looking back thirty years to
that first rehearsal we had in
your mum's front room in Cheshunt
I remember thinking to myself "this boy
is going to be big, real big".
 Seriously, could any of
us back then (apart from Peter
Gormley) have even fantasized this incredible
thirty years?

 love Hank

So its 30 years....well
Congratulations Cliff --
Just hang in there--
You'll make it!-----
 Love Brian

155

Dawn French, along with Jennifer Saunders, and the act French and Saunders, is a highly rated satirical surveyor of contemporary life.

Maureen Lipman is one of Britain's best loved theatre names with performing and writing credits.

Victoria Wood is one of Britain's most funniest commentators on life. Her television and live shows have been much heralded.

Clare Davidson is a stage director, drama school lecturer and has voice coached famous pop and film stars.

re: Cliff Richard

I've never met him, but he looks as though he'd be great at snogging

—From Dawn French—

Maureen Lipman

"I suppose it has to be said that Cliff Richard's curling top lip during his rendition of "Living Doll" illicited the first scream from my erst-while prim lips and that to this very day I'm full of admiration for him and would like to have a copy of the picture he must have hanging in his attic".

Best of luck with the book.

Kind regards

Maureen Lipman

Maureen Lipman

Victoria Wood

Re Cliff—

i've never met him

but Dawn French says hes

great at snogging.

Victoria Wood.

Having wondered what you might be like as a person I suddenly found myself in your company — and loved every minute of it. Not just a pop personality you obviously think and care deeply and spiritually.

Loving thoughts

Clare Davidson

and the sales for *Private Collection* have taken my breath away. Second, the last tour was a sell-out after a matter of days. Third, there are constant demands that could take me years to fulfil.

I would like to do something unusual or different but I must be careful not to dabble, that's always a constant temptation. Nor must I play for safety. Perhaps I want someone to make me an outrageous offer! This is a time in my life when I can afford to be crazy! I don't think it would matter. I'm delighted to be even in the top 20 amongst all the new people. I enjoy making the top 30! That might worry some people, not me. I don't have to deal in negatives, worrying how some people might react. I do believe that my positive approach has won me friends, and has been an important element in my survival. I believe in being honest and it's the people around me have always kept things straight. I believe I have won through on my principles; they may not appeal to everybody, but I've never been ashamed of them. I've never been afraid to say openly and clearly that I am a Christian.

You know often through the years people have written me off, some still do! When I was one of those rockers people said I would vanish with them. Some of the people who said that back in the late 1950s must be more than a little surprised that I rate only second to Elvis in the hit achievement listing. To me Elvis was, and still is *numero uno* and I'm chuffed to be up there with him! But Elvis died prematurely and if I can continue going then I shall catch up with him and maybe even overtake him.

And then the Beatles. Ah, it was said, this is the end for Cliff. I think if people look carefully at what really did happen during the Beatle years then they will find that I still had massive hits, appeared countless times on radio and TV, toured and featured extensively in magazines. You know I've never claimed that I'm better than someone else, rather I've said I'm equal to others. I've been in quite a mix of company over the years: hard rockers, punks, new wave, the disco-dance people and so on. I've survived through it all.

Yes, I have done more than most, perhaps more than any British pop star; I'm not going around bragging, but of course I'm pleased. And I am glad to see have seen off some writers who have slagged me, mis-reported me, and tried to make me what I am not.

I still get moved by the enormous good will and kindness that I am shown. I was last winter when EMI put on a special celebration and I was presented with a solid gold disc that had all my hits printed on it. It was wonderful. I felt so happy and I was knocked out that so many people who had worked with me during my time with the company were there. It was a fabulous gesture from EMI.

I've survived but I'm going to stay around for quite a while yet. Keep writing my story, Tony.

Luv!

Cliff

CLIFF'S HIT SINGLES AND ALBUMS

UK SINGLES

1958	Aug	1	Move It/Schoolboy Crush (DB 4178)
	Nov	2	High Class Baby/My Feet Hit The Ground (DB 4203)
1959	Jan	3	Livin' Lovin' Doll/Steady With You (DB 4249)
	Apr	4	Mean Streak/Never Mind (DB 4290)
	Jul	5	Livin' Doll/Apron Strings (DB 4306)
	Oct	6	Travellin' Light/Dynamite (DB 4351)
1960	Jan	7	A Voice in the Wilderness/Don't Be Mad At Me (DB 4398)
	Mar	8	Fall In Love With You/Willie and the Hand Jive (DB 4431)
	Jun	9	Please Don't Tease/Where Is My Heart? (DB 4479)
	Sept	10	Nine Times Out of Ten/Thinking of Our Love (DB 4506)
	Nov	11	I Love You/'D' In Love (DB 4547)
1961	Feb	12	Theme For a Dream/Mumblin' Mosie (DB 4593)
	Mar	13	Gee Whiz It's You/I Cannot Find A True Love (DC 756)
	Jun	14	A Girl Like You/Now's the Time To Fall In Love (DB 4667)
	Oct	15	When The Girl In Your Arms Is The Girl In Your Heart/Got A Funny Feeling (DB 4716)
1962	Jan	16	The Young Ones/We Say Yeah (DB 4761)
	May	17	I'm Looking Out The Window/Do You Want To Dance (DB 4828)
	Aug	18	It'll Be Me/Since I Lost You (DB 4886)
	Nov	19	The Next Time/Bachelor Boy (DB 4950)
1963	Feb	20	Summer Holiday/Dancing Shoes (DB 4977)
	May	21	Lucky Lips/I Wonder (DB 7034)
	Aug	22	It's All In The Game/Your Eyes Tell On You (DB 7089)
	Nov	23	Don't Talk To Him/Say You're Mine (DB 7150)
1964	Jan	24	I'm The Lonely One/Watch What You Do With My Baby (DB 7203)
	Apr	25	Constantly/True True Lovin' (DB 7272)
	Jun	26	On The Beach/A Matter of Moments (DB 7305)
	Oct	27	The Twelfth of Never/I'm Afraid To Go Home (DB 7372)
	Dec	28	I Could Easily Fall (In Love With You)/I'm In Love With You (DB 7420)
1965	Mar	29	The Minute You're Gone/Just Another Guy (DB 7496)
	May	30	Angel/Razzle Dazzle (DB 762)
	Jun	31	On My Word/Just A Little Bit Too Late (DB 7596)
	Aug	32	The Time In Between/Look Before You Love (DB 7660)
	Oct	33	Wind Me Up (Let Me Go)/The Night (DB 7745)
1966	Mar	34	Blue Turns To Grey/Somebody Loses (DB 7866)
	Jul	35	Visions/What Would I Do (For The Love Of A Girl) (DB 7968)
	Oct	36	Time Drags By/The La La La Song (DB 8017)
	Dec	37	In The Country/Finders Keepers (DB 8094)
1967	Mar	38	It's All Over/Why Wasn't I Born Rich? (DB 8150)
	Jun	39	I'll Come Running/I Got The Feelin' (DB 8210)
	Aug	40	The Day I Met Marie/Our Story Book (DB 8245)
	Nov	41	All My Love/Sweet Little Jesus Boy (DB 8293)

1968	Mar	42	Congratulations/High 'n' Dry (DB 8376)
	Jun	43	I'll Love You Forever Today/Girl, You'll Be A Woman Soon (DB 8437)
	Sep	44	Marianne/Mr Nice (DB 8476)
	Nov	45	Don't Forget To Catch Me/What's More (I Don't Need Her) (DB 8503)
1969	Feb	46	Good Times (Better Times)/Occasional Rain (DB 8548)
	May	47	Big Ship/She's Leaving You (DB 8581)
	Sept	48	Throw Down A Line (CLIFF and HANK)/Reflections (DB 8615)
	Nov	49	With The Eyes Of A Child/So Long (DB 8648)
1970	Feb	50	The Joy Of Living (CLIFF and HANK)/Leave My Woman Alone/Boogitoo (CLIFF and HANK) (DB 8657)
	Jun	51	Goodbye Sam, Hello Samantha/You Can Never Tell (DB 8685)
	Aug	52	I Ain't Got Time Anymore/Monday Comes Too Soon (DB8708)
1971	Jan	53	Sunny Honey Girl/Don't Move Away (with Olivia Newton-John)/ I Was Only Fooling Myself (DB 8747)
	Apr	54	Silvery Rain/Annabella Umbrella/Time Flies (DB 8774)
	Jul	55	Flying Machine/Pigeon (DB 8797)
	Nov	56	Sing A Song Of Freedom/A Thousand Conversations (DB 8836)
1972	Mar	57	Jesus/Mr Cloud (DB 8864)
	Aug	58	Living In Harmony/Empty Chairs (DB 8917)
	Dec	59	A Brand New Song/The Old Accordian (DB 8957)
1973	Mar	60	Power To All Our Friends/Come Back Billie Jo (EMI 2012)
	May	61	Help It Along/Tomorrow Rising/Days Of Love/Ashes To Ashes (EMI 2022)
	Nov	62	Take Me High/Celestial House (EMI 2088)
1974	May	63	(You Keep Me) Hangin' On/Love Is Here (EMI 2150)
1975	Mar	64	It's Only Me You've Left Behind/You're The One (EMI 2279)
	Sep	65	(There's A) Honky Tonk Angel (Who Will Take Me Back In)/ Wouldn't You Know It (Got Myself a Girl) (EMI 2344)
1976	Feb	66	Miss You Nights/Love Is Enough (EMI 2376)
	May	67	Devil Woman/Love On (EMI 2485)
	Aug	68	I Can't Ask For Anything More Than You, Babe/Junior Cowboy (EMI 2499)
	Nov	69	Hey, Mr Dream Maker/No-one Waits (EMI 2559)
1977	Feb	70	My Kinda Life/Nothing Left For Me To Say (EMI 2584)
	Jun	71	When Two Worlds Drift Apart/That's Why I Love You (EMI 2663)
1978	Jan	72	Yes! He Lives/Good On The Sally Army (EMI 2730)
	Jul	73	Please Remember Me/Please Don't Tease (EMI 2832)
	Nov	74	Can't Take The Hurt Anymore/Needing A Friend (EMI 2885)
1979	Mar	75	Green Light/Imagine Love (EMI 2920)
	Jul	76	We Don't Talk Anymore/Count Me Out (EMI 2675)
	Nov	77	Hot Shot/Walking In The Light (EMI 5003)
1980	Feb	78	Carrie/Moving In (EMI 5006)
	Aug	79	Dreamin'/Dynamite (EMI 5095)
1981	Jan	80	A Little In Love/Keep On Looking (EMI 5123)
	Aug	81	Wire For Sound/Hold On (EMI 5221)
	Nov	82	Daddy's Home/Shakin' All Over (EMI 5251)
1982	Jul	83	The Only Way Out/Under The Influence (EMI 5318)
	Sept	84	Where Do We Go From Here?/Discovering (EMI 5341)
	Nov	85	Little Town/Love And A Helping Hand/You, Me and Jesus (EMI 5348)
1983	Apr	86	True Love Ways/Galadriel (both with London Symphony Orchestra) (EMI 5385)
	Aug	87	Never Say Die (Give A Little Bit More)/Lucille (EMI 5415)
	Nov	88	Please Don't Fall In Love/Too Close To Heaven (EMI 5437)
1984	Mar	89	Baby You're Dynamite/Ocean Deep (EMI 5457)
	Oct	90	Shooting From The Heart/Small World (RICH 1)
1985	Jan	91	Heart User/I Will Follow You (RICH 2)
	Sep	92	She's So Beautiful/She's So Beautiful (inst) (EMI 5531)
	Nov	93	It's In Every One of Us/Alone (inst) (EMI 5537)

1986	May	94	Born To Rock 'n' Roll/Law Of The Universe (inst) (EMI 5545)
1987	Jun	95	My Pretty One/Love Ya (EM 4)
	Aug	96	Some People/One Time Lover Man (EM 18)
	Oct	97	Remember Me/Another Christmas Day (EM 31)
1988	Feb	98	Two Hearts/Yesterday, Today, Forever (EM 42)
	Nov	99	Mistletoe & Wine/Marmaduke (EM 78)
1989	May	100	The Best Of Me/Move It/Lindsay Jane (EM 92)
	Aug	101	I Just Don't Have The Heart/Wide Open Space (EM 101)
	Oct	102	Lean On You/Hey Mister (EM 105)
1990	Feb	103	Stronger Than That/Joanna (EM 129)
	Aug	104	Silhouettes/The Winner (EM 152)
	Oct	105	From A Distance/Lindsay Jane 11 (EM 155)
	Nov	106	Saviour's Day/Oh Boy Medley (XMAS 90)
1991	Sep	107	More To Life/Mo's Theme (Instrumental)
	Nov	108	We Should Be Together/Miss You Nights (Live) (XMAS 91)
	Dec	109	This New Tear/Scarlet Ribbons (EM 218)
1992	Nov	110	I Still Believe In You/Bulange Downpour

UK ALBUMS

1959	Apr	Cliff
	Nov	Cliff Sings
1960	Oct	Me and My Shadows
1961	May	Listen To Cliff
	Oct	21 Today
	Dec	The Young Ones
1962	Oct	32 Minutes And 17 Seconds With Cliff Richard
1963	Jan	Summer Holiday
	Jul	Cliff's Hit Album
	Sep	When In Spain
1964	Jul	Wonderful Life
	Dec	Aladdin And His Wonderful Lamp
1965	Apr	Cliff Richard
	Jul	More Hits By Cliff
	Aug	When In Rome
	Nov	Love Is Forever
1966	May	Kinda Latin
	Dec	Finders Keepers
1967	Jan	Cinderella
	Apr	Don't Stop Me Now
	Oct	Good News
1968	May	Cliff In Japan
	Aug	Two A Penny
	Sep	Established 1958
1969	Jun	The Best Of Cliff
	Oct	Sincerely
	Nov	It'll Be Me
1970	Jul	Cliff Live At The Talk Of The Town
	Oct	About That Man
	Nov	His Land
	Nov	Tracks 'n' Grooves
1972	Nov	The Best of Cliff Volume Two

1973	Dec	Take Me High
1974	Jun	Help It Along
	Nov	The 31st of February Street
1976	May	I'm Nearly Famous
1977	Mar	Every Face Tells A Story
	Sep	40 Golden Greats
1978	Feb	Small Corners
	Sep	Green Light
1979	Feb	Thank You Very Much (Cliff and The Shadows)
	Sep	Rock 'n' Roll Juvenile
1980	Sep	I'm No Hero
1981	Jul	Love Songs
	Sep	Wired For Sound
1982	Aug	Now You See Me . . . Now You Don't
1983	May	Dressed For The Occasion
	Oct	Silver

A second album – Rock 'n' Roll Silver – was included as part of a limited edition box set.

1984	Sep	Cliff and The Shadows
	Nov	The Rock Connection
1987	Sep	Always Guaranteed
1988	Nov	Private Collection
1989	Oct	Stronger
	Oct	The EP Collection – Ballads And Love Songs
1990	Nov	From A Distance – The Event
	Dec	From A Distance – The Even' (limited boxed set)
1991	Nov	Together With Cliff
1993	Apr	Access All Areas